D0815935

HOUSE OF PLENTY

CAROL DAWSON AND CAROL JOHNSTON

HOUSE OF
PLENTY

THE RISE, FALL,

AND REVIVAL OF

LUBY'S CAFETERIAS

UNIVERSITY OF TEXAS PRESS, AUSTIN

Requests for permission to reproduce material from this work should be sent to:
Permissions
University of Texas Press
P.O. Box 7819
Austin, TX 78713-7819
www.utexas.edu/utpress/about/bpermission.html

○∞The paper used in this book meets the minimum requirements of
ANSI/NISO Z39.48-1992 (R1997) (Permanence of Paper).

LIBRARY OF CONGRESS CATALOGING-IN-PUBLICATION DATA

Dawson, Carol
    House of plenty : the rise, fall, and revival of Luby's Cafeterias / Carol
Dawson and Carol Johnston. — 1st ed.
        p.   cm.
    Includes bibliographical references and index.
    ISBN-13: 978-0-292-70656-9 (cloth : alk. paper)
    ISBN-10: 0-292-70656-1 (alk. paper)
    1. Luby's Cafeterias, Inc. — History. 2. Cafeterias — United States — History
I. Johnston, Carol. II. Title.
TX945.5.L83D39 2006
647.9573 — dc22   2006009113

CONTENTS

□ □ □

HOUSE OF PLENTY

1

BLOOD SACRIFICE IN TEXAS

□ □ □

The first word that flashed in the senior police officer's mind as he peer-ed with an expert eye at the mess on the far side of the threshold was "homicide."

Dark blood pooled across the room, drenching the carpet. A man dressed in blue pajamas with blue jogging pants pulled up over the bottoms sprawled face down on the floor beside the bed. Next to his left hand, as if released in final surrender, lay a large kitchen knife, its steel blade lacquered crimson, its handle printed by a wet grip.

The man had plainly been dead for some time now. Holes in his throat and neck gaped wide, but no longer bled. That there were several wounds was immediately obvious to the police observers; that the neck and chest of the man had been attacked with a determined savagery was also evident. Other smaller gashes on the body—fourteen in all, revealed when they turned the man over—told of a less drastic if no less painful assault. But of the five big stab wounds in the neck, three were serious enough to have alone proven mortal. And of the total of nineteen cuts, not a single one bore the characteristic marks, locations, and angles of self-defense.

Clearly this had to be the work of a vicious murderer, a person or persons unknown who had plunged the knife into the unresisting victim with such frenzied force that it looked, according to one police officer present, "as if he'd tried to cut his heart out."

Yet other than these fiercely inflicted stab wounds, there was no sign of a struggle. Room 214 of the Motel 6 on Interstate 10 in San Antonio, Texas, remained as tidy and neat as when the maid had last cleaned it. The bedspread still lay undisturbed. Nothing was disheveled, as it would have been had a scuffle of any kind occurred. The lamps and furniture all stood in their normal positions. The luggage rack, closet, and dresser drawers were empty of suitcases or clothes. If anyone else had penetrated this plain, simple second-floor chamber, they had left no clue at all behind.

Yet despite the reflex assumption of murder during these first moments of horrified perception, such a state of forensic purity was not completely unexpected by the police and their accompanying EMS technicians. The caller who had dialed 911 a few minutes after 6:30 a.m. on March 13, 1997, and alerted them to go to the motel had already warned them of the reason for her call: she had awakened at 6:30 to find her husband missing from bed. His bag for the business trip he was scheduled to make in an hour or two was still packed and ready in place. So was his briefcase. But his car was gone. Perplexed that he would have departed without saying good-bye and forgotten to take his important luggage, she had wandered to the kitchen. There she discovered a note addressed to her, carefully planted on her desk. The handwriting was her husband's. His note expressed love for her and for their three children. It also informed her of his whereabouts and requested that she not try to find him, but instead to send an ambulance.

Immediately she picked up the phone.

Later it would be discovered that the dead man, 49-year-old John Edward Curtis Jr., had left his house, driven to the Motel 6, and checked in sometime between 10:00 and 10:30 p.m. the night before. Then he had returned home, written the message for his wife, rejoined her in bed, and left again around 1:00 in the morning to go back to Room 214. There the mystery stalled. There was no sign of abduction. If he had been lured or coerced from his house, all traces of the coercer were now apparently obliterated. The desk clerk was quite certain Curtis had checked in alone, and seemingly of his own volition. Only one conclusion seemed inevitable.

But even as the EMS technician examined Curtis and pronounced him dead a few minutes after 7:00 a.m. on March 13, the police officers continued to stare in baffled disbelief at his body. Surely no one could inflict such protracted and ruthless injury on himself. It was unheard of, this display of wild, furious violence. What burden of guilt, what act of atonement, could such a terrible form of death represent? What buried secrets could possibly prompt this severe a self-punishment?

In the days that followed, their questions would hover unanswered. For the next few weeks, as the autopsy results came in and the last hours of John Curtis's life were painstakingly scrutinized, the enigma of his gory demise would haunt officials and the press as poignantly as it did his loved ones. In particular it would disquiet the board of directors and the 13,000 employees of Luby's Cafeterias, Inc., as well as the many people who had invested in Luby's public stock. The initial buzz of disturbance on Wall Street would increase to a frightened drone. For only two months before, John Curtis had been named president and CEO of the Luby's corporation, the largest cafeteria chain in the nation. And he had committed this grisly act on the eve of his very first board of directors' meeting—literally within a few hours of his ascent to the chair at the end of the table.

The word *suicide*, derived from the Latin *sui* for "of oneself" and *cide* for "murder," is seldom so floridly demonstrated. An overdose of sleeping pills, a poisoning, hanging (the second most common means of suicide in the United States after firearms), a leap from a bridge or building, or even the single shot from a gun muzzle held to the temple or jammed in the mouth do not suggest quite the extremity of malicious abuse and determined annihilation that stabbing does. Even the four-letter arrangement in "stab" evokes a special chill: it sounds like the action it describes. Stylistically, the concept of stabbing can make us far more uneasy than other kinds of assault; there is something primal about it, smacking of an assassin sneaking silently up behind his victim in a night-drenched alley. It is a very intimate, hands-on, *human*-scale mode of death. Usually, in cases of murder, one or two—perhaps three—thrusts complete the job. With suicide fewer are necessary, or even physically possible, except when the perpetra-

tor has entered a state of shock. In cultures that have traditionally con-
doned suicide using sharp blades as an indirect type of execution, such as
Romans receiving imperial orders to cut their veins, or societies in which
a historical niche existed for suicide as an honorable solution to shameful
circumstances, such as the Japanese hara-kiri (belly-cutting), or seppuku,
the one strong, straightforward slash was considered sufficient to expiate
all the victim's sins. According to psychiatrists, stabbing as a method of
suicide is, anywhere in the world, extremely rare. The act of self-stabbing
implies an unsurpassable hopelessness coupled with ferocity; it is the
quintessential self-murder. Even Juliet would have preferred Romeo's poi-
son rather than her final, resigned recourse to his dagger.

So why did John Curtis choose it?

To all who knew him, especially his wife Kathi and his three children—
Aimee, twenty-six; Daniel, twenty-five; and Adam, sixteen—Curtis was the
most unlikely candidate for suicide that they could think of. The man who
had groomed him for the chief executive role at Luby's Cafeterias, Inc.,
former president and then current chairman of the board Ralph "Pete" Erben, echoed the same sentiment. "He was the last person in the world you'd
expect to do such a thing," Erben said later. "Uncharacteristic" was how
Erben described Curtis's act to the press, adding, "I don't know if there are
adequate superlatives to describe him as a man. Very bright, very conscientious . . . a real sense of dignity." A deeply religious Christian with unpretentious habits, Curtis was devoted to his family, and maintained very close
connections with each member. The only items of jewelry he owned were
a silver James Avery key chain and a Seiko watch. The community and his
Luby's colleagues knew him as a quiet, solid person of intelligence and reserved mien, a model of stability. He had trained as an accountant, earning
his degree at Texas Tech University, before taking his first job at Bielstein,
Lewis and Wilson in the 1970s. He then went on to work for Tejas Airlines
before joining the Luby's staff in 1979. For the next 18 years he applied himself steadily to his tasks, making his way slowly up the corporate ladder.
Everyone who knew him liked him. His days and hours were all predictable and accounted for; he had no secret life, no hidden vices that any later
investigation would reveal. Every Sunday he and his family attended services at the Tree of Life Fellowship in New Braunfels, Texas, where he enjoyed a close, confidential friendship with his pastor. Until three years be-

fore his death, he and his family lived in a modest home in New Braunfels, and he commuted the thirty miles into San Antonio for work. When he received a substantial pay raise, giving him a six-figure salary, they moved to a small but tasteful house in a gated community in San Antonio. Kathi had known and loved him since the sixth grade.

On announcement of his death, the public's instant assumption was that the condition of the company was to blame for Curtis's decision. The toxicology report from the autopsy showed no drugs or alcohol in his system. The only pharmaceutical product he had been ingesting was an asthma medication called Serevent, made by Glaxo Wellcome, which he had recently started taking twice a day. Data from the clinical trials proved that Glaxo researchers had noted no psychosis or depression induced by the drug. Other than the broken sleep he had occasionally complained of to his wife after his promotion to the position of Luby's president and CEO, Curtis exhibited no signs of depression at all, no changes in his usual demeanor. Only one category of comment, made both to Kathi Curtis and to Pete Erben, indicated unease of any sort, and in corporate terms it certainly didn't seem to be of a nature to pressure someone into suicide: Curtis had felt troubled by two recent closures of Luby's stores, and the futures of the now unemployed personnel. Naturally, therefore, the first concern was: what would the corporate books divulge? Was there a nasty surprise pending exposure at the board meeting that Curtis had just dodged by taking his own life? Why else would he resort to such a bizarre and extravagant avoidance technique?

The answers to all these questions are not simple. The fact that Curtis was not about to announce a loss at the meeting, but rather a small but decent gain in earnings, and that the company seemed to be in fine fiscal health, considering its recent expenditures, only served to render his suicide all the more opaque.

But the answers do, in all probability, lie within the context of the company for which he had so lately assumed responsibility. To find them, and understand them in all their moral weight and complexity, one must go back through the long history of an ideal American business to its beginnings, and probe the legacy that Curtis had shouldered for such a brief span of time. One certainty will emerge in the following chapters: the death of John Curtis, like two other important events in the history of Lu-

John Curtis

by's Cafeterias, Inc., that preceded it, was bound up with the structure, personalities, and traditions of Luby's. All three events marked crucial changes, not only at Luby's, but in American society at large. And all three signified a particular, and universal, "tipping point."

□ □ □

Like many of its kind, this archetypal American story would seem, on the surface, to start as a straightforward tale—wholesome, and ripe with optimistic struggle that yields triumphant returns. But under the surface it is wrought with all the most riveting dramas and inner complexities of the human condition. And it so happens that the story's pattern, in many ways, duplicates the pattern, in miniature, of our country's history for the last century.

This is because Luby's has always been more than just a business. It has proven itself to be the incarnation of a unique product, one for which our country is so famous that during the past seventy-five years its title has become a catchphrase all over the globe. Numerous books have been written to promote and/or dissect this product. One television network evening news program recently devoted an entire year to the analysis of its substance. But the product is not an artifact of any manufacturing industry, or engineering know-how, or crop cultivation. Instead, its name unites two ephemeral concepts into a shape so apparently solid that nowadays it is taken for granted as a natural resource. The product in question is, of course, the American Dream. And Luby's Cafeterias, Inc., the earliest real cafeteria chain to be established in the United States, is one of its physical manifestations.

For a company—any company—to become the very essence of an idea is a rarity. For that idea to be so sweeping and fundamental presents a staggering challenge. No other country in the world has such a commensurate dream attached to its national identity; there cannot be said to exist an Irish Dream, or a German Dream, or an Indian or Japanese or Iranian Dream, or any other dream at all with the same magical furnishings of hope and plenitude as ours. The Old World long ago gave up on self-reinvention and the possibility of riches from nothing but hard work, fortitude, ambition, and vision that so fervently grips our civic imaginations. More often than not, immigrants have come to America because this is the only place left where we all can choose to make our own luck.

According to interpreters as disparate as Dan Rather, Martin Luther King Jr., and Edward Albee, the American Dream is centered within the words written by Thomas Jefferson in the Declaration of Independence: that "all men are created equal," and therefore equally deserving of "life, liberty, and the pursuit of happiness." For James Truslow Adams, the man who first coined the term in his 1931 book, *The Epic of America*, "The American Dream" is "that dream of a land in which life should be better and richer and fuller for everyone, with opportunity for each according to ability or achievement. . . . It is not a dream of motor cars and high wages merely, but a dream of social order in which each man and each woman shall be able to attain to the fullest stature of which they are innately capable, and be recognized by others for what they are, regardless of the fortuitous circumstances of birth or position." Freedom of opportunity—all types of opportunity—seems to be the keynote.

And over and over, our hopes have been justified. Our Dream has borne fruit. We've seen it played out countless times, seen it embodied in the very concrete forms that hold us fixated upon it, that keep us, and those millions of immigrants, dreaming it. From religious sects persecuted in other countries to Microsoft, from the Enron Corporation executives to Andrew Carnegie, from ghetto delinquents turned state legislators to illiterates turned bestselling cookbook writers—all are living proofs that a belief can be as real as a material entity, even if it is later abused. But for most Americans today, such people's stories almost always share one common denominator that towers over all others: money.

Not that making a fortune is the only endpoint. *That* dream can be found anywhere in the world. No: the American version is far more complex. For within it lie embedded certain values that have grown to be inextricable from its framework—specifically, those Judeo-Christian virtues upon which we've always based the visions of our better selves, the people we strive to be. Integrity, generosity, charity, equality, fairness, service to one's fellows and to the larger community: these are intrinsic to the Dream's armature. Most importantly, the Dream lies within the reach of everyone. In theory, according to the national mythos, anyone can own it; anyone can achieve it. The quest for it is a constitutional right, an entitlement upon which we are nurtured from birth.

And what public institution expresses the heart of the Dream as well as a cafeteria? No mythical street paved with gold could compete with the immediacy of good, hot food displayed in profusion, ready for harvesting onto your very own tray at a cheap price. It is the "equalizing" place where rich and poor alike can go for a casual, satisfying meal. Based on all the above definitions, it can truly be said that Luby's Cafeterias, Inc., has for ninety-five years not only represented the American Dream. It has *been* the American Dream. A Dream come to life, a microcosm of Middle America, complete with the goodness, strong characters, fine relationships, sense of family connection, and ensuing wealth and prosperity for its founders and personnel that all human beings crave. And of course, the darkness that every dream, no matter how noble, also contains—the corruptions and nightmare moments, the terrors and evils that are invariably part of a national history, and that make any dream a fully rounded reality.

This microcosmic view includes the lives of multiple generations of men, women, and children who have worked at Luby's, eaten at Luby's, literally grown up within its walls, and in more than two dozen cases, died violent, tragic deaths there. For, among these last, the suicide of John Curtis is merely the most recent.

2

PLANTING SEEDS

☐ ☐ ☐

You cannot improve on time spent eating a good meal.
CHARLES JOHNSTON

This story begins with a phantom.

Like most phantoms, he began his existence as a normal human being born of flesh and blood. However, once his ghostly status effectively commenced—an event that took place several decades before his death—his presence in people's minds quickly dwindled to little more than the whispery echo of a few words. It is true that during his later years he struck his occasional observers as a dapper, reticent, benevolent, and gentlemanly fellow; but after the year 1927, when he retreated into the sanctuary and privacy of home life for the rest of his time on earth, he so rarely made himself available for observation that the opportunities of those few witnesses were cursory and superficial at best. As a result, other than the tangible records of his career, we have only the sketchiest reports of his personality and actions upon which to rely. Thus Harry Luby, who achieved success and retired wealthy at an absurdly young age, has proven to be one of the most elusive entrepreneurs to ever found a business empire. So unassuming was this maverick flame-starter that even within his most intimate circle of business cronies, kinfolk, and acquaintances, he became not so much famous for his modesty as almost erased because of it.

Yet, paradoxically, this phantom is also the man whose brilliant idea, aggressive growth strategies, and fair-minded business practices not only made a number of people incredibly rich, but wound up influencing four generations of Americans and changing the public dining habits of our nation forever.

Today, the surviving individuals who knew Harry Luby during his long lifetime puzzle a little before groping through their memories to offer a glimpse, any clue at all, that will lend shape to their dim impressions. Most often they remark on his affability, his soft-spoken reserve, his genteel demeanor. To retrieve even these morsels of concrete information seems a triumph of effort; soon they shake their heads apologetically and give up. So mostly what's now left of Harry Luby's reputation is his amazing creation, his innovative vision, his legacy of beneficence, and the multitude of personal fortunes to which these combined factors gave birth. Of his direct descendants, only a solitary granddaughter remains. And of the man himself, only his surname lives on, as a sign above the highway or in the shopping mall parking lot, as a brand seared on the consciousness of the many employees who have benefited from his philosophy, or as a watchword among business legends. And, of course, as a whole way of life for millions of his fellow countrymen.

This is because, despite such a wholesale disappearing act, it's accurate to say that Harry Luby possessed real genius. This gift, born perhaps of his innocent hopes and ambitions—born perhaps of the traumas of his childhood—went far beyond both his visionary knack, and his willingness to work very hard in a newly created field only so he could retire early to a life of quiet, almost frugal leisure. It lay in instinctively finding the right path, and then attracting the right people to fall in step on that path behind him. From small-town neighborhoods to the oil field trail across the first third of the twentieth century, from grocery stores and orchards, meat companies and football fields, he lured relatives, friends, and acquaintances like the Pied Piper, leading his followers toward futures of unexpectedly lavish rewards— rewards that he indulged himself scarcely at all. As a man whose principles of generosity would eventually create a large pool of millionaires and form the guidelines of a major modern corporation, he reigned supreme.

So why does such a charismatic figure remain so mysterious?

"I was a student at San Jose State University, nineteen years old, when I came to Texas for the first time," says George Wenglein, retired president and CEO of Luby's Cafeterias, Inc. "During previous summers I'd worked in my hometown of Ukiah, California, picking fruit. My father was a cabinet maker there. I had six sisters, and I was the boy in the middle. But one of my older sisters had recently married Bob Luby. Bob Luby was Harry Luby's only child, and he and my sister Georgia had met in San Francisco, fallen in love, gotten married, and were now moving back to Dallas to open up a new business on Live Oak Street. So I went down with them to spend the summer working there for a change. The year was 1937, and we were all still deep in the Depression.

"When I arrived in Dallas, before I even started work, Bob Luby's father Harry took me on a shopping trip downtown to buy some clothes. This was because I was about to start working for him and his son, and also because I was his son's new kid brother-in-law. First he drove me around and around, searching through the city blocks for a parking meter with some time still left on it so he wouldn't have to drop a penny in the slot to buy us a space. After a long time of this hunting—at least twenty minutes or so—he finally found one with some time to spare. Then he parked his car, and together we walked into a department store. Once inside, this man whom I hardly knew turned to me and beamed a big smile.

"'Now, pick out whatever you want,' he said. 'Anything at all. And don't worry. I'm paying for it, it's all on me.'"

The name of the store, George noted at the time, was Neiman-Marcus.

As shoppers throughout the country recognize, Neiman-Marcus owes its fame to its prominence as one of the most expensive emporiums in the United States. Thus Harry Luby, a man who disliked spending so much as a cent on a parking meter if he could avoid it, introduced George Wenglein in one beautiful moment both to the magnanimous embrace of the Luby family circle and to his own prosperous future.

Yet—perhaps precisely *because* his benefactor's presence was so low-key and nondescript—this is George Wenglein's chief active memory of the man who started the very first cafeteria chain in the United States.

Harry and Julia Luby

□ □ □

Who was Harry Luby really? Why, when those who knew him try to describe him, does his personality yet seem so evasive? "A gentleman," George Wenglein recalls, "who, even long after his retirement, dressed always in a suit and a bow-tie. Day or night. But he never said much." "A wisp of air," says another person connected to the Luby's organization. "Very quiet. And when he took off his hat, he always held on to it with both hands." Clearly, although Harry Luby never *seemed* to dominate anyone's attention, the fact that he managed to change the course of so many lives speaks of his powerful influence. What he lacked in forcefulness he made up for in his determination, his phenomenal thinking powers, and his dream.

Harry Luby was born in 1887, the only son of Alec Luby, an affluent businessman in Illinois. Unfortunately, Harry's mother's name is lost to history. He had three sisters, but their birth order is unknown. The Luby family, of Irish descent, occupied a comfortable position in their community. Harry's father owned a sawmill, a general store, and several other concerns.

But the sweetness of such a life was about to turn bitter. Unfortunately, when one of the many epidemics afflicting the United States during that period scoured through the state, Harry's mother and two of his three sisters became its tragic victims.

With half the family wiped out in one blow, the two remaining children, now the sole hopes of a father devastated by this loss, felt the effect maim their existence. Their father's hurt ran so deeply that even his financial luck changed. The house filled with his sadness—a sadness that refused to go away.

As Alec Luby's despair grew following the deaths of his wife and two daughters, his fortunes sank accordingly. The timing of his disasters couldn't have been worse. An economic depression now gripped the region. Doomed to suffer a streak of trials as monumentally grim as Job's, he watched helplessly as, one by one, his businesses slid from his hands. Soon he and his two children were left almost destitute.

For the rest of Harry's childhood, he and his last sister, Bess, endured their father's fiscal failures and emotional hardships. It was not a happy way in which to grow up. Against all odds, Bess retained her lively and vivacious nature, eventually becoming what one member of the family has called "a ripsnorter." But Harry, a gentle boy, was already by disposition far more reserved and inward than his sole remaining sibling. As he matured into a gentle, meek man, he couldn't escape the haunting anguish of that early loss of family, financial security, and sense of well-being. Perhaps the sorrow of his sisters' and mother's fates was inextricably wedded in his mind to the desperate financial plight he now saw his father mired in; perhaps he felt that the balm of solvency would also somehow heal the wound of his family's loss. Whatever the case, throughout his youth he longed to put the bleak atmosphere of his father's home behind him forever. By the time he reached adulthood, he had vowed to pursue a life of stability and contented domestic certainty. And in his opinion, the only way to accomplish this goal was to grow rich enough to retire early and never have to worry about money again.

But Harry's real aim was not quite so raw as pure material acquisition. Desire is always far more complex than it appears. Money alone could never fully supply the solace he missed so badly, although the careful shepherding of it would remain a discipline embedded within him for the rest of his years, as demonstrated by George Wenglein's lone anecdote. Harry Luby's plans for wealth must be achieved only with certain attitudes in play, and must bear a certain ethos as an intrinsic part of their workings, for them to be able to confer the healing that could lead him back to true happiness. He wanted to find something to do that would unite people, soothe and comfort them, tie them together into a sense of prosperous community, the way he had longed for the restoration of his family's old place in their community before death and ruin stripped it away, the way he had longed to be soothed and comforted while he was still a bereft and grief-stricken child—the way, possibly, that he still longed to be reunited with those loved ones he had lost. He wanted to find the way to redeem the sadness of his boyhood home.

He also wished to provide people with a needed service—a useful expansion to their lives. So he set out to seek the right profession in which to accomplish this. His first attempt, which in retrospect seems a full 180 degrees off the most direct track, was as a retail clothing merchant.

Tailor shop, Springfield, Missouri, ca. 1909

In 1908, at the age of twenty-two, Harry opened a men's haberdashery shop in downtown Springfield, Missouri. It was the kind of shop, specializing in hand-tailoring, that was designed to be run by one or two persons only, and it didn't take long after the opening for Harry to discover just how far off the track he had strayed. The work was unrewarding in every aspect. He found little satisfaction in supplying the public that straggled in through his door with gentlemen's suits, shirts, overcoats, and undergarments. He possessed no real affinity with cloth, no particular talent for style, and was insufficiently aggressive to summon the pressure tactics necessary to turn himself into a winning salesman. Most importantly, he quickly saw that he wasn't going to make much money, and certainly not enough for early retirement, running a struggling new small business in a small Midwestern town. Harry felt discouraged and dissatisfied, but he wasn't sure yet what to do about it.

As it turned out, in all likelihood his first choice of vocation wasn't quite the dead-end it might appear. One saving grace made the whole experience worthwhile. For it was in the course of this first venture that Harry met a young woman named Julia Kotchie. Julia was the daughter of a tailor, and therefore a natural acquaintance for Harry to make in the circles he now inhabited. Luckily for him, she was also feisty, attractive, adventurous, and a hard worker. The very opposite of a pale wraith or a shy and timid maiden, Julia was quite capable of filling the room with her vitality, her cheekiness, and her strong opinions. She made the ideal antidote to Harry's muted reserve.

As a child Julia had been crippled by a heavy flowerpot that fell off a high porch and crushed her foot. Because she came from a family of devout Christian Scientists, no doctor had been called after the accident. Instead, the foot was merely wrapped and bound in bandages, and left to mend as best it could. As a result, the mishap and avoidance of treatment sentenced her to wear stout corrective shoes for the rest of her life, and to endure chronic pain. Despite such a handicap, or perhaps because of it, Julia had a larger-than-usual reservoir of determination and courage from which to draw strength, and was willing to brave risks beyond the usual sphere of a small-town tailor's daughter. Soon romance began to leaven the drudgery of the clothing shop. Harry felt love's power at work, relieving

Street scene, Springfield, Missouri

the ache that had tormented his loneliness since boyhood. It wasn't long before Julia consented to become his wife.

And that was when *his* luck changed.

The first two years of the clothing business were hard. The young couple possessed very little to fall back on other than their devotion to one another. But one talent Julia brought into Harry's life was the direct result of a childhood spent doing the chore her crippled condition made her peculiarly fit for: she was a splendid cook. Instead of wandering the neighborhood with her friends, or playing outdoor games of hopscotch and skipping-rope like most girls, she mastered the arts of the kitchen, taking pride in baking pies and cakes, bread and rolls, preparing vegetables and roasts for her family. In Julia's hands Harry would never starve for lack of delicious food. Every morning, she provided him with pots, plates, and thermoses filled with soups, stews, and other hot meals to eat in his shop for lunch.

Often the merchants up and down the block dropped in to say hello and chat when trade was slow enough to allow socializing. Noontime especially would find them visiting Harry's haberdashery to compare the morning's traffic. While there they would incidentally catch a whiff of the savory odors emanating from the containers Julia had filled. There was no public place with comparable food in which to eat in that neighborhood of downtown Springfield at the time. Thus, the requests began: would it be possible for Julia to cook a little extra beef stew or squash casserole for a couple of bachelors, and include it when she dished up Harry's lunches? Could she perhaps spare a slice of that mouth-watering apple pie?

She was only too glad to comply. No doubt her youth, freshness, amiability, good looks, kind hospitable heart, crisp shirtwaist blouse, and neatly pinned hair made these meals an even more appetizing break from the daily grind. She was the ideal hostess—just the kind of zesty girl from whom a single man would want to receive a meal.

Soon the popularity of Julia's cooking swelled to such a pitch that she was catering to a sizable portion of the Springfield merchant nucleus. Men would flock to the haberdashery shop to taste the products of her kitchen, and order an extra helping for the next day. For as long as the shop remained open, she fed the hungry compatriots flocking to its door.

But business remained slow. Not yet a father, but already conscious of his new responsibilities and the financial obligations of a family, Harry had begun feeling very discouraged, and more and more disinclined to throw his energies and his personal future away on a project yielding only small dividends. The amount of work necessary to build this artisan-based type of business into even a minor success seemed excessive to Harry. His disenchantment reached a nadir.

Then in 1909, the year after he first established the haberdashery, Harry Luby went on a buying trip to Chicago. And there, like Paul on the road to Damascus, he had his revelation.

□ □ □

Throughout the months leading up to and following Harry Luby's Chicago junket, several significant developments occurred in the social fabric of the United States and of the world. The first airplane flew across the English Channel. The NAACP was founded. The wireless telegraph, or as we now know it, the radio, was invented, and the first effective cure for syphilis was discovered. Christian fundamentalism suddenly became an established and recognized force in the United States and abroad, severely splitting the American population over conflicting views of science, contemporary experience, and knowledge throughout the next nine decades, and affecting everything from governmental to regional educational policies.

Also in 1909, Robert E. Peary and Matthew Henson became the first explorers to reach the North Pole. The first movie review, a report on D. W. Griffith's film *Pippa Passes*, appeared in the *New York Times*. In 1908 chlorine was added to public drinking water, in Jersey City, New Jersey, to purify it and prevent the water-borne typhoid, cholera, and dysentery epidemics that had plagued the nation for so long, and by 1909 many other cities and states were adopting the practice. Instant coffee hit the market. The concept of deliberately controlled metropolitan growth received official acceptance with the convening of the First National Conference on City Planning. And during that same year of 1909, the architect Daniel Burnham published his *Plan of Chicago*, a groundbreaking design for the Windy City that incorporated regional perspective and wide-ranging integration of transportation systems, parks, schools, streets, neighborhoods, and other public facilities.

The notion of efficiency as a premier virtue had now married with the most recent modes of mechanization, and Chicago became the poster city to demonstrate the new style of twentieth-century living. Chicago was modern—maybe even more modern and up-to-date than New York City. Chicago had flair. Chicago strutted its culture, entrepreneurial spirit, and forward thinking. Chicago represented real progress—meat packers, food reform, incipient gangsters, infant skyscrapers. Chicago had it all.

So when Harry Luby entered its precincts, with wide-open eyes and ears alert to the jangle of the up-and-coming, he stumbled across his destiny in an unexpected spot nestled within this show town of surprises: in a little café called The Dairy Lunch.

The Dairy Lunch was a simple place, unpretentious, with a small number of tables and chairs inside, along with the most rudimentary of arrangements. But like most simple places and ideas, it was also elegant. Its elegance lay not in its decor, appointments, or ambience, but in its productivity. Instead of ordering from a menu, the customers chose their meals from a variety of dishes that were displayed on a counter. They then served themselves, heaping their food onto plates set upon trays that they carried to a table, thereby eliminating any middle-person wait-staff.

Harry was fascinated and delighted. Never before had he seen a restaurant that allowed its customers to walk down a line gathering their own entrées and side dishes. The recent invention of the Ford assembly line was displayed here for the most basic human consumption, as neat and handy as any car factory. He was as drawn by the low cost of the procedure (which benefit was passed on to the clientele) as he was by the new-fangled democratic efficiency of it. To him, The Dairy Lunch must have shone as the very epitome of the new era. Immediately Harry started dreaming of ways in which to refine its methods and presentation. But it would be a while longer before he could put his dreams into action.

Over the next year, Harry closed his unprofitable haberdashery shop and decided to try his hand at tilling the soil. He got a farm just outside Springfield, plowing and sowing, attempting to resign himself to the unaccustomed physical labor that went with his new vocation. However, his hopes for something more interesting, while dormant, did not die. In an extravagant moment of confidence he ordered a catalog from a restaurant supply house, perusing it in his spare evenings. The seeds of a new kind of café continued to take root and grow.

Then one day in 1911, in the middle of his farming toil, he saw a man in a business suit trudging toward him through the fields. The restaurant supply house, as eager to pursue potential customers as he was to find a new branch of endeavor, had sent out a sales representative to push their wares in person.

It must have struck Harry Luby as a sign from fate. Abandoning all his former caution, he placed an order with the salesman. Within a few months he had rented a couple of small commercial rooms in town, built a simple twelve-foot counter, arranged a few tables and chairs, and opened The New England Dairy Lunch. The total cost of the operation's setup was $1,200. The two cooks he hired were professionals, but the chief chef and menu planner was Julia. As for the unusual name of his establishment, located so far from the Northeast coast, he borrowed "The Dairy Lunch" straight from his Chicago inspiration. His signature recipe provided the rest of the title. Among the few other culinary treats he offered was the New England Boiled Dinner, a slow-cooked dish similar to a pot roast but more complex, rich with peppery beef brisket, potatoes, carrots, beets, onions, cabbage, green beans, and rutabagas, all united by an appetizing sauce. The excellence of the food and the thrifty prices made the restaurant an instant winner.

Hungarian Goulash

Cut Short ribs, brown in fat, sprinkle well
with flour and mix well. Add water to cover
Salt and pepper. Add buttering onions.
When done, add paprika. Cook noodles and
serve in long pan, ribs in one end and
noodles in the other.

New England Boiled Dinner

1 tray carrots (cut like stew)
1 tray onions (buttering onions)
1/2 tray turnips
1 1/2 tray new potatoes
6 heads cabbage
green beans
beets
Cook and season all vegetables separately.
When done arrange in long pan as follows:
green beans
new potatoes
carrots
onions
beets
turnips
cabbage

Vegetable Dinner

Cook green beans, season with ham. When
half done add carrots, new potatoes, buttering onions, and whole kernel corn. Cook
until all are tender.

Chicken Pie

Dice chicken in small pieces
Dice potatoes in small pieces
Place layer of chicken in baking pan and add
layer of potatoes. Pour thickened chicken
broth to cover. Cover over with pastry
dough or biscuit dough cut with doughnut
center and place on top. Place in oven
to brown. Cut into 24 orders.

*Recipes for Hungarian Goulash, New England Boiled Dinner,
Vegetable Dinner, and Chicken Pie*

□ □ □

The first twelve years of the new twentieth century marked a period of numerous social and industrial revolutions. And 1911 was particularly charged
with evolutionary change. The Progressive movement of reform begun in
the 1890s in New York City was by that year sweeping through the country,
shaking the patronage and nepotistic systems of appointments and corrup-

tion that had long held local and statewide political frameworks to ransom and tarnished the principles of democracy upon which the Constitution had been founded. The Pure Food and Drug Act, passed by Congress under the aegis of President Theodore Roosevelt's administration, was already altering and improving commercial food processing standards for upcoming generations in ways never before conceived by either consumers or producers. The women's suffrage movement also was in full sway, and during that same year of 1911 California became the fifth state to grant women the right to vote.

Transportation was changing, too, and altering the way Americans regarded their country's breadth. In December 1903, the Wright brothers achieved the first motorized airplane flight. In 1908, the same year that Harry Luby had begun to search for a new and better method of making a living, Henry Ford produced the first Model T automobile in Detroit through the innovation of the assembly line, a format that would eventually change the face of industry in every manufacturing sector. It also enabled a much greater portion of the general public to buy a lower-priced car, thereby providing quicker transportation for a formerly static population. This innovation both necessitated the building of new and better road systems to crisscross the landscape (at the time the country boasted a total of only ten miles of paved roads), and introduced another new industry imperative: the oil boom. The watchwords of modernity were wider availability, cheaper accessibility, and increasing mobility. And although the first motorized cross-country trip had just taken fifty-two days to complete, suddenly anyone could go anywhere if they wanted to, or so it seemed. And once they got there, services needed to be already in place to take care of them.

Springfield, Missouri, Harry Luby's newly adopted home, was a quiet town of about 35,000 people in 1911. Situated in the foothills of the Ozark Mountains, it possessed a beautiful environment on the cusp of two worlds: the old eastern United States and the recently settled West. Because of this geography it formed the most likely axis for the area. The Springfield economy depended chiefly on fruit, grain, livestock, and lumber cultivation, but there was also a large mining enterprise; and the city ranked fourth in the state for manufacturing activity. According to the 1900 United States Census, African-Americans and foreign-born minorities made up only 10 percent of the population. The other 90 percent were chiefly of European descent.

Thus, in the early years of the century, by the most idealized standards that ruled the demographics of the period, Springfield seemed like a solid, idyllic, backbone kind of town that had thankfully outlived its chief notoriety as the site of the very first Old West "walk-and-draw" gunfight (fought to the death on South Street, next to the Springfield City Square, between Wild Bill Hickok and a professional gambler named Dave Tutt on July 21, 1865). It was prosperous without being too flashy. It possessed a few claims to culture, with a small college, a music conservatory, two newspapers (one for each major political party, Republican and Democratic), and four large private parks. It was blessed with a strong merchant community, an important railroad hub, several busy factories, and plenty of respectable tillers of the soil. It was, in other words, the perfect setting in which to pursue the American Dream.

And it made a dandy test laboratory for the next typically American social revolution. But who could have guessed that would take the form of quick food?

The brand-new concept that had captured Harry's imagination was one that would eventually help democratize the privilege of "dining out" for even the least prosperous of American families over the course of the twentieth century. As the Springfield downtown merchants had already discovered, at that time, especially in a provincial "Middle American" town, one only had two choices if one wished to eat away from home: the very expensive formal dining room of a hotel, or the rough-and-tumble, greasy-spoon atmosphere of a saloon. There was certainly no venue at all to which one could bring one's family for an easygoing outing; no casual, yet wholesome and respectable place to treat your mother-in-law to a lunchtime meeting. A vacuum existed in the social context. A need required filling. What could be more typical of this country's get-up-and-go attitude than that someone identify the need and provide its solution?

In 1909 few people in Middle America had ever thought of actually opening a cafeteria, much less one specifically aimed toward the general public. Admittedly, there were by then a few cafeterias in various large, primarily coastal, cities. Some had been set up for working women at certain urban YWCAs, and there was a cafeteria in Los Angeles called Boos Brothers, as well as one called simply "The Cafeteria," opened in 1905 by Helen Mosher, and the small serve-yourself café in Chicago that was Harry Luby's inspiration. The word itself was the brainchild of John Kruger, who in 1893 had established the first dual-gender self-service café at the World's Columbian Exposition in Chicago (as opposed to the Exchange Buffet, opened in New York in 1885, which catered to a strictly male clientele and required them to buy their food at a counter and eat it standing up). Kruger had encountered smorgasbords while traveling in Sweden, but labeled his new business a "cafeteria" based on the Spanish name for a coffee shop. These places, however, and their soon-to-come imitators had the customers picking up their dishes and juggling them in their arms toward a table—a practice that earned them the nickname "grab joints." Then a pair of brothers named Child developed a group of nine cafeterias in New York, and changed the destiny of self-service eating. Their first cafeteria (opened in 1898, and also catering chiefly to working women) utilized the sliding tray upon which customers could place their plates, soup bowls, and side dishes—an innovation that is still in use to this day, unchanging and largely unimprovable. The Childs Cafeterias in New York were temples of hygiene during a particularly germ-conscious period that followed multiple epidemics scourging the country: diphtheria, typhoid, whooping cough—the same kinds of epidemics that had decimated Harry Luby's family. Customers entered a pure white environment—white walls, white tables, white floors, white waitresses dressed from head to toe in starched white uniforms—and thereby assumed they would be buying a pure and sanitized meal as well. To offset all this sterility, a cluster of crystal chandeliers hung from the ceilings, and one Childs even had a five-piece orchestra to soothe and enliven the diners' spirits.

The Horn & Hardart Automats, by contrast, employed vending machines with glass doors in which the customers could insert a coin in a slot and retrieve the dish of their choice from inside a small container. From a partnership founded in Philadelphia in 1900, the first New York City Horn & Hardart Automat opened in 1912, one year after Harry Luby's New England Dairy Lunch, and was the nearest relative to the cafeteria style of serve-yourself dining in America. But the purely Yankee innovation of the

Colonial Hotel, Springfield, Missouri. This is an example of one of the only venues for dining out available at the time.

assembly-line format had made it possible to introduce the cafeteria style across the nation—a radical departure from traditional European restaurant service, and one particularly well suited to the American temperament, pocketbook, work schedule, family life, and democratic attitude.

Yet almost all these original self-service cafeterias were restricted to a single city, or a single state. Certainly no one had yet considered franchising such a modern mode of dining by making it into a multistate chain of operations. But Harry Luby intended exactly that—to expand across a number of state lines. Thus, thanks to Harry, for the first time, many Americans throughout the central part of the country would now not only enjoy the luxury of a cornucopia of excellent food displayed ready for their selection but could also comfortably bring their children "out to eat" as well, without worrying waitresses.

□ □ □

Within only a few weeks, it became apparent that Harry and Julia's new venture was a brilliant triumph. The public flocked in to try this novel format of dining and to sample Julia's recipes, and kept returning when both proved irresistible. Ironically, the location of the cafeteria was at 404 South Street, about one block from the spot where Dave Tutt died of bullets from Bill Hickok's gun.

Despite having no training in food preparation or marketing and only the slimmest financial resources, Harry's success surpassed everything he had dreamed. His secret lay in the fact that he didn't suffer from excessive ego: according to his son Bob, he was willing and determined to learn the business one step at a time. His skill at cutting costs also stood him in good stead. In particular, he was a just and considerate employer; in years to come, Bob would remember how humbly he dealt with his employees.

Never a man to embrace conflict willingly, Harry tended to gently persuade hirelings into performing their jobs and carrying out their responsibilities rather than ordering them to do so. Although this technique was not always effective and sometimes led to discouragement and frustration that would later be observed by his family, it apparently didn't occur to him to assert a bosslike authority. In such behavior lies revealed the regard in which he held all people: everyone was naturally and constitutionally equal in Harry's eyes, and an attitude of mutual cooperation and mutual gain was the only one he wished to prevail under his sponsorship. It was during this time that Harry Luby developed his readiest catchphrase, one that would come to mark all his undertakings: "Share the work, share the risks, share the profits."

So in 1912, only one year after establishing the first cafeteria, he and Julia were opening a second New England Dairy Lunch location in Springfield. And at this time, they changed the names of both their restaurants to The New England Cafeteria.

□ □ □

Despite his sad childhood, at least Harry had not been deprived of secondary kinships by the epidemic. For all the scarcity of his own immediate relatives, another Luby branch filled in the gap left by the missing members—numerically if not emotionally. Alec Luby, Harry's father, had a brother named Joseph, who, together with his wife, Rose Perkhiser Luby, parented a brood of thirteen children. Although one died in infancy, twelve of these children survived into adulthood. Another (the youngest boy, Wes) perished at the age of twenty-six from old injuries received in a football game. The remaining eleven—seven boys and four girls—provided a pool of connections that would help Harry to sustain his undertakings throughout the oncoming decades. Even after he left Illinois to start life in Springfield, Missouri, he had maintained regular communications with his first Illinois home place. So the loneliness that he had felt within his diminished family after his mother and sisters passed away must have been at least partly relieved by this large and boisterous squad of first cousins. Certainly the loyalties, comradeship, and mutual business enthusiasms that braided them together in later life were the products of a strong family bond originating in their early years. And the kind of business that Harry founded would eventually tie them all in ways that would never be broken—not even by death.

All these cousins lived in the town of Mattoon, Illinois, and their house-

Frank, Clyde, George, Mac, Ralph, and Earl Luby

hold bustled with a rowdy life unlike any other that Harry experienced during his melancholy boyhood. The forthright Irish Luby temperament came out in full force amongst their personalities—both boys' and girls'. Soon after their marriage, Harry and Julia added to the group a son of their own. He would grow to feel the kinship with these cousins and appreciate it as strongly as his father did.

Born in 1910, the year before his father's grand inaugural project, Robert "Bob" Luby was to be Harry and Julia's only child. The years to come provided him with a nomadic childhood, as his parents moved from city to city and state to state, opening cafeterias in new locations. In order to develop a strategy for growth and expansion, Harry once again had to pick the smartest path to follow. He looked around, noting the changes and trends affecting the now mobilized population of America. Then he had his second inspiration—or rather, the luminous recognition of a link in a larger pattern. The very thing that was making the country's newfound mobility possible—the very substance fueling the motorcars that Henry

Opal Spaulding, Hazel Stone, Joseph and Rose Luby,
Helen Blodgett, and Lola Johnston

Ford's assembly line put together—was oil. Oil production had become the latest, boldest industry spreading its exploratory fingers across the eastern half of the country, enticing workers to follow its lead, creating boomtown after boomtown throughout the states. And each new drilling center needed convenient dining facilities.

Companies in Harry's home state of Illinois had been drilling for oil for heating and lighting uses since the first wells were established in the 1850s, so the concept of the industry was hardly new to him. And Standard Oil had long been a presence in Missouri for the same reasons, although by 1911 it was officially dissolved, the casualty of a U.S. Supreme Court antitrust ruling handed down in 1909, the year Harry went to Chicago. But now, since Texas and Oklahoma had entered the competitions and cheap automobiles were creating a much larger demand for gasoline to quench their thirsts, fields were opening up everywhere. So Harry and Julia took to the oil trail. In a western-moving progression, they started cafeterias to service the new boom sites. And each cafeteria they built was one further evolutionary step removed from the original Springfield store.

Some of Bob Luby's earliest memories were acquired within the confines of his parents' cafeteria premises. He recalled as an eight-year-old arriving home daily from school to play in the basement of the second St. Joseph, Missouri, branch, the fifth cafeteria his parents had generated. The year before, he had lived in Joplin, and the year before that, in St. Joseph also, when that town's first store opened after Harry and Julia initially embarked on their journey out from Springfield.

Three years later, the Lubys left Missouri altogether, lured out of state for the first time to Muskogee, Oklahoma, where the oil fields were flourishing and creating business opportunities in many directions. There Harry opened a cafeteria with his first cousin Earl Luby as a partner, launching a precedent that would continue for the rest of his career, and infect the entire Luby family with the cafeteria fever. Then Harry and Julia, along with the young Bob, transferred to Ardmore the following year to open another store, leaving Earl to run the Muskogee branch. In 1921, only ten years after the New England Dairy Lunch made its debut, they entered Texas and started a cafeteria in Beaumont—the eighth of its kind.

The stay in Beaumont lasted one year. From there Bob Luby and his parents resided sequentially in Shreveport, Louisiana (for two years), and Waco, Texas. Below is a chronological list of their establishments, which also constitutes the expansion of one of the nation's first food franchises:

Springfield, second location — 1912
St. Joseph, Missouri — 1914
Joplin, Missouri — 1915
St. Joseph, second location — 1916
Muskogee, Oklahoma — 1919
Ardmore, Oklahoma — 1920
Beaumont, Texas — 1921
Shreveport, Louisiana — 1922
Waco, Texas — 1924
San Antonio, Texas — 1927

The result of this continuous moving, of course, was that Bob attended a number of schools before graduating from high school in San Antonio, Texas, in 1927. His family's migrations mapped the trek of the oil industry and of free enterprise across the midsouthern states — each new move signifying a larger leap in the development of the cafeteria's methods and surroundings.

Almost all the locations flourished. But at least in one instance, the social conditions in a town became too prohibitive for operation to continue. After the Ku Klux Klan — an organization that was gaining much greater force and political power in the South and Southwest during the early 1920s — demanded that Earl Luby join their ranks during his presence in Muskogee, Oklahoma, Earl knew he had a real dilemma on his hands. There could be no doubt about his choice, however. Upon his refusal to capitulate and don the white hood and robe, the Muskogee Klan members threatened both him and his business, warning him that they would "shut him down." Sensibly, Earl locked the doors and fled. The Muskogee store was the only one of Harry's ventures into the new concept of franchised cafeterias that ended his partnership with failure. As for Earl Luby, his move to manage the Ardmore store proved merely the first in a progression of increasing expansions. Eventually he moved to Dallas, Texas, relinquishing the Ardmore management to Julia Luby's sister Sadie and her husband, Ray Pressler, in order to cofound the Luby's No. 1 on Browder Street with Harry. After some years he would come to own several cafeterias outright, and represent the second strand of a three-strand division of Luby's tradition, only one of which has finally extended to the present day.

But there were to be no other adverse encounters during the widening spread of Harry Luby's cafeteria gospel across the United States. As far as Harry was concerned, the policy of expansion that he adopted during the early years—specifically the first fifteen years of his franchise—was as simple and elementary as his original twelve-foot hand-built counter: he would organize an operation in the new location, using more advanced and sophisticated plans, pushing his latest ideas to their limits. Before leaving the most recent store to move on, he would sell it, either to individuals from within his large contingent of first cousins or to other buyers. Usually he would retain a partial ownership, a modified partnership, guaranteeing him a percentage of the profits, thus insuring his ongoing franchised participation, and incidentally making his cafeterias the very first franchised restaurants of their type in America—in fact, a chain.

The reasoning behind this policy was also simple. Harry felt that the modifications he wished to execute in the next new store would have proven disconcerting to his already-established clientele. His customers had grown used to the way their particular cafeteria was run. They liked it. They knew what to expect. Therefore, their patronage was assured. To change things within a preexisting New England Dairy Lunch meant taking the risk of alienating them and losing their business. This way, he was able to keep their loyalties, and simultaneously help out family members who wanted to go into business for themselves.

His terms of sale were always benevolent. Invariably they demonstrated the same trust he himself earned from everyone—staff, customers, and purveyors. (The term *purveyors* is one used universally in the food industry to refer to suppliers.) "Pay me when you can," he once declared to a buyer who was concerned that he hadn't enough money both to run his newly acquired cafeteria and to reimburse Harry outright for the chance to do so. Harry possessed enough faith in the continuing prosperity of the store to know that he would get his money sooner or later, meanwhile providing the buyer with a profitable income. It was not his intention that anyone should suffer while working off their debt to him. On the contrary, he wished for his buyers to find the same comfortable level of return that he had, without groaning under a large financial burden.

Harry also began, in this period, to help some of his other cousins start their own individual cafeterias. Soon no less than eight out of eleven of his Mattoon-based first cousins—four of the boys, and all four girls—found their destinies intertwined with Harry's big idea and eventually grew intrigued enough to entrust their energies and their lives to the Luby's cafeteria concept.

It was to prove a sound investment.

□ □ □

Over those first early years during the migrations of the Luby family, Harry experimented with names for his stores. After trying out The New England Cafeteria, he affixed his own name: Luby's New England Cafeteria. Ultimately the stores adopted the Luby's Cafeteria name.

Whenever one of his cousins followed Harry's entrepreneurial example and entered the business on his or her own, with or without Harry's fiscal participation, Harry generously endorsed their use of the Luby's name as well. As a result, several Luby's opened in various Texas cities independent of Harry's managing hand, albeit with his help and encouragement and occasional financial affiliation. It wasn't long before Houston (Clyde Luby and his son Don Luby), Dallas (Earl Luby, Lola Luby Johnston, Hazel Luby Stone, and Helen Luby Blodgett, along with Harry), San Angelo (Clyde, Don, and Mac Luby), Abilene (Ray and Sadie Pressler, after leaving the Ardmore store), and Galveston (Clyde and Don Luby) were all homes to Luby's Cafeterias, independent of Harry's franchise.

The Luby family in its various branches had clearly decided that life and prosperity were more promising in the Lone Star State than back in the Midwest. Not one cousin who made the leap into cafeteria proprietorship remained in Illinois. By now other cafeterias had started appearing throughout the South, stores that would eventually develop into chains— notably Britling's, the first location of which opened in Birmingham, Alabama, in 1918; as well as Picadilly out of Baton Rouge, Louisiana; Morrison's out of Mobile, Alabama; and the S&W Cafeteria out of Asheville, North Carolina. Later on, in the 1940s, would come Furr's, started in Hobbs, New Mexico; and Wyatt's, out of Dallas.

But Texas, at this time, was still brand-new ground for cafeterias. So, by the late 1920s, most of the Lubys had turned thoroughly Texan. And the most Texan of all was Bob Luby himself, the only son of Harry and Julia.

No matter where else he was to roam in the future, Texas would always draw him back to its heart.

3

GROWING SEASON

□ □ □

Pigs get fat. Hogs get slaughtered.

CHARLES JOHNSTON

The oil route caravan that Harry and Julia Luby had embarked on sixteen years before reached its final destination in 1927, in a basement premises below the Texas Theater in downtown San Antonio. This was the spot where Harry planted his last self-started cafeteria. Shortly afterward, he turned the manager's position of the new store over to Julia's brother, Hugh Kotchie, and then achieved his dream of retiring from active participation in all his stores. Since, according to his son Bob, he had quit work "just as soon as he thought he could live comfortably for the rest of his life," it marked the pinnacle of his many feats that he could look forward to such a long lifetime stretching ahead in which to live comfortably. For he was only thirty-nine years old—and yet, during that brief sixteen years, he had established no fewer than eleven new cafeterias in four different states. He and Julia, already quite affluent, would grow a great deal more so over the next several decades, thanks to their investments and continuing partnerships in successful cafeteria ventures. Bob Luby was now finishing his education at Main Avenue High School and well on his way to an autonomous adulthood. No younger children waited in the wings for attention. The cafeterias were all well tended. The obstacles were now removed to a life of utter leisure.

At the time of Harry's retirement, an unprecedented, almost maverick prosperity was apparently blessing much of the nation. He had just helped to found the Browder Street Luby's Cafeteria in Dallas in partnership with his cousin Earl, and they were doing a landmark business. During these years Dallas had a population slightly under 330,000, and was the largest city in which Harry had undertaken to install one of his brainchildren. The Browder Street store, thereafter to be known as Dallas No. 1 among the Luby family, was the first cafeteria partnership in which Harry was not an on-site presence. Eventually he would enter into eight such partnerships, with locations in San Antonio, Fort Worth, Dallas (including a second store on Main Street and a third on Live Oak Street), Corpus Christi, El Paso, Harlingen, and Abilene.

The Jazz Age reigned. Times were changing so rapidly now that people welcomed every novelty and quick convenience with enthusiasm. The automobiles Henry Ford had launched from his assembly lines had multiplied; now he and a number of competitors produced hundreds of thousands, and many people owned cars who had never known the luxury of a horse-drawn carriage, or even a buckboard. After the armistice was declared ending the First World War, entrepreneurial spirit had seized America with a vengeance. Now Prohibition gave rise to a new gangster class; the cottage industries of bathtub gin distillation and bootlegging flourished; the stock market rocketed more and more wildly as speculators thrust fortunes into wildcat schemes. Fads, appliances, and inventions flooded the consumer's sight, accompanied by an industrial advertising drive to convince people to abandon their traditional values of careful saving and frugal purchases in favor of buying items they neither needed nor could afford. Inevitably, more and more credulous Americans' spending began to exceed their earnings, enabled by the innovation of credit debt, or "buy now, pay later" plans. Stocks were purchased on margin also, with the plan of putting 10 percent down for ownership and paying the other 90 percent later when the shares were sold at a gain, thereby ruining the integrity of the transactions, and ultimately contributing to the historic collapse on Wall Street. "The key to economic prosperity," a General Motors executive announced in 1929, prior to that fateful October 29 that nearly destroyed the nation's, and indeed the Western world's, economies, "is the organized creation of dissatisfaction."

Culture, of course, changed along with practical conditions. The end of the Great War also ended the country's repressive moral attitudes toward many aspects of life—particularly sex. Women's skirts grew shorter than ever before in the history of Western civilization—shorter than a Scotsman's kilt. The chance glimpse of a well-turned ankle was no longer the longed-for ideal to agitate a man's breathlessness; now the goal had climbed to a gartered thigh. The film censorship code had not yet been implemented into law, and silent movies reflected a preoccupation with the brazen "immorality" that accompanied the shifts in national consciousness and practices, often graphically depicting subjects that would later be categorized as verboten, such as premarital intercourse, adultery, drug addiction, and homosexuality. Clara Bow oozed the sex appeal that got defined for the first time on the silver screen in her movie *It. Our Dancing Daughters*, starring a long-legged Fort Worth, Texas, flapper named Joan Crawford, warned of the wanton dangers of indulging in smoking cigarettes, drinking cocktails, chasing men, and dancing the Charleston, the shimmy, and the Black Bottom—and of being a flapper. Materialism and greed kept escalating to a hotter scale. Fast wealth became the rule and the goal. New-made millionaires abounded.

But the wealth of the country still resided in only 0.1 percent of American families' homes, and these families had an income equal to the bottom 42 percent of the population. From 1923 to 1929, as manufacturing output per person-hour increased by 32 percent, corporate profits rose by 65 percent. But workers' wages only grew by 8 percent.

Still, at Luby's Cafeteria, workers could eat well on a pittance, and feed their families well too.

Harry and Earl Luby opened the new premises on Browder Street in Dallas two years before Black Friday and the onset of the Great Depression. Quickly their business grew flush with excited customers. Their competitors were small lunchrooms, hotel coffee shops, restaurants, cafés, and the occasional hamburger stand. Another competitor that would in time grow into a venerable Dallas institution, without ever branching out into other locations, also opened in 1927. Someone else had finally caught on to the simple beauty of the cafeteria idea. But the Highland Park Cafeteria was more suburban, catering chiefly to the housewives and their children who lived in the elegant precincts of Highland Park and University Park.

Soup recipes from Lola Luby Johnston's recipe book

Soup

Vegetable Soup

Put plenty of bones in pot and cover well with water. Add diced carrots, chopped onion, diced potatoes, chopped celery, and allow to cook at least 1 hour. Add 1 gallon can tomatoes or more and cook at least 1 hour longer. Salt.

Split Pea Soup

1 gallon can split peas, wash and cover with water. Add ham for seasoning and salt. All Allow to cook at least 2 hours or until thick. (Never add thickening.)

Cream of Spinach Soup

Heat milk in top of double boiler. When warm add chopped spinach, salt and butter and heat until hot and the spinach is tender.

Cream of Tomato Soup

Heat milk in top of double boiler. Heat tomatoes to boiling point and add 1 T soda to 1 gallon tomatoes. Mix well and add to hot milk. Season with salt and butter. Strain in soup bowl.

Potato Soup

Dice raw potatoes small, cook until tender with a little chopped onion. Drain and add to hot milk that has been heated in double boiler. Salt and add butter. Allow to cook together for at least 10 minutes to season well.

Harry and Earl Luby, however, held the position of lunch-line providers to all of professional downtown Dallas, with their large array of hot entrées and home-style desserts. In a period when many kinds of innovators and bootleggers, mob bosses and industrialists, stockbrokers and wheeler-dealers were springing up from the masses to take their places on the American scene, Harry and Earl had become the kingpins of the sliding tray, the new lords of plenty—the fairest, most honest businessmen in town.

```
                    Chicken Noodle Soup

        Heat chicken broth to boiling, thicken a
    little and add cooked noodles, salt and 1/2 t.
    currey powder dissolved in some of the hot soup.

                     Chicken Rice Soup

        Heat chicken broth to boiling and thicken
    a little and add cooked rice and 2 fresh tomatoes
    diced.

                      Navy Bean Soup

        Pick and wash two-thirds gallon can navy
    beans.  Cover with water well, season with
    ham and chopped onion.  Cook until beans are
    tender.  (3hrs.)  Be sure and have plenty broth.

                      Lima Bean Soup

        Pick and wash beans and cover well with
    water.  Add butter for seasoning and chopped
    onion.  When beans are about tender add a few
    canned tomatoes chopped fine (no juice.) and
    finish cooking.  Have plenty broth.

                      Oyster Soup

        Heat milk in double boiler.  Heat oysters
    (do not boil) and add to hot milk.  Season with
    butter and salt.  Never allow milk to boil for
    anything.
```

□ □ □

Harry Luby's philosophy didn't encourage either his or his partners' and employees' stakes in the millionaire race. Modesty, in the promotion of a stable, steady business base and an economically reasonable service to the community, was still and always his profile for success. The cafeterias he owned demonstrated his notions of fair dealing by offering the most lavish compensation policies in the food business. Each employee was paid a solid wage, and every manager received a mind-boggling 40 percent of the net income of the store he managed, leaving the remaining 60 percent to the collective or individual ownership.

This went against all accepted labor precepts of the 1920s on a franchised scale. In any other chain restaurant, managers could expect to be paid a regular wage like the other staff members, usually a small one. Only as recently as 1886 had organization of the American Federation of Labor in the United States been generated in response to the growing abuses committed by captains of industry against their workers, and the big labor disputes and strikes that had cost the lives of many men, women, and children.

But Harry Luby did not need AFL president Samuel Gompers's suggestions of cooperative negotiation between management and labor in order to heed his workers' requests or complaints, or to attend to their needs. He had worked too hard himself for that. And he was far too humane to pinch pennies—not when it came to employees and fair deals. He also understood a basic principle, which would prove to be one of the main keys to success for himself and everyone associated with him: in hard times and good, employees were usually willing to work just as hard as the person who hired them if they were justly rewarded for their efforts.

Harry, at age thirty-nine in his new home in San Antonio, felt content. He had attained everything he had strived for: a happy family, a wife so lively she put everyone else in the shade, and a stable, pleasant future. Meanwhile, the No. 1 store he had just opened in Dallas along with Earl Luby was to become a model of the Luby's future. Its name was still the New England Cafeteria, and would not be changed to Luby's for several years. But already its clientele comprised an intriguing cross-section of the public, prophetic in its multilevel strata of social positions. All of down-town Dallas came through the doors to walk down the cafeteria line. Em-ployees from AT&T and Dallas Power and Light took happy advantage of the ready meals and convenience. The entire legion of shop girls and salesclerks from Neiman-Marcus trooped in daily to sample the dozen sal-ads from the extra-long salad counter, the meat loaf and roast beef and fried chicken, the cobblers and cakes and pies. Just as the very first cafete-rias in existence had been started at the Kansas City YWCA in the 1890s to cater to the needs of working girls looking for a cheap place to eat, so the Browder Street Luby's continued this traditional role.

But there was certainly nothing very staid about certain other customers who entered the Luby's line. Multimillionaires rubbed shoulders with the more ordinary middle- and working-class folks at the steam tables. Every noon, John Carpenter, the chairman of the Southland Life Insurance Company and owner of some of the most valuable real estate in North Texas, sat down to eat his unvarying lunch of corn sticks and a bowl of veg-etable soup (which he always smothered under half a bottle of Heinz ketch-up), while perhaps at the very next table, several of the prostitutes that had marked out downtown as their territory were stoking their boilers for the coming evening's trade. These particular working girls practiced their trade not by walking the streets but by cruising them in their cars. One of the more vivacious of their number, known to the Luby's staff as "Bubbles," often dropped in for lunch with one or another of her many sugar daddies in tow. Earl and his employees called these men "red sugar daddies," due to the smears of lipstick with which Bubbles would have decorated their cheeks, mouths, and collars. In the early 1930s and then again later in the decade, the racing fraternity from the horse track at Fair Park would often dine at Luby's. During the three years leading up to the 1936 Texas Centen-nial World's Fair, the sport of horse racing was dormant in Dallas due to the demolition of the Fair Park track to make room for the Cotton Bowl football stadium, as well as the elaborate buildings and exhibition halls constructed for the celebration that marked 100 years of Texan independence from Mexico. But the track was rebuilt a couple of years later, and racing lumi-naries from all over North America, including the prominent Canadian thoroughbred owner A. G. Tarn and the world-famous jockey Johnny

Longden, liked to settle down to a plate of steaming home-cooking in the fragrant Luby's atmosphere.

The booming Dallas underworld, at that time still in the crude infancy of its wild career, also favored the Luby's cuisine. Benny Bickers, a notorious gambler, swung around to the back parking lot between the Baker Hotel and the cafeteria's rear entrance almost daily after his lunch to entice the kitchen staff into playing the numbers racket. Bickers and his friend Benny Binion, who got his hair cut at the barbershop next door on the corner of Browder and Commerce streets, were regular customers at both the Browder Street cafeteria and the Main Street Luby's (known as No. 2), which opened in 1931. Their rise to eminence in their field would later bring them a nastier form of renown; after Binion was accused of murdering his chief rival in gangland fashion, with a sawed-off shotgun, he beat the rap and wound up controlling gambling all over Dallas, operating from his and Bickers's Top of the Hill Casino just outside the city limits, and frequently consorting with fellow Dallas nightclub impresario Jack Ruby. Binion and Bickers ultimately co-owned casinos in Las Vegas as well, alongside their associates L.A. mobsters Mickey Cohen and Jack Dragna. (Both Bennys would be interviewed by the Warren Commission during its investigation into the slaying of President John F. Kennedy.) But the 1930s were still early days in the hectic careers of the two men, and the Baker Hotel parking lot was a likely outdoor casino in which to push their vocations. According to George Luby, the son of Harry's cousin George Luby Sr. (who began his own cafeteria career in 1932 by traveling down to Texas from his home in Mattoon, Illinois, to spend all four of his high school summers working at the Browder Street store), the cooks and busboys and other workers often won big sums of money in their crap games and numbers racket sport with Bickers and Binion. Of course, they lost their hard-earned money even more frequently.

At least they didn't have to spend it on food. All Luby's employees, in accordance with Harry's edict, ate their meals free of charge. This rule changed only under the pressure of rising costs in the 1960s, after which they paid half price for all food items. Until then, every busboy and busgirl, cook, pot washer, and line server lived in the culinary lap of luxury.

But the Depression began to take its toll on Dallas, eroding the prosperity that had captured the imaginations and pocketbooks of so many citizens. As it did all over the nation, so hunger crept up on the local populations of Texas. Harry's humanitarianism suddenly found itself challenged and stretched in many more directions than before. No longer was it merely his staff at the cafeterias who needed generous treatment. People were starving, homeless—and he was in the food business. So Harry instructed the managers of every cafeteria in which he owned an interest to feed the public, which meant anyone who came to the doors hungry, whether they could pay for their meals or not. "If you can't afford it," he told Boyd Morrow early one morning at the train station in San Antonio, where he was seeing Morrow off to his first management position, "then feed them and send *me* the bill." The policy was the same in Waco, Dallas, Beaumont—everywhere the cafeteria was in business. At 7:30 p.m., after the doors had closed for the evening, the line of down-and-outers formed to receive all the dishes that were left over from the day's service. Then they sat and ate their fill. No one got turned away. Earl Luby, Lola Luby Johnston, and all Harry's other partners and associates followed this policy. In the case of Earl Luby, the denizens of downtown Dallas could often see him on Commerce Street, handing out silver dollars to those he identified as down on their luck.

One Dallas personality named Pappy Dolsen, who was eventually to own several flourishing nightclubs and host a radio show of his own, depended so much upon Luby's benevolence that he later claimed that the cafeteria and its owners literally saved his life during those lean years. He would have starved to death, he said, if it hadn't been for Luby's. Another famous entrepreneur of Dallas, the supreme master of marketing and retail Stanley Marcus, went to bat for the cafeteria when one man (the only person in many decades of operation to do so) claimed to have contracted food poisoning from something he picked up on the line. Marcus's salesgirl employees, after all, dined there every single day—even trusting the honesty of the institution enough to jump up en masse and leave all their purses behind during one exciting noontime, when a gas explosion that killed nine people and injured thirty-nine rocked the Baker Hotel basement next door, and frightened everyone away from the Luby's premises. Each purse was later accounted for and restored to its owner, with its contents undisturbed.

The Browder Street Luby's Cafeteria
stood between these two hotels, the Baker and Adolphus, in Dallas.

A Luby's, Main Street, Dallas, Texas

Other stores had their own tales to tell of Luby's altruism. In Waco one young man who had stumbled and thumbed his way into town from the countryside without a nickel in his pocket, stepped into the New England Cafeteria on a sunny morning, drawn by the delicious smells that wafted out onto the sidewalk. He knew he couldn't pay for a meal, but his hunger was so stark, and his longing so intense, that he felt compelled to pick up a tray anyway and travel down the line, selecting his stomach's desire among the entrées. When he reached the cashier, he sheepishly glanced down at the tray loaded with crockery and food and admitted, "You'll have to take this back. I can't actually pay for it. I'm sorry. I just couldn't resist having it in front of me for a few minutes. But I tell you what—if you'll accept my watch in earnest for it, I'll pay you back as soon as I can." To which the cashier replied, "I'll have to talk to the manager." The manager came forward. "Son," he said, "we don't want your watch. But you look honest. I've got orders from the boss not to let anyone leave this place hungry. Go ahead, take your food to a table and eat. You can come pay us back later, when you get a job."

Years later in 1949, when Bob Luby and his partner went to Waco to open a new store, they suffered a small setback on the very eve of their first day. During the final preparations, a piece of counter glass got shattered. It was the close of the business afternoon, too late to get it replaced. Bob, his partner, and their new Waco manager, Maynard Koplan, didn't know what to do. The opening was only hours away. Koplan rushed to the local glass shop just as it was shutting its doors. The company refused to take the job—that is, until the owner heard it was for Luby's.

Immediately, he yelled to one of his men to cut the necessary piece of glass and bevel the edges, a task that took about ten minutes altogether. When Koplan expressed his appreciation for the special treatment, and asked how much money was due on the bill, the owner replied, "Nothing." The greatest thing that had ever happened to him, he said, was the day Luby's management had trusted him enough to feed him for free— without even accepting his watch as collateral. At last he now had an opportunity to repay the kindness.

But the complex inevitabilities of human nature hold true. No matter what or where the venue and circumstances might be, there is always a sour apple somewhere around. Thus, the exception to this happy lineup of

Four-year-old Charles with his father, Charles,
and mother, Lola Ethel Luby Johnston, ca. 1914

grateful Depression guests was a particular couple whom the Luby family fed at the Browder Street cafeteria in Dallas. Every single night this husband and wife would join the line of poverty-stricken supplicants, filling their trays with free dinners. A few years later, this same couple not only retrieved their fortunes; they became rich and prominent in the community. After the reversal occurred, they also remained loyal Luby's customers—the most regular, and the worst, most bitter complainers that the Browder Street store ever served.

Such ingratitude was an insignificant bother in the face of so much magnanimity. The example Harry Luby set remained permanently ingrained in those who observed it. "He touched me in more ways than you can imagine," Boyd Morrow was to tell an interviewer later. The best aspect of this virtue was that Harry's influence would percolate down not only to his son Bob, but into other younger-generation branches of his family—especially to his second cousin Charles Johnston, the son of his first cousin Lola Luby Johnston.

Charles Johnston (like Bob Luby, an only child, and born in the same year as Bob, 1910) got his introduction to the cafeteria business inside the Browder Street store. He was not yet twenty when he came down to Texas from Colorado, where he had grown up. Where Bob Luby inherited his father's ingenuity and business acumen, Charles was to prove the legatee of Harry's "people" skills—his sincerity, willingness to listen to suggestions and complaints, and amiable personality—the grease that would later help to lubricate an empire. Like Harry before him, Charles would eventually inspire devotion and dedication in his future employees equal to the highest degree of loyalty that could be found in a workplace.

One early hourly worker said of Harry Luby, "I walked in off the street and Harry Luby had never seen me before. But he greeted me like I was his banker, and he treated me that way from then on. He had a great respect for human dignity, and it extended from the pot washer to the produce vendor." His cousin's son Charles was just as kind and respectful—and it would make all the difference to the continuation of Luby's success.

Throughout the 1930s Charles Johnston continued to work in the Browder Street cafeteria for his Uncle Earl and his cousin Harry, learning the grunt work as well as the finer nuances of the trade. In 1931, at age twenty-one, he met the beautiful and lively Gertrude "Trudy" Cunningham, a native of Oak Cliff in Dallas, when he happened to be in her part of town picking up a barrel of pickles to deliver to the kitchen. The eighteen-year-old Gertrude was working in her own uncle's barbershop on Jefferson Street at the time. Apparently Charles thought he could double up on his errands and squeeze in a haircut. Soon their romance—begun, as Charles was often later to quip, over a pickle barrel—sweetened to the point of commitment, and the pair eloped to Norman, Oklahoma, where the marriage laws were looser than in Texas.

After his wedding, Charles brought his new wife into the Browder Street premises to work beside him. At first the two worked on the line, washed turnip greens, cleaned and sliced liver, prepared salads and desserts, and swabbed grease traps and silverware like all the other members of the staff. It wasn't long before Charles proved to be as good a cook as any person Harry had ever hired. In fact, Charles had a passion and a gift for food. So

Young Gertrude in high school

did Gertrude. After a while, she began to help supervise the entire kitchen, while Charles acted as cashier during the lunch hours and jack-of-all-trades before and after.

A day in the life of a cafeteria during this period was filled with countless chores. Everyone did the hard jobs, from the manager on down to the pot washers and cooks. Such a routine could be found exemplified by the Browder Street and Main Street branches in Dallas.

The morning would begin at dawn (or before dawn in winter), with the purchases of fresh vegetables at the market and the receiving of meats ordered from purveyors. Meat came whole; every manager started his training by learning to expertly butcher and fillet sides of beef, pork, and entire fish, as well as how to turn out a good pastry, how to wash, peel, and chop vegetables cleanly and thriftily, and how to mix salad dressings. By mid-morning, when the custards were baking, the stews stewing, and the soups simmering, a brief break was permitted. The staff relaxed, smoked, and chatted before resuming the last preparations for the day's service. At the end of the day, after service was concluded, everyone without exception put his hand to clean the filthy grease traps, the most unpleasant task of all.

The system for tallying the price of a meal for a customer was purely mental in those days, requiring a sharp eye and the arithmetic skills to quickly sum up the contents of a tray at a glance. Most items were priced uniformly within their category. Thus, the cost of entrées ran from eight to fifteen cents; bread, whether cornbread or dinner rolls, was three cents per piece; vegetables cost three to seven cents; and all desserts were five cents. One could eat a large meal for a quarter. The cashier at the end of the line had to add each customer's trayful within a second or two, announce the total, get paid, and make change in rapid succession to keep the line moving. A small push bell, such as the ones found on old hotel reception desks, resided next to the cashier's hand. Whenever customers left their tables after eating, the cashier would ring the bell to alert a busboy or busgirl to remove the dirty dishes. Back in the 1930s, a city was a very different aural world from the one we know now. The sounds on the street outside would fall strangely on our ears. Firemen manually clanged a big bell mounted on the side of the truck whenever they rushed to a fire. Automobile Klaxons shouted *ahhooo-gah*, or their horns squawked, beeped, or blared in the traffic; newsboys bellowed out the daily headlines, urging passersby to "read all about it," street vendors hollered advertisements of their wares, from "hot tamales" to "roasted goobers, get your hot roasted peanuts here." And, indoors at Luby's, the lunchtime conversational clamor was punctuated with the silvery music of the bell's chime.

At some point in the 1930s, Charles Johnston acquired a small interest in the Browder Street store, pooling his investment with Harry's and Earl's. But by the time the Main Street store opened in 1931, several other cousins of Harry's had moved to Texas to stake their futures on the cafeteria line. Charles's parents, Lola Luby Johnston and Charles Edwin Johnston, bought a one-third partnership in Luby's No. 2. So did Lola's sister Hazel Luby Stone, along with her husband, Russell Stone. Also included were Lola and Hazel's sister Helen Luby Blodgett and, of course, their brother Earl, each holding a one-sixth interest in the partnership. Now the second of what would become three branches of the multiple franchise of independent Luby's Cafeterias was established. The branches consisted of Harry's original ventures; Earl's Dallas-based holdings, together with and separate from Harry's; and the other stores that were beginning to proliferate across the wide landscape, chiefly owned and operated by other siblings and/or cousins.

This three-branched tree, the limbs of which at first sprang so similarly from the trunk of Harry's idea, would eventually grow and flourish in very different directions, based on the philosophies that governed the owners. Harry's philanthropic views, for example, were not consistently reflected in his fellow family members' practices. The revolutionary formula that he had devised—a 40 percent annual net-profit income bestowed upon the manager of each store in the belief that such generosity would in turn generate superior income to the owner/60 percenters—didn't always appeal to the other partners and independents. They were not necessarily willing to compensate their management so lavishly; they were not willing to treat staff with the same kind considerations. And this departure from Harry's basic strategy, while the very foundations of a long-term entity were being laid, would yield not only different success and longevity rates for each of the three branches but different moral results as well. In this way, Luby's Cafeterias became an interesting gauge of the correlation between high ethical conduct and financial reward.

4

FIRST HARVEST

Portrait of a Budding Magnate

□ □ □

*I always like to know the "doers" of a business, the people
who make it happen. The reason I like to meet them is to let them
know how much I appreciate their ability. At the cafeterias, my most
admired employee is the dishwasher, a talent that I never had.*

CHARLES JOHNSTON

Long before he went off to college, Bob Luby set his heart on going into
the cafeteria business. Julia Luby tried to warn him that this might be a
foolish decision. Often she spoke of the many other professional choices
he could make, despite the fact that her own sisters, Sadie Pressler and
Bess Ragland, and their husbands had now joined forces in the industry
and were busy making their livings on the line. "My mother," Bob said
later, "tried to talk me out of it, since she knew all about the hard work and
long hours. Back then you opened at seven in the morning and closed at
eight-thirty at night, six days a week. On Sunday you came back for half a
day for extra cleaning."

But her gentle parental advice wouldn't deflect him. He had spent his teenage years following precisely that regimen during his out-of-school hours, and knew very well what he would be in for. The innovation his father had pioneered inspired in him a vision of where such savvy could travel, and how far.

As for college, he looked upon its opportunities as a large intellectual cafeteria, with dishes of all kinds—a view that perhaps reflected his earliest conditioning and entrepreneurial environment. Despite the fact that he was majoring in business administration, which had no foreign language requirement and therefore suited his strictly monolinguistic talents, he wished to acquire a broad education, "a little bit of everything," without specializing in any one field. The University of Texas in Austin seemed ideally equipped for this approach.

One of the goals that Bob looked forward to achieving was the further implementation of refinements to the business operations that his father had developed. For instance: the old, simplified form of accounting, in which the day's earnings were kept in a can of dried beans or the three-gallon ice cream freezer secreted in the kitchen and taken out when it was time to pay purveyors and staff in cash, was a bit too primitive for what Bob envisioned in a future cafeteria empire. Decor was another challenge he wished to meet—to create a pleasantly consistent atmosphere for diners. Training programs also intrigued him. But first he had to dip his toe in the water.

He was so eager to wet that toe that he dropped out of college only halfway through, in 1931, seizing the chance to join with Boyd Morrow, a former Baylor University student who had worked his way through college at the Waco branch of Harry's New England Cafeteria as a busboy, and with Ralph Luby in opening a new cafeteria in Corpus Christi, Texas. But after a brief stint on the Gulf Coast Bob returned to the University of Texas to complete his B.A., graduating in 1934. He felt that all America was calling to him, and he listened hard. He intended to accomplish three goals at once. He would gamble by entering into business in a bigger way than before; he would spread the gospel of Luby's throughout the land; and he would see and experience more of America than the Mid- or Southwest.

So, in partnership with his aggressively enterprising second cousin Earl,

Bob followed Horace Greeley's famous advice and went west—all the way to California. It was Earl Luby's idea for the two to try their luck in San Francisco. If you were going to go west, Earl and Bob reasoned, you might as well go as far west as the ocean's edge allowed. So Earl left the young Charles Johnston in charge of the Browder Street cafeteria in Dallas while he journeyed out to push his San Francisco gambit. Charles would remain there for the rest of the 1930s, up until the outbreak of World War II, running that store with his wife, Gertrude, and acquiring more management experience. He had automatically won his cousin Bob's liking as well as respect for his honest, amiable personality and manner. The two West Coast adventurers wouldn't meet back up with Charles for quite a while yet. But cooperation can take place across thousands of miles, and the arrangement worked out so well for Earl and his Dallas partners that Bob took special notice, mentally filing his observations away for later.

The location Bob and Earl found for the new cafeteria they jointly established lay in the basement of the Sutter Hotel at 191 Sutter Street. The Sutter stood on the corner of Kearny, just a few blocks from Union Square in the heart of downtown San Francisco. Chinatown sprawled right next door. Nearby were a number of elegant stores, small shops, and the prosperous financial district.

But timing is as important to any budding business endeavor as the apparent blessing of location. The year Bob and Earl landed in the City by the Bay was a stormy one, full of change. Construction had just begun on both the Golden Gate Bridge and the Oakland Bay Bridge, the two enormous projects that would unite the urbanized peninsula with the Marin County headlands and the other mainland across the bay, making the city less dependent on the ferry system. Shipyards and Italian fishing boats littered the shores. The port, one of the most important in the United States, was lined with large wharves catering to shipping and ocean liners for passengers to Asia and elsewhere in the Pacific. Military installations included an army base, the Presidio, and an old pre–Civil War–era brick and granite bastion, Fort Point, looming over the throat of the Golden Gate where the powerful white-topped waves lapped against the stone and concrete quay. Naval activity was spread from San Francisco across to Oakland, and up and down the coast.

Altogether the city had a reputation for eclecticism, sophistication, a legacy of wealth, frontier maverick energy, vice, and radical thinking. Its wild, gold rush–era Barbary Coast area had been the first place to introduce the precursor to cafeteria-style eating, when the many bars and saloons would provide smorgasbords of free dishes to entice drinking customers and accompany heavy beer and whiskey sessions. Bob and Earl's new venture was to be a more civilized and domesticated, tee totaler's continuation of that tradition.

But they happened to be starting it up right at the height of a major civic conflict. Because of the concentration of shipping-related vocations and trade, and because San Francisco had always been a labor-oriented hot spot with a strong union history, the residents took labor action for granted as an inevitable right. Therefore, in early May 12,000 longshoremen went on strike at the docks. On July 3 riots broke out across the streets after the strike moved from the waterfront personnel through the other unions to the warehouse district. The riots were to last for three violent days and pit unionists against the police force, leaving twenty-four people wounded and two dead. It ended after Bloody Thursday, and led to the General Strike that paralyzed the city's functions for another three days.

Bob and Earl Luby couldn't have picked a more colorful landing place in all America in which to plant their hopes. Four years prior to their advent, Dashiell Hammett had published *The Maltese Falcon*, and had followed it with *The Thin Man* only two years later. Downtown San Francisco was now Sam Spade territory. It was also a simmering international melting pot, a nexus of cultures as rich and flamboyant as New York City. Consequently, all kinds of ethnic foods, including, of course, fresh seafood, Italian and Asian cuisine, Russian, Hungarian, French, and other European dishes, as well as traditional all-American meals, were readily available to the local population. It remained to be seen whether good, old-fashioned southern-style cooking would hold an equal appeal.

It didn't.

Quite shortly after the two partners opened their doors inside the Sutter Hotel in early 1935, it became clear that heavy southern meals, with their arrays of fried meats and chicken and richly seasoned vegetables, didn't suit northern Californians' appetites or palates. Although they must have served every single Texan in the Bay Area at one time or another, it seemed there were simply not enough Lone Star expatriates to consume all their surplus. The hotel basement location was not the most favorable for business either. Soon Earl saw the writing on the wall and left Bob to go back to Dallas. Bob persevered for two years, until it was obvious that the problems originally generated by the Great Maritime Strike of 1934 could not be overcome. Then he, too, decided to return to Texas.

But he wasn't giving up. Shipping home all that remained of the dead enterprise, the kitchen equipment, he calculated that it would cost five thousand dollars to set up another cafeteria on Live Oak Street in Dallas, in the midst of a tried-and-true customer base, and that he could make ten thousand dollars a year selling meals on the same price scale that had been fixed for several years now.

"That was a nice markup," he would later conclude.

Harry Luby loaned him the necessary money, since all the assets Bob possessed were tied up in his San Francisco equipment. He had nearly lost those too. Labor disputes, the kind that troubled the city, had in the end proven to be Bob's downfall. His landlord, according to Bob a true gentleman, appreciated his efforts to keep the cafeteria going and to pay everyone what they were owed. He told Bob, "By rights this equipment in here now belongs to me. But I think you did everything you could do, and therefore you may keep it." A grateful lessee found the Live Oak Street premises back in Dallas, moved the furnishings in, and got to work.

But in the course of his West Coast sojourn, he had also won another prize. One day, while serving up entrées on the line in the Sutter Hotel basement, he spotted a tall, dark-haired, slender beauty moving toward him on the opposite side of the counter. Instantly he was smitten. "See that woman?" he said to the counter girl standing beside him. "I'm going to marry her."

The woman's name was Georgia Wenglein. She had grown up in the small agricultural town of Ukiah, California, 120 miles north of the Bay Area, with the rest of her large family, and then taken a job in San Francisco with Standard Brands. With all the determination in his nature, Bob wooed her and fulfilled his romantic prophecy. When he traveled home to Texas, Georgia Wenglein Luby went with him—as did her brother, George.

George Wenglein, who had had no food-service experience in his hometown of Ukiah, except for picking fruit at harvesttime, had studied engineering at San Jose State University. He was only nineteen years old when his new brother-in-law talked him into moving to Dallas for the summer. "'If you want, you can come down to Texas and work for me for the summer and help me out,'" George quotes Bob as saying. "'If you like it and decide that's what you want to do, you can stay on. If you don't, I'll still pay you for the summer's work, and you can go back to college.'" George concludes the story with four fateful words: "I never went back."

Eventually George became a partner in the Live Oak store, known as Dallas No. 3, along with another talented friend, John Lee. Both Wenglein and Lee would remain active pioneers in the Luby's organization for the rest of their working lives. It proved a smart decision for everyone concerned; on a good day, the Live Oak store made as much as $175, and there were many good days ahead. Dallas, and most of Texas, as it turned out, loved both cafeteria eating and southern food. Even if the partners only had 200 such profitable days per year, it meant one single store could earn a gross of $35,000 annually—a phenomenal profit for the Depression years.

But no matter what other moneymaking improvements Bob experimented with in his ventures, one precept that Harry had instituted remained locked adamantly into place. This was the benevolent philosophy of compensation for management. Every manager would always earn 40 percent of the net profit for the store he oversaw. And this policy made immense practical sense, as well as providing an example of generosity. As Charles Johnston was to express it years later, when defending the tradition to company CPAs, board members, and others who declared themselves to be baffled and appalled at such munificence, "The advantage of giving management a large percentage of a store's profits should be obvious. You don't have to wake the person up, dress him, and show up to do his job for him."

Two years after his return, Bob opened yet another Luby's branch, this time in El Paso, along with his aunt Bess and uncle R. E. Ragland, his brother-in-law, George Wenglein, and his father as an inactive investor/partner. George, now twenty-three years old, took all the money he had made at the Live Oak store and funneled it as his equity into the partnership, marking his first real ownership of a cafeteria. The process of assimilation into the Luby family ethos and endeavors had been repeated; the nature of the lively Lubys and their business successes proved once again infectious. By the end of the decade, Bob Luby was the coproprietor of two flourishing cafeterias, 650 miles apart. The prospects he and Harry had foreseen—of a uniquely American idea that consolidated a gradually swelling financial prosperity with strong, close family foundations, intensive but satisfying work, a sense of beneficial service to a community, and mutual camaraderie among all the staff and owners involved in the businesses— were getting realized.

But Bob understood that the ideal could grow richer yet, and embrace many more participants. Now that the Depression was nearly over, the future seemed bright. But a new obstacle was thrown across his path: in December 1941, the Japanese bombed Pearl Harbor.

With war now officially declared by the United States, Bob, along with his peers, felt the urgent call to defend his country.

5

RECRUITING NEW HANDS

FOR THE SECOND CROP

The Band Begins to Gather

□ □ □

The first person from the new El Paso cafeteria to answer the summons to fight for his nation's future was George Wenglein. In 1942, at age twenty-eight, he said good-bye to the food business and his sister and brother-in-law and enlisted in naval flight training school. That left the thirty-two-year-old Bob to run the El Paso store.

But Bob, in turn, had already heard the call to duty. His first wartime decision was to hire a young Fort Worth–born salesman and golfing partner named Arthur S. Kidd, whom he had met and befriended through Swift & Company, the meat purveyor servicing the Dallas stores, to take over the managerial duties in George's place. Ironically enough, in doing so, Kidd defected from one dynamic family culture to join another. Art's father had worked for Swift for forty years. Art himself had been Swift's representative for nine years, since 1933, when at the age of twenty-two he had started calling on Luby's in Dallas to take their orders. Swift & Company was a Kidd tradition. Mr. Kidd was sorry to see his son depart from it, but Art's friendship with the Luby's group of young men, combined with the chance to improve his position and prospects in the world, were reasons enough to justify the jump. Even though Art knew the work would be hard, the Luby magnetism once again proved irresistible. And indeed, Art Kidd promptly demonstrated his worth, his firm grasp of the business, and the rightness of his choice, by keeping the El Paso cafeteria not only open but running profitably throughout the rest of the war, despite the acute hurdles of rationing and labor shortages.

After installing Art Kidd as the new El Paso manager, Bob regretfully sold the Live Oak cafeteria. Then he joined the Army Air Corps. There was simply no way he could run Live Oak from a distance, and he didn't have anyone else primed and waiting in the wings to take over. George Wenglein was already out of the picture, and John Lee had also just donned a naval uniform. Lee worked in Naval Food Operations in Dallas for his first year's duty, and then shipped out, bound for the Pacific theater. Of the active partnership, there was no one left at all. Bob's cousin Charles Johnston, now thirty-two, had volunteered for military service as well, leaving his wife, Gertrude, and Browder Street behind to enter the Army Air Corps. In fact, almost all the young men of Luby's were patriots on the march.

For the war's duration, Bob would be stationed in California as an intelligence officer. But he had no intention of forgetting his peacetime occupation. For the first time since graduating from college, he wasn't embroiled in the trenches of a business. Therefore, he could enjoy a new and unaccustomed luxury: to reflect from a distance, from a perspective uncluttered by work pressures, schedules, cooking and supply issues. He would devote every spare minute to honing his intellectual and problem-solving skills.

For the next couple of years he seized the military interlude to review the difficulties and challenges inherent in the food business, and to carefully rethink his dream. These concerns included planning how to set up future cafeterias that would be run along more efficient lines and shorter hours. "I thought about the operation and how it could be simplified and upgraded," he said later. "I envisioned a cafeteria that would serve the highest quality food, pay good wages, and not require working dawn to dark." The contrast between his daylight activities and his cafeteria fantasies must have been a vivid one; his misgivings about the long hours required by the food business, and methods with which to resolve such issues, probably competed strangely with the need to defeat the Japanese in the Pacific theater. "I used those years in the Air Corps to think," he said later, "and to make contacts for the business I hoped to start once I was discharged."

But as he was destined to discover before the war was over, his best contact had already been made. Soon he would have the opportunity to assess just how fortunate that already-existent connection could be.

Meanwhile, another neophyte was entering the Luby's ambit. Herbert Knight, a sixteen-year-old farm boy from rural Freestone County, Texas, moved to Dallas in 1943 to attend business school. In order to pay for his tuition, he took a job busing tables in the Main Street store owned by Harry Luby's cousins.

It wasn't very long before another bus-person got transferred to that same store. Her name was Ina Faye; she was pretty, charming, and seventeen years old, and she had a bright and sassy intelligence with plenty of pragmatic good sense. She was also from Herbert's home county. And in the course of their daily duties, Herbert followed in the footsteps of Charles Johnston and Bob Luby: he found himself falling in love while doing cafeteria business.

It was more than an adolescent crush. The wartime milieu, one that often forces people to grow up more quickly than they normally would, seemed conducive to a mutual understanding. The two teenagers worked together from early morning to the restaurant's close, taking their breaks at the same time as the rest of the staff, listening on the radio to the war news interspersed with the music of Benny Goodman, Glenn Miller, and Vera Lynn while they all sat around the dining tables, wondering about the future. Their bosses—Lola Luby Johnston; her husband, Charles Edward Johnston; siblings Helen Luby Blodgett, Hazel Luby Stone, and Russell Stone; and of course, Earl Luby—maintained the "one big happy family" atmosphere that encouraged courtship and made it easy for true romance to bloom once again under the Luby's roof. Often Russell Stone and Charles Johnston would take off in the early afternoons to go watch a newsreel at the nearby theater, leaving the women to run the kitchen. According to Herbert Knight, Lola Johnston, a genuine spitfire by nature, did all the pastry creations, desserts, and baking. Hazel Stone cooked the "ranges"—the meats and vegetables that would fill the bulk of the meal. Helen Blodgett oversaw all salad preparations. The men computed and paid the bills, doling out cash from the front register for everything but the meat account. By the time Herbert had worked there eight months, he had finished school and gotten promoted from busboy to full-time employee. His chief tasks included butchering, all types of kitchen work, and acting as cashier. At only seventeen years of age, he became an official assistant manager. He was, in effect, one of the first management trainees to be hired from outside the family circle. And he was already engaged to be married.

Then he, too, heeded the call to arms and signed up for the U.S. Navy.

Luckily, Herbert survived the war without getting wounded. In 1946, exactly one day after his discharge from the military, he married his sweetheart, Ina Faye.

Lunchtime at Dallas Luby's No. 2, 1954

Herbert Knight and Frank Luby, 1954

The nineteen-year-old didn't need to look far to find himself a job with a future. As always, Luby's took care of its own. The shape of civilian life now lay before him and his bride as graphically clear as a pie chart: his first duties after rejoining the cafeteria staff would, in fact, include cutting pies.

Meanwhile, Bob Luby had been planning great advances. The next step took place in 1945. It was during that year that Bob Luby happened to run into an old friend and relation while on his way to an intelligence course at a Florida school, 3,000 miles away from his station in California. And it also just so happened that that Luby family member had also been pondering the possibilities of a future cafeteria empire. Charles Johnston had spent the war years so far running an army post exchange in Florida. The two cousins were delighted to see one another, and even more delighted, in the course of their discussions, to find that their ambitions matched as beautifully as their talents complemented each other. Putting their heads together, they compared notes on the refinements they had separately been envisioning for a chain of cafeterias—an enterprise that would embrace Harry Luby's principles and make everyone involved wealthy in the bargain. After hours of lively exchange, Bob told his cousin his verdict. With all their most recently developed ideas in place, he said, "I believe we can work reasonable hours with multiple management" — the most important keystone to his plan — "pay the best wages in town, and offer the best food and service at a good price. And if that doesn't work, then I'm getting out of the cafeteria business."

"Count me in," Charles replied. Solemnly they both shook hands on the new perspective. By the time the visit concluded, they had agreed to meet up in Texas as soon as the war was over, and get rolling.

When Bob returned to California, one of the first things he did was to arrange a rendezvous with Wenglein. George had now trained as a navy pilot. Like John Lee, he was about to head for the South Pacific. No one could guess in those days who would live through the bloody conflict and who wouldn't. The future was uncertain, but of course everyone hoped and longed for a golden life of new vigor once the fighting ended. Bob sat George down, outlined the plan he and Charles had developed, and asked him if he wanted to be in on it. George's answer rang out a resounding *yes*.

So did John Lee's, once Bob approached him with the same question.

Bob Luby and Charles Johnston, 1950

John Lee's people-managing skills had already been identified by the others. But just as important was the keen discrimination of his nose and taste buds. Lee's highly evolved sense of taste set him apart from most common folks, just as his culinary flair marked him out as an ideal food business practitioner. Creative recipes spilled out of him; it seemed he was a born chef. He was particularly inventive when it came to improving the more mundane dishes, like pan-fried steak. Turning a simple but boring standby into a crowd-pleaser was his specialty. And his gift for delicacy when dealing with employees, for framing what might sound like a critical comment into a kindly and helpful piece of advice, was a priceless asset. People listened to Lee. They welcomed his supervision. They instinctively recognized his humane touch, the way he made sure any customers, no matter how meager their purse, would, with a manager's beneficent recommendations, be able to choose a good and nourishing meal for themselves. Naturally Bob Luby and Charles Johnston were eager to nail him down for their grand scheme.

But there still remained a few more gaps to fill. In order to build an empire, one needs a full cabinet ministry. Not the least post at such a table is the chief of finance. Within the corridors of his California military posting, Bob had encountered just the right person.

Norwood Jones was one of Bob's fellow officers at Santa Ana Army Base. He also was a Texan, a Dallasite born and bred. Best of all, he already possessed considerable accounting experience and financial expertise. When Bob explained his ideas to Jones, he accepted the invitation to become an ally.

And now, as the war years came to a close, the band of men and women who would form a young, new generation of Luby's entrepreneurs was almost fully assembled. They would soon transform the mom-and-pop aspect of the cafeteria business into a large and elaborate machine, fulfilling every single one of Harry Luby's original prerequisites—fulfilling, in fact, the American Dream.

6

THE $60,000 INCUBATOR

□ □ □

Seldom can there be there found in the business world a more balanced and auspicious partnership than that of Bob Luby and Charles Johnston. The unlikelihood of this fact is, in retrospect, one of the most striking aspects of it. To meet the two cousins face to face, one might not have imagined such a coupling could be very effective, or even possible, so different were their personas. One might have received an impression of lopsidedness, perhaps, at the very least. Bob, a blunt-spoken dynamo of honed ambition, strong opinions, and flamboyant style, held within him a cool business drive that cut through obstacles like the proverbial knife through soft butter. He was no diplomat, but he could decode intricate financial riddles, slice the tangles of commercial red tape, and spring from point A to point D by rising completely above the hurdles of points B and C. He had inherited his mother's feisty and determined nature and her willingness to take risks, and it showed in the matter-of-fact and often abrupt way he handled relationships.

Charles, for his part, acted as the gentle, kindly listener with a deft way of guiding people through their questions and confusions. He was the quiet, unassuming one, the genial fellow who, to an outside observer, might have at first seemed overshadowed or even dominated by his charismatic cousin. But appearances are so often deceiving. Charles had what it took to dull the potential thorns the two would otherwise have encountered among employees, purveyors, and contracted artisans, almost before they arose. He took the time to salve difficult "people" issues when Bob had no patience for dealing with them. His thoughtfulness, circumspection, and sharp intelligence were invaluable assets. So, despite their disparate personalities, Bob and Charles performed beautifully as crankshaft and piston, interlocked and working in tandem to produce power to spare. Each, in his own way, possessed both opposite and apposite talents to contribute toward their organization. United, they made a formidable team.

Perhaps the most outstanding force they shared and both brought to their infant endeavor was the optimistic confidence of servicemen who had just returned triumphant from a wartime victory. The same was true of their cohorts. All the young lions attached to this project felt charged with an impetus toward the modern, prosperous America opening before them. It was an attitude that infused large numbers of Americans in the mid- and late 1940s. They had trounced the ruthless Axis Powers, the Germans, Italians, and Japanese. Now they were going to get things done at home, and they were going to do them right. The Depression was over. The clouds of war had dispersed. Fresh opportunities loomed everywhere. Returning military personnel had a new maturity fostered by their combat experiences, new skills combined with a travel-based worldliness that they had not possessed before, new discipline, new energy to burn in improving their statuses, and a new sense of democratic entitlement that many, especially those from working-class backgrounds, might previously never have dared to claim. Having fought for their country, now they had earned the chance to benefit from their sacrifices. The nation did not lie in shambles, the way most of Europe did; there was no slow and weary scramble upward from the bombed-out ruins of cities or societies. Nor was there any political oppression to hold them back, and little economic disaster from which to have to reconstruct a viable industry. The similarities between America after World War II and the country's early days of pioneer settlement are inescapable: these men shared the same drive as their immigrant ancestors, plunging into a wilderness full of promise and possibility.

So the band of collaborators waiting to create an empire was already boostered with the best possible fuel. And they had acquired the tools for building.

The first facility Bob and Charles set up made use of that very same military legacy that had granted these psychological rewards. The two partners pursued and won a contract to open a large cafeteria for the Veterans Administration's Dallas office at Love Field. Although this was an institutionalized setting, and seemingly a far cry from the Browder Street, Main Street, and Live Oak Street Luby's environments, the reality of its routine differed very little from those cafeterias. The same tasks had to be performed; the same types of food had to get served in the same ways (although not necessarily the same *quality* of food, a circumstance that in itself could teach a lot about why better food would, in the long run, generate a better profit); and the same attention to detail and long, hard hours were required to run the business efficiently.

The idea behind the Love Field operation seemed elegant in its simplicity: the place would act as a "boot camp," a refresher course and training ground both for the friends who had already tried their hands at the food business before the war, such as John Lee and George Wenglein, and for their more recently enlisted comrades who needed to learn the basics of the industry they had just agreed to enter.

This was a smart strategy. After nearly half a decade in the armed forces, even old hands like Bob and Charles, who had, after all, grown up in cafeterias, felt a little rusty and out of date. Here lay the chance to put some of the refinements and notions they had been developing during the war years into practice before bursting out onto the civilian scene, where consumers would have to be lured and seduced into giving the cafeterias a try. A test tube situation with a captive customer base was the ideal spot in which to perfect their procedures without losing a large portion of the capital they were ready and willing to risk. And Bob Luby and Norwood Jones, in particular, had good reason to aim for thorough experimentation, for they had both made very extensive sums of money by investing heavily in the stock market during the war. Their philosophy at the time had been that if the Allies won, stock prices would skyrocket; and if the Axis countries won, according to Luby, "the world was going to pot anyway." So there seemed little to be lost by the gamble. Luby had been so successful in his choices that he now held a big enough fortune to allow him to follow in his father's footsteps. He could retire at an early age and, as he put it, "settle down in California and maybe do some teaching." His own father had retired happily at thirty-nine; Bob himself was only thirty-six. But the overwhelming difference between Bob and Harry resided in one stark fact: Harry longed to relax in private ease, but Bob itched for work. "I *loved* it," he later told Steve Barnhill, the writer that Luby's Cafeterias, Inc. would hire in the 1980s to chronicle some of its early history. "Even after I got back in the business, I still thought that when I got a few cafeterias going I might go out to California and retire. But I was having too much fun!"

It required only a very brief stint of operation before Bob and Charles were able to assess the success of their ideas, and to launch several managers, both old hands and novices, on a path that would insure a great chain of cafeterias. The Dallas VA cafeteria had furnished a wonderful laboratory in which to test a number of innovations developed during the war, such as products like frozen fruit and fish. The only real hitch in the Love Field site was just how competent and "managerial" the newcomers were turning out to be. It was a clear-cut case of overqualification and top-heaviness—too many bosses in one spot—when it came to getting the menial jobs delegated and done. But menial labor was an intrinsic part of hands-on management, and no one complained. As was the inevitable Luby's way, included among these newcomers were several recruits from the team's own families—for instance, Gerald W. Lee, who was John Lee's younger brother, and Charles's wife Gertrude's younger brother, J. W. Cunningham Jr. They knew better than most rookies what kind of dividends lay in wait for them once they finished their Love Field training and moved on to manage impending cafeterias: that all of Harry Luby's initial principles would remain intact, essential bolts in the framework of Bob and Charles's business, and that the main one would rule their futures. Each and every manager would receive a full 40 percent of net income earned by his store. Guaranteed.

The occasional head-butting between alpha males was worth it.

□ □ □

Soon the partners reached the conclusion that the time had arrived. The first new-generation Luby's Cafeteria was due for its inauguration. But where to fling open the doors?

Bob and Charles knew for sure that they wanted to stay in Texas. They knew they needed to establish themselves in a city large enough to support a regular group of customers used to cafeteria convenience—preferably also a city with military installations making up a part of its fabric, because as a bigger-scale employer the military provided a dependable economic foundation, as well as a steady pool of patrons. In addition to the already initiated, they needed to introduce the cafeteria mode to a wider segment of the new populations pouring into urban settings now that the war was over. These days, people were going to want to "eat out" much more than they had in the past. The poverty that had plagued millions of families before the war was gone. Americans now earned much bigger incomes. Some of them now possessed a great deal of disposable income, and they were ready to spend it. The idea of going downtown to take in a movie on a weeknight, and grabbing a bite of dinner before or after the show, may have been a novelty to many (such as those who actually needed to be educated in the pursuit of leisure activities that hadn't been available in their previous, often rural, communities). But in this carefree and relieved post-Depression, postwar milieu, they eagerly adopted the habit. Yet, in a holdover from their prewar lives, they still wished to be assured of good value for their money—in this case, high-quality food at lower prices. For Luby's purposes, they needed to be inducted into the cafeteria culture.

Others, most especially the surging tide of returning members of the armed services, presented one particular challenge the partners would have to meet. Millions of army and navy veterans had sworn that after four full years of languishing in endless queues for meals, health attention, inspection, etc., they would never stand waiting in a line again once they came home to civilian life. This resistance, in fact, appeared perhaps the biggest barrier that Bob, Charles, and their colleagues would need to overcome. The Luby's mission was to create an experience so enticing, so satisfying, that servicemen would welcome the chance to move through a line and consider themselves so well compensated that the reminder of their old, drudging routines would in no way diminish their appetites.

Nobody who was watching the team from outside the Luby's circle believed they could do it.

At last, a city got picked in which to prove the observers wrong. It was the final stop on Bob Luby's childhood and growing-up migration: San

Antonio. The choice made excellent sense. Bob was very familiar with it. Harry and Julia Luby had lived there; they still had many useful connections and ties there; and Harry, of course, intended to be one of the backers for Bob and Charles's merry band of entrepreneurs. No fewer than five military posts occupied the area: Fort Sam Houston for the army, and four air force bases. The city was growing quickly. So when Bob and Charles found a location in a cavernous basement on the corner of Presa and College streets—almost literally "across the alley from the Alamo," as the popular Mills Brothers song was lilting on radios all across the country at that very moment in 1947—they seized the chance to lease it. And much to the surprise of all the skeptics who voiced their regrets for the folly of such an extravagant mistake, this unlikely venue would become the partners' San Antonio Rose.

In addition to Charles Johnston, Bob Luby, and Harry Luby, the financial partnership for the Presa Street store now involved Norwood Jones, John Lee, and fresh from her Dallas success, the redoubtable Helen Luby Blodgett, Charles's aunt. But they were not nearly as nervous as the outsiders who doubted the store's potential. Even the partners' architect, Addis Noonan, shook his head sadly and commiserated with the young men. "Robert, I feel terrible about all this," he said to Bob Luby. "You guys are wasting your money. So I'm not going to charge you my regular fee. I'll just bill you my costs." One of the carpenters working on the site echoed Noonan. "I hate to see you fellows lose all your money this way. You'll be broke in sixty days." The cafeteria was costing eight times more than any of its predecessors—a whopping $60,000, a fortune for the period. Also, the basement was huge—more than twice the size of any previous cafeteria. When finished, it would seat 180 diners at a time, and the critics argued that that would never happen. Shortages still kept a tight vise on various supplies across the country. So, although rationing restrictions had been officially lifted in 1945, it was still tricky to find certain building materials, food items, and so on. Sugar especially was a problem. Whoever heard of a Luby's without a sumptuous array of desserts? The partners were reduced to using pewter and a poor grade of copper for plumbing fixtures, and some equipment, such as the walk-in refrigerator for the kitchen, had to be obtained from army surplus. Still other necessities couldn't be purchased at all, like a stove exhaust fan, which in the end was built by a machine shop nearby. And the geographic location itself prevented any reasonable hope of a successful dinner service. Downtown San Antonio during the lunch hour might be fine for a business clientele, even though the immediate blocks were somewhat shabby and down-at-the-heel. But during those years the neighborhood grew utterly deserted once the sun went down. Discouragement bared its teeth at every turn. Obviously, the partners' investment would get thrown away.

So imagine how dumbfounded everyone was, when, on opening day, January 28, 1947, the basement was thronged with customers.

The wall-to-wall crush started first thing in the morning and went on until closing that night. "We had more business than we ever expected, almost more than we could handle," a gleeful Norwood Jones described later. Even the self-assured, full-speed-ahead partners hadn't anticipated such a turnout. And it didn't let up. Day after day, evening after evening, the place filled to capacity as the word spread like wildfire. Servicemen—those queue-haters and line-scorners—were consenting to wait for thirty minutes or longer in order to sample the high quality of fresh, hot food offered along the Luby's counters. The phenomenon caught on as the meals' cheap prices eroded objections. And another condition also contributed to this surprise twist in Luby's fortunes: what no one had factored into their dire predictions was that San Antonio was wrestling with a housing shortage. Many families that had just moved there had been forced to take up temporary residency in hotels downtown. So the seedy metropolitan area, no longer abandoned at nightfall, was indeed suddenly transmuting into a comfortable, respectable domain in which entire middle-class households would saunter peacefully up and down the blocks, bringing a new vivacity to once-empty streets, and grateful that such a welcoming destination existed at the end of their strolls. The cafeteria became an informal gathering place for them all.

Once again, Luby's was providing an inestimable service to a newly forged community.

7

SALAD DAYS

□ □ □

If your business requires long hours and strict rules, be prepared to pay your management big money, or get a real thrill out of retraining!
CHARLES JOHNSTON

One year later, in 1948, Bob and Charles opened their second San Antonio cafeteria. The leap from the Dallas VA Love Field contract to downtown San Antonio to the new site, all within three years, was a triumph of swiftness for any group of men so recently sprung free from fighting a war. The whole team had a lot to be proud of. And with the second cafeteria, they had had the foresight to take an innovational turn worthy of Harry himself. Unlike all its historic predecessors, this new store was not a downtown shopping/business-crowd eatery. Instead, in its location it resembled one of Harry and Earl Luby's earlier rivals—specifically, that godsend of easy family dining for the busy housewife and her brood: the Highland Park Cafeteria in Dallas.

Wooing a similar clientele to that of their supremely successful competitor seemed a great idea for broadening a customer base and making

Luby's a household word among the baby-booming families sprouting all over the country. It was time to get neighborly. It was time to treat the suburbs to Luby's convenience and good taste. Those newcomer folks who had been sheltering in inner-city hotels throughout the San Antonio housing shortage were snatching up homes for themselves just as fast as the homes could get built. New residential districts were being developed. A new postwar America was recarving the shape of the city. A new lifestyle was evolving, and its adherents needed accessible local services.

So Bob and Charles decided to create the prototype of the future "community" Luby's. They bought a lot on Broadway in the prestigious new neighborhood of Alamo Heights, and then commissioned Addis Noonan (the architect who had felt so pessimistic about their chances on Presa Street the year before that he had waived most of his standard fee) to design a free-standing building for it. Noonan was astounded. Not only did he express shock over their unexpected success, but because of the benevolence he had demonstrated with the previous project (an attitude that fit well with the Luby ideal of obliging generosity), he would now be destined to receive every Luby's design job in the future, and to author the look of all Luby's Cafeterias for the next several decades. The same kind of loyalty was extended to a dairy company that had behaved compassionately when Presa Street first opened by supplying its milk on altruistic long-range credit terms in order to help the partners as much as possible on their supposedly losing scheme. For the next number of years, Luby's would serve only Knowlton's milk, refusing to purchase any other.

Once the new Broadway store got completed, George Wenglein and John Lee acted as joint managers. Bob and Charles, meanwhile, were already working hard, planning greater expansion from the not-so-plush surroundings of their mobile executive "office." This office—a small capsule in which every task from bookkeeping to traveling to El Paso to oversee the cafeteria branch there to scouting for future plum locations across the state—was none other than the front seat of their Studebaker. Together they lived in it most hours of the day. By this time they were almost joined at the hip anyway, two inseparable alter egos as energetic as any roving pair of Texas Rangers ever had been—Bob spinning off on some grand idea, and Charles reining him back with thoughtful analysis; the outspoken Bob blurting his strong convictions, no matter whom he offended, and the agreeable Charles smoothing the ruffled feathers afterward; Bob plunging brazenly into a new deal or a business proposition with Charles following behind, delicately calibrating the negotiations into a win/win outcome. Bob, the dashing young go-getter whose handsome Luby looks and incandescent smile still to this day glow out from his photographs with a magnetic verve and charm—and Charles, the mild, gentle presence, distinguished by his wide oval dome of a forehead, and the kindly eyes beaming good-naturedness and trustworthiness from behind his spectacles.

Deep in the heart of the Piney Woods, Tyler was the next stop on the Texas-sized chart of their ambitions.

Tyler is a town that lies nestled in the northeastern part of the state, not too far a drive from the Louisiana border, and its population is saturated in the Old South culture of that region—a very different demographic from the Hispanic influences in San Antonio or the cowboy/Hispanic in El Paso. The store that Bob and Charles built there began serving lunches and dinners to East Texans in 1949. Its kitchen focused more on traditional southern cooking than it did on the enchiladas and guacamole to be found in the first locations. For its opening, many people connected to Luby's pitched in to work, including wives, aunts, and mothers. Georgia Luby (Bob's wife), Gertrude Johnston (Charles's wife), Helen Luby Blodgett (Charles's aunt), and Lola Luby Johnston (Charles's mother) all arrived to make the salads and pastries and teach the employees, newly trained over multiple weeks by the San Antonio fleet of managers, how to prepare them. This process was eventually to occur with every new opening. The family aspect of the endeavor persisted as the business spread.

Then, for the store after Tyler, the cousins dropped way down to the south part of the state, near the border with Mexico. There, in the town of Harlingen in the fertile Lower Rio Grande Valley, they established a cafeteria to be managed by Ken Weaver, the husband of Charles's first cousin and the son-in-law of Opal Luby Spaulding. J. W. Cunningham Jr., Gertrude Johnston's adored younger brother, was made assistant manager.

This hiring proved to be crucial to the fortunes of at least one partner's family, as well as the partnership itself. It was the first, and for a long time the *only*, misstep in an otherwise beautiful sequence of decisions. For, unbeknownst to the principals, who in all good faith were building a solid business structure founded on the rules of fairness and integrity that Harry Luby had first chartered, Cunningham's appointment would lead to severe repercussions on the whole utopian work atmosphere of the Luby's organization.

Of all the states within the Continental U.S., the shape of Texas is probably the most universally recognized, owing to the frequency of its iconic appearances. Many millions of non-Americans throughout the world know what Texas looks like, even if they don't know it's Texas. Now the partners-in-chief owned cafeterias located on three distant compass points in the sprawling landmass, which at that time was the largest state in the Union. With the El Paso store already prospering, the points representing the Luby cousins' holdings formed a gigantic triangle across that familiar silhouette that outlined their territory. The headquarters in San Antonio occupied the central point within the triangle. The 600-mile line from Tyler to Harlingen when joined to the 705-mile line from Harlingen to El Paso and the 660-mile lateral stretch back over to Tyler added up in reality to nearly 2,000 miles of roads the cousins had to traverse regularly just so they could keep up with their far-flung cafeterias. The direct top middle point of the compass, due north from Harlingen, pinned down the town of Wichita Falls, adjacent to Oklahoma. By no means the northernmost point of Texas, Wichita Falls nonetheless marked the pinnacle of the cross made by the lines from the other points.

But Wichita Falls already had a Luby's. It had been started by a family member, and was a good example of the scattering of independent cafeterias owned neither by the Earl Luby partnership clusters nor by the Harry/ Bob/Charles line—the third branch of the tree. And as such, it would remain the *only* Luby's in Wichita Falls, demonstrating another strong principle to which Bob and Charles would unswervingly adhere: wherever a previously established, independent Luby's cafeteria already existed, they would never invade. They would not present competition to any other member of the family, or any other Luby's owner, by planting their own Luby's name in the same town.

Meanwhile, they were also holding true to several of Harry's other tenets, especially the ones regarding compensation for staff and management. For the pay at Bob and Charles's Luby's cafeterias was indeed the highest rate per specific job to be found anywhere in the food industry—at least anywhere in Texas and its adjoining states. And Bob and Charles were now actively training several managers directly on the job, with the promise of the 60/40 net profit split once they got assigned their own stores.

Setup of the salad counter

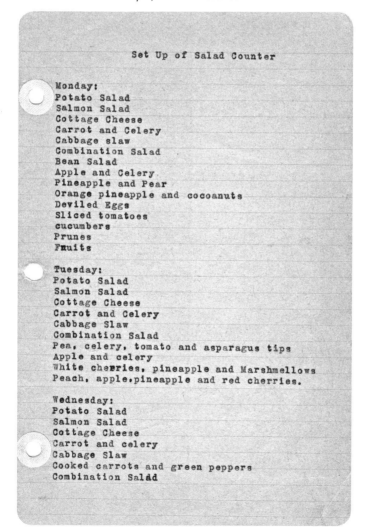

```
           Set Up of Salad Counter

    Monday:
    Potato Salad
    Salmon Salad
    Cottage Cheese
    Carrot and Celery
    Cabbage slaw
    Combination Salad
    Bean Salad
    Apple and Celery
    Pineapple and Pear
    Orange pineapple and cocoanuts
    Deviled Eggs
    Sliced tomatoes
    cucumbers
    Prunes
    Fruits

    Tuesday:
    Potato Salad
    Salmon Salad
    Cottage Cheese
    Carrot and Celery
    Cabbage Slaw
    Combination Salad
    Pea, celery, tomato and asparagus tips
    Apple and celery
    White cherries, pineapple and Marshmellows
    Peach, apple,pineapple and red cherries.

    Wednesday:
    Potato Salad
    Salmon Salad
    Cottage Cheese
    Carrot and celery
    Cabbage Slaw
    Cooked carrots and green peppers
    Combination Salåd
```

The manager's workday began at 7:00 a.m., when he unlocked the door to the cafeteria, and ended often after ten or eleven at night. Throughout the hours in between, he performed a cascade of tasks: the first one was to remove the day's cash from its secret hiding place, which was often the dried bean can in those early stores, and put it in the cash drawer of the register. Next he "pulled boxes." This meant he opened the refrigerators, inspected the big pans and trays of leftovers and fresh inventory from the

```
      Lima  Beans, celery and pimento
      Apple and celery
      Peach , pineapple and marshmellow
      Banana, pineapple and orange, 3/4 cups sugar


      Thursday
      Potato Salad
      Salmon Salad
      Cottage Cheese
      Carrot and Celery
      Cabbage Slaw and Diced Apples
      Combination Salad
      Pea, sweet pickle and cheese AY salad
      Apple and Celery
      Mixed fruit--pears, pineapple and white cherries
                    marshmellow
      Peaches pineapple, and red cherries.

      Friday:
      Potato Salad
      Shrimp Salad
      Cottage Cheese
      Carrot and celery
      Cabbage, diced pineapple,pimento
      Combination Salad
      Kidney Bean, --sweet pickle, celery, boiled
                    egg and little onions
      Apple and celery
      Orange and pineapple and cocoanut
      Sliced tomatoes

      Saturday:
      Potato Salad           Cabbage, pimento and diced
      Salmon Salad                  apple
      Cottage Cheese         Combination Salad
      Carrot and celery      Corn, celery, pimento,
                             apples and
      Pineapple and          cherries
      Marshmellow
```

prior evening's service, and chose from among them the ingredients with which he could whip up an exciting array of dishes. Then he brewed a pot of coffee, and wrote down the menu while he sipped it. According to Herbert Knight, who became one of the highest profit-earning managers Luby's ever produced, the creative use of leftovers was key to the success of the cafeteria. Most good managers either possessed or learned this ability, a knowledge they shared then with many careful, frugal housewives across

```
                    Apple Salad

  8 medium size apples (unpeeled and dices)
  1/ 1 1/2 coffee cups white raisins (washed)
  4 slices American Cheese
  (1/4 inch slices diced small).

     Mix with mayonaise

                  Apple Salad

  8 medium size apples (peeled and diced)
  2 handful celery
  1 cup seeded white or pink grapes

     Mix with mayonaise
```

the nation in the forties, fifties, and sixties but one that would now separate them from most managers, as well as the general population. Today, in most restaurant settings, leftover dishes get thrown out when they're not bought. Loss from waste is a persistent problem. But back then, innovation could make or break a kitchen budget. And the manager's entrée options were only as limited as his culinary imagination. Roast beef from the night before could be ground, seasoned, and mixed with rice for a savory offering of stuffed bell peppers; the fruit—apples or cherries or peaches—carefully scooped out from yesterday's now-soggy pie shells could get reused in puddings, cakes, and cobblers; baked fish made excellent croquettes when shredded and mixed with spring onions, spices, and breadcrumbs. As Knight points out, "People don't know how to do that anymore. Fewer people cook in this [present-day] culture because they eat out; therefore, they lack the ingenuity and skills to incorporate previous dishes into new ones." This knack, Knight says, was one of the factors that made the 60/40 percent split work so well, and kept it to everyone's advantage—even the consumer's, whose purse and taste buds reaped the benefits of the manager's expertise.

It was also up to the manager to watch the dirty plates coming back into the kitchen. If plates came back from bused tables to the dishwashers' section with an unfinished portion of a particular recipe—say, baked squash, or a chicken casserole—for three days straight, the manager immediately made a beeline for that pan on the line, and began to investigate why the dish wasn't pleasing the customers, knowing it wouldn't sell well later unless something was put right. The cooking method, the flavors, and the raw materials—all got scrutinized. To expedite this process, every manager carried a special badge of office at all times: his official tasting spoon. He would sample each dish before it appeared in public, rejecting those not up to standards of excellence. The more particular and refined his sense of taste, the more successful the manager proved. The best were never seen without these instruments jutting from a pocket. This is the foundation for the ongoing tradition that a Luby's manager who has passed away is buried with his spoon tucked in his front pocket.

Placement of food was also important to sales, according to Tommy Griggs, another of the management trainees who came to San Antonio in the early fifties via his employment in the Abilene Luby's cafeteria, which his brother, Lee Griggs, bought from Sadie and Ray Pressler in 1946. Kitchens cooked up the necessary projected amounts of each dish based on gauging customer preferences and consumption rate. But projections didn't always hold true. The answer to that problem lay in rejuggling the food counter. If, for instance, there seemed to be an unexpected surplus of beef stew, the manager could put it in an extra-large pan early in the line so that the customer would see it first. If, on the other hand, the kitchen was running out of stew, it was better placed at the line's end, in a small pan.

The next step in the manager's morning task roster, after he had made the coffee and composed the day's recipes, was to lay out the foods for the cooks to prepare. Then he would change the water in the steam tables and light the gas burners underneath them. Deliveries of meat, produce, dairy products, and dry shipments would by now be arriving at the back door, to be checked off and examined. When the cooks came in, the manager supervised their procedures the same way a head chef would in a gourmet restaurant, making sure each dish for the serving line was meticulously concocted and finished. If one of the cooks, or indeed any other employee, failed to show up for work, he filled that person's place—prepping vegetables, kneading yeast dough for rolls, roasting meats, busing tables, washing dishes. Sometimes the day became grueling in its demands before it even properly started, which was why managers' problem-solving reflexes had to be so quick and their bodies so physically vigorous. For this reason, Bob Luby developed a partiality to hiring former high school and college football players as potential trainees. As he later confided to Herbert Knight, "They can think on their feet." A whole parade of football veterans recruited for these gifts would eventually become top managers and executives in the organization—Alvin Beal, Harold Day, Vernon Schrader, and Ralph "Pete" Erben, a star of the Baylor University team who would one day reach the ultimate goalpost in the Luby's administration—that of president and CEO. The early tests for management trainees were therefore typically as strenuous as fall training: the hands had to learn skills for the toughest jobs first. Butchering meat and skinning liver were foremost on the list, followed by cleaning grease traps, washing vegetables, making all salads and sauces, baking all breads, cleaning up all surfaces from floors to tables to walls and ceilings, operating and emptying the dishwashers, and scouring the toilets. If candidates didn't like doing these chores, then Bob, Charles, and the other pioneers didn't want to pay the expenses of their continued training. As Kent Weaver, whose father was the son-in-law of Opal Luby Spaulding and the first head of the Harlingen store, now puts it, "Once you went to the general manager level, it became really obvious

Salad dressing recipes

Salad Dressings

Poppy seed dressing

$\frac{1}{4}$ cup sugar
1 tsp. salt
1 tsp dry mustard
1 TBlsp. grated onion
1 cup salad oil
$\frac{1}{4}$ cup vinegar
1 Tblsp poppy seed

    Mix sugar,salt and mustard then add onion and vinegar. Add oil one spoonfull at a time beating constantly with a rotary, stir in poppy seed. Makes 1$\frac{1}{2}$ cups

Rocqueford cheese dressing

    4 green peppers chopped fine
    2 "a." fruit bowls sweet pickle relish
    7 oz. blue cheese(grated fine)
    2/3 gallon mayonaise

Clear garlic dressing

    4 cups salad oil
    1$\frac{1}{2}$ cups vinegar
    3 tsp. sugar
    4$\frac{1}{2}$ tsp. salt
    1$\frac{1}{2}$ tsp. dry mustard
    12 buttons of garlic(pressed)

      Combine ingredients in bottle or jar
      shake vigorously.

Shrimp cocktail sauce

    6 Tblsp. worchestershire
    10 Tblsp. red hot sauce
    2 Tblsp. onion juice
    2 Tblsp. lemon juice
    2 Tblsp. horseradish
    6 Tblsp. sweet relish
    1 Gallon catsup.

Sour cream dressing

    4 cups mayonaise   2/3 cups sugar
    1 cup vinegar   1 Tblsp. black pepper
    2/3 cup sweet cream
        Mix thoroughly after adding each.

whether you had the discipline, intellect, and leadership skills to run your own business."

As the morning progressed toward noon, the staff would get the chance to grab a brief midmorning break. This was always a social time, with radios or even a Victrola momentarily dominating the kitchen floor inside the circle of smokers and idly chatting tea-ladies, busboys and busgirls, cooks,

```
                    Oil Mayonaise

8 eggs
1 1/2 gallons oil
1 heaping cup sugar
1/2 cups salt
5 serving spoons mustard
3 cups vinegar

        Beat eggs light add oil slowly then add
above mixture (makes 1 3/4 gallons.)

                Thousand Island Dressing

1 cup chopped green peppers
1 onion (chopped fine)
4 pimento chopped
2/3 round pan of mayonaise
2 cups catsup

                    French Dressing

3 cups sugar
1/2 cups salt
2 serving spoons Paprika (level)
4 cups vinegar_____together
4 serving spoon mustard
8 cups Salad oil
        Let oil run in on sugar, salt and paprika
and put vinegar and mustard in by spoonful until
oil has run through.    (Makes 2 gallons).

                    Tartar Sauce

1/3 round pans of chopped sour pickles
3 onions (medium)chopped fine
fill rest of pan with mayonaise
```

```
                         Roasts

Baked Ham & Grits
Roast Pork & Apple Sauce
Roast Beef
Veal & Dressing
Roast Pork & Dressing
Corned Beef & Cabbage

                         Stews

Beef Stew
Hungarian Goulash
Short Ribs & Potatoes
Short Ribs & Dumplings
Short Ribs & Spaghetti
Casserole of Veal
Barbecued Short Ribs & Rice
Barbecued Spare Ribs
Baked Spare Ribs with Kraut & Noodles
Brains & Eggs
Chop Suey & Rice
Ruebenola & Rice
New England Boiled Dinner
Vegetable Dinner

                         Chicken

Chicken Pie
Chicken & Dumplings
Chicken & Baked Dumplings
Luby's Special Chicken
Chicken en Casserole
Fried Chicken
Turkey & Dressing
Chicken & Rice
Noodles & Giblets
Giblets & Rice or on Toast
Chicken a la King
```

Meat entrées

line servers, and dishwashers. Managers usually seized the lull to catch up on paperwork, place orders with purveyors, and/or speak with an employee who had some problem, complaint, or needed a reprimand. Then toil recommenced and the kitchen resumed its complicated choreography, which was, as Herbert Knight puts it, like "a circus on concrete; everyone had their own trapeze." The workers took their proper places, coordinating

```
                Sauce for Barbecued Short
                         Ribs

     1 gallon can tomatoes
     1 gallon water
     3/4 cup worchestershire sauce
     3 cooksp. red hot
     2 cooksp. chili powder
     1 cooksp. chili quick
     2 cooksp. mustard

                     Chop Suey

     3 large bunches celery (cut large)
     3 large onions (cut rather large)
     1/2 can bean sprouts
     1/2 can mushrooms (chopped)
     1/2 can water chestnuts (chopped)
     1 cup chop suey sauce
     4 lbs. pork loin (cubed)
     1 cup salad oil
     Cook celery, onions, bean sprouts, water chest-
     nuts and mushrooms in water to half cover vege-
     talbes, until barely tender. Fry pork in salad
     oil until browned, add to the above when done.
     Thicken a bit and serve with rice.

                    Brains & Eggs
     Soak 5 lbs. brains in salt water at least 15
     minutes. Clean and wash. Put in beater and whip.
     Melt 1/2 lb. butter in roast pan, pour in whipped
     brains and cook in oven, stirring often, until
     half done, add 3 dozen eggs, beaten and finish
     cooking. Do not let them cook too dry.

                   Reubenola & Rice
     4 T butter
     1 can mushrooms
     3 bunches celery (cut like chop suey)
     3 large onions (cut like chop suey)
```

Recipes for Chop Suey, Brains & Eggs, etc.

their distinctive movements with one another in mutual precision, and is-suing the loud warning "Behind you!" if someone else got too close. One slip, one person out of position at the wrong moment, or missing altogether, and the whole timing was thrown off. Accidents could occur—collisions of busboys' loaded arms with full tea carts, hoisted pans on their way from the ovens to the steam tables spilled over employees, fires flaring. The manager had to be ready to step in, fill the empty spot, and evenly maintain the timing to prevent safety disasters as well as promote productivity.

Once meal serving started, at 11:00 a.m., the manager constantly watched the line and checked its length to make sure the kitchen was corresponding with it, the way two cogs mesh in a gearbox. "If it was pretty long," George Wenglein explained, "you'd have the cooks fill the grill with steaks and put more baskets of fish into the fryer so you'd have it ready by the time the people got to the counter. The object was . . . to anticipate demand so that the food was freshly cooked." The line's length presented another problem tackled and solved by Luby's. On Sundays after church, for instance, the line could grow so long that it might trail out the doors and around the block. This was not acceptable care of customers, who, chances were, felt uncomfortable standing out in the weather. So, years before Disneyland ever opened to the public, the Luby's organization invented the double-back line. The team of Bob, Charles, and their cohorts also kept a sharp eye on timing the customers' turnover to its maximum efficiency. If everything ran according to plan, the journey through those full-house Sunday lunch lines would take exactly twenty minutes, from entry through the front doors, to the wait in both double-backs (the standard number arranged), to the promenade along the food counter, all the way to the checker at the end. Managers also needed to be ready to tally up food tray contents and present the total bill at a moment's notice as competently as the usual cashier, so the line could keep moving.

One Sunday, a lady fainted dead away at the cashier's desk in San Antonio right after she had picked her drink to add to her meal. So deft was Henry Jones, Norwood Jones's brother, who happened to be manning the register, that he reached out and grabbed her before she could hit the floor and supported her with his left arm, all the while continuing to ring up the oncoming customers' trays with his right hand—never missing a beat.

After lunch service had finished, it was clean-up hour. This lasted anywhere from sixty to ninety minutes. The dining room and kitchen both received a good scrub-down. All pots, pans, and dishes were washed. Then the staff took one more midafternoon break before the whole process got repeated for supper. Since pot-washing was one of the most arduous jobs in the cafeteria, managers had to be in especially hardy condition if they replaced an absentee pot washer. An anecdote from those early days aptly demonstrates the difficulties inherent in the drudgery, as described by Norwood Jones:

There was a gas burner under the rinse side of the pot sink that kept the wa-ter at one hundred sixty-five degrees. So it was not only hard work, but it was awful hot. We had a great big fellow who took the job of pot washer at Presa Street one day, and after a few hours at the sink he was wringing wet. The dirty pots were coming at him at a pretty good pace. A pot washer al-ways wore long rubber gloves that came up to the elbows. Right in the mid-dle of our busiest meal, this man ripped off the rubber gloves, threw them across the kitchen, and stormed out. On the way out he hollered, "I didn't have to work this hard in the penitentiary!"

He didn't even come back for his half day's pay.

□ □ □

Family primacy, so central to the core of the Luby's philosophy, was also naturally emphasized among the organization's management policies. Be-cause managers worked such long hours, the partners/owners felt concern that they should have happy domestic lives to go home to, which would incidentally spur their incentives for hard, stable, dedicated labor through which to earn those six-figure incomes equaling those of the local doctors and lawyers. So married managers were preferred to bachelors, even though some of the team principals themselves, in the early fifties, had not yet married. Managers should also get to spend as much quality time with their families as possible. That was why, on weeknights, a manager's wife and children were encouraged to show up at his store to eat dinner with him. In this way they shared an evening meal like a "normal" household, albeit in a commercial backdrop, and the father could hear about his chil-dren's school days and interests and generally participate more in their lives. When the supper line started service, the wife and offspring arrived in their nicest clothes (after all, no manager wanted his family to be seen scruffily or dirtily dressed!), passed down the line like any other customers, and spent the next hour immersed in the husband/parent's work atmo-

Luby's wives and children. Left to right: *Ruth Kidd holding*
Nancy Kidd; Gertrude Johnston with Carol and Barbara;
Georgia Wenglein Luby holding Martha; and Alice Wenglein.

sphere—the manager's own small kingdom. For this space of time, the
assistant manager often took over the GM's kitchen duties. It was also he
who oversaw the store on the GM's one day off per week. Wives themselves sometimes worked in the stores, but were never made managers.
The two cousins' rationale proceeded like this: men were the chief bread-
winners. Expansion was triggered by the maturation of managers ready to
run a new store, rather than by building the store first and then training
someone. Movement, through transfers, was part of the initial management training period. Women couldn't be mobile, because their husbands
couldn't get uprooted from *their* jobs. Therefore, Luby's couldn't afford to
hire any women for upper-tier positions. The postwar fifties mentality, that
a wife should be cared for at home while she nurtured the children and
ran the house, permeated the cafeteria culture.

In these practices and attitudes, Luby's very firmly reflected the mores
of Middle America on a microcosmic scale. Not until the 1970s would this
policy change, and the first women receive management training. It is

probably no more than an ironic coincidence that many of the band of pioneers, those original Luby's Cafeterias, Inc. "movers and shakers" (including Bob and Charles, both Norwood and Henry Jones, and Art Kidd), fathered only daughters—mostly one each.

But to return to the manager's daily routine, just in time to end it: once his family went home, he resumed his temporarily abandoned work schedule. This meant seeing the dinner service through, closing the doors at 8:00 p.m., supervising all cleanup operations (another sixty to ninety minutes' worth), assessing the leftovers, closing out the cash register, adding up the day's remuneration, and seeing the rest of the staff out the door before locking up and turning out the lights. The manager was always required to be the last person to leave the premises. Then he would go home just in time to sleep before starting a new morning.

On the whole, the proof of a good manager's worth could be measured by the harmony amongst his underlings. And it is to the Luby's partners' credit that their stores seldom had any malcontents lurking inside the uniforms, which testified to the art of the managerial diplomacy, and the keen judgment with which the pioneers picked their trainees. Walkouts, such as that of the hot and disgruntled ex-con pot washer, rarely occurred, and mutinies, except for one floridly violent incident in El Paso, were unheard-of. Very few staff members ever complained or felt disaffected about their lot. For the most part, employees stayed at Luby's for many years—often for the entire course of their working lives. For example, Annie Musgrove, who began cooking at the Presa Street store when it first opened in 1947, continued to cook there for more than thirty years, and was honored for her outstanding tenure in 1977. Also in San Antonio, a tea-lady named Genevieve Hayes worked first at the Broadway store for twenty-eight years until its closure, then at another store, for a total of thirty-two years' duration. Genevieve literally became the "poster girl" tea-lady for Luby's; her photograph was featured in the promotional literature for decades, and to this day she holds fast to her Luby's stock fully knowing that it will continue to rise like the phoenix from the ashes of its former lucrative glory. Another employee, Juanita Gonzales, still works in one of the two Waco Luby's, as she has for the past thirty-one years, first as a line server and later as a cashier, with time off only to bear and partially raise her children. Loyal

Waco customers (including one of the authors of this book) have watched her life progress season by season, her dark hair turn gray, her youthful, cheerful smile deepen through middle age, as they've exchanged familiar greetings with her across the steel countertops and tables.

This trend of steadfastness, for at least the last five decades—throughout the second half of the twentieth century—remained a truth about Luby's, and its source lay in the high wages, the advantages, and eventually, the stock options even the most menial employee was bestowed with once the company went public—plus the considerate, respectful, familial treatment of all hirelings as first established by Harry Luby himself. Occasionally the notion of family even got carried to a sacramental crescendo. One cashier, when she became engaged, asked if her marriage ceremony could take place in the Main Street store managed from 1954 until 1968 by Tommy Griggs. Permission was of course granted. Then she asked for Tommy to act in the stead of a father and give her away to her groom. He was thrilled to comply, although the duty wasn't in his GM job description. Other sacraments of life, and life's end, were honored too. On more than one occasion, when someone died while still in Luby's employ, the company paid for the funeral.

For this reason, also, very little stereotypical petty crime, such as pilfering, occurred among the Luby's staffs. When it did, it got handled in an unusual manner. Managers were urged to ignore certain problems rather than confront them head-on. The difference in approaches could mean either the loss or retention of otherwise outstanding employees. For instance, Annie Musgrove, the same cook mentioned above for the longevity of her career, often through the years kept a large covered pot full of some mysterious contents on the shelf above her work station in the Presa Street store, for no discernible reason. One day a young, zealous trainee had occasion to notice the pot. His suspicions alerted, he asked her to fetch it down to her table and open it. Annie refused. The trainee grew strict. "It's just water," Annie said, "nothing else." He stood on tiptoe and lifted the lid; yes, she was telling the truth. But why water? Just as he was about to haul the pot down and expose the meager little cache of leftovers she habitually secreted behind the pot, Charles Johnston, who happened to be passing by at the time, intervened, took him aside, and murmured in

Annie Musgrove and Charles Johnston

his ear to drop the subject. Later on, Johnston, chuckling, asked Herbert Knight, "Herbert, do you know the difference between an assistant manager and a general manager?" He answered his own question. "The general manager knows when to be looking the other way."

Or, as Rick Gozaydin, a highly successful later-generation manager, puts it, "The magic of Luby's that kept those people working there was the passionate involvement of the general manager who ran that store."

On the single violent occasion, that of the incident in El Paso, the assistant manager of the store (another young former football player recruit), broke with accepted managerial advice and directly confronted a loyal, steady worker, who was not performing his job quickly enough to meet the restaurant's strenuous schedule. The AM was temporarily in charge of the store on the GM's day off. Meanwhile, the worker, a long-serving pot washer disgruntled because there was no hot water with which to efficiently clean the pots, was conducting a one-man open rebellion. A very large man with a stolid disposition, he stood belligerently beside the sink with his brawny arms folded across his chest, frowning his dissatisfaction at the momentary lapse in the plumbing. When the assistant manager gave him an order to get busy, the pot washer refused. Unfortunately, the aggressive impulses sharpened on the football field rose up in the AM, and he issued a gruff ultimatum. Still the pot washer dug in his heels. So the AM, temper inflamed, punched him and knocked him down to the floor.

As soon as he could recover himself, the injured pot washer retaliated. The next thing anyone knew, a full-scale brawl had ensued, with fists flying, blood spouting, and tables crashing. By the time the fight was broken up, the assistant manager had fired the pot washer, who left the premises in a state of bewildered disbelief that this event could have happened, and happened to *him*, at, of all places, Luby's.

But the proof of the company policies and attitudes was yet to come.

For the next few days, the assistant manager found himself trapped in workplace purgatory. All the other employees, with whom he had previously gotten along well, now froze him out. Backs remained turned; greetings remained unreturned; orders were obeyed in sullen silence, and helpful suggestions were ignored. Disdain, unhappiness, and disrespect contaminated the kitchen atmosphere. The situation was worse than any Luby's Cafeteria had ever faced. Morale had bogged down to an all-time low. The AM had no idea what to do about it, yet clearly these conditions couldn't continue. His general manager, who had of course heard all about the fracas, indicated his sharp regret at losing such a valued employee. The pot washer had clearly been in the right in making his complaint; the assistant manager should have addressed it. And certainly he should not have started the brawl over the pot washer's resistance. But the general manager said nothing about what had actually happened. He didn't need to; his hush was ominous enough. The AM knew he was gravely at fault, both for the oversight and for the ensuing fight. The fallout from his mistakes demonstrated by contrast just how good a work environment Luby's employees ordinarily enjoyed.

But the AM recognized impending doom when he saw it. He had lost all his authority. He understood that steps would have to be taken either to restore it or to expel him from his position.

Early one morning a week after the incident occurred, a delegation of the owning partners walked unannounced into the El Paso kitchen. Bob Luby, Charles Johnston, George Wenglein, and John Lee had flown across the state to stand before the abashed assistant manager, and let him and the staff know the violence had not passed unnoted. Word had gone out, and now a decision had been reached.

In front of the entire kitchen staff, Bob Luby told the AM he wished to speak with him in private. He took him into the manager's office. Once there, he said, "This is bad. We've talked about it. We've trusted you, and you've done very well up until now. But this is a bad situation, and you've created it." The AM knew he meant every word. There had been several occasions when the general manager was ill, and the responsibility for the store had fallen on his shoulders. He had stepped up to the plate, performing so well that the partners had sent him an extra $500 check at the end of the month as a token of their appreciation. Now he had breached that trust by unleashing his bad temper.

"We've lost a solid, steady employee through your behavior. Now we're unable to get him back. But we've decided to give you another chance. This kind of thing must never ever occur again."

"No, sir," said the assistant manager.

"All right. Now, there's not going to be another word said. Do you understand me?"

"Yes, sir," the AM replied.

"Then let's go."

At that, Bob Luby opened the door, placed his arm around the AM's shoulders, and walked him back into the kitchen. He made no speeches; in fact, he made no reference to the incident at all. But the staff, who also trusted their bosses implicitly because of the organization's fine treatment and integrity, saw the arm's embrace. Bob Luby kept the AM close for another moment.

Then he gave the AM a final pat on the back, and the partners said good-bye and left the building.

And that was all it took. The ice was broken. Immediately balance was restored to the kitchen; everyone resumed normal conversation with the A.M. They knew the partners took the matter seriously; they knew the assistant manager had not gotten off lightly, and that their concerns were respected. But they also knew, from that one cross-state journey, and Bob Luby's simple action, that those concerns had been weighed, a conclusion had been drawn, and the solution wordlessly stated. The partners were willing to believe in the AM's reformation. Therefore, the staff should also.

From that moment on, the assistant manager's authority was reestablished. And because of the bitter lesson he had learned, and the way in which the Luby-Johnston duo handled his problem, he altered his approach to all his future interpersonal and professional communications. Today he counts himself a better man—not just in the workplace, but in every other area of his life.

Because the commitment to good practice and fair relations was so reliable in the Luby's administration, all employees were eager not to betray their faith, and to maintain an honest, cheerful milieu. The irony therefore is all the more biting that the first big, serious crime ever to get committed under a Luby's roof, as will be revealed in the next chapter, was perpetrated by an actual blood-tie family member—a resentful, aspiring assistant manager who, in the words of one observer, "didn't have what it took to become a general manager."

8

THE WORM IN THE APPLE

□ □ □

*You can't separate a person from his or her ethics. The same person who
goes to work, goes home.*

CHARLES JOHNSTON

Over the next few years, in the early 1950s, the fact that Luby's Cafeterias
began to spring up over the Texas landscape with great regularity was purely a testament to the hard toil, acumen, and gutsy determination of Bob,
Charles, and the team they had assembled. No partner or "executive" in
the group shirked even the most menial chore; each was happy to demonstrate to trainees how to scrape the sludge out of clogged pipes or mop the
dirtiest floor, and to lend their hands to any cafeteria needing an extra pair.
Their reputations for absolute integrity in all their dealings preceded them.
Everyone connected to the food industry, from bankers, purveyors, and
suppliers to contractors, employees, and the general public, knew the word
of Luby's management was solid gold.

By 1954 there were three San Antonio locations, all built through funds generated by the earlier stores. The following year a Luby's opened in Beaumont. Now seven cafeterias adorned the state map. But the partners weren't getting rich yet. They plowed every extra cent they made back into expansion.

It was in that year, 1955, that Bob Luby and Charles Johnston decided it was time to set up a real office rather than depend solely on one boxed in by a dashboard and cramped by a steering wheel. They also wished to turn over the bookkeeping to a professional who would meet that responsibility exclusively. Since they were still using old-fashioned methods to distribute payrolls for the stores' employees—gathering up the week's cash takings, and counting out the money due into vegetable bowls designated to each worker—it was time to grow a little less primitive.

So they leased a room above the Broadway cafeteria and hired Henry Lee, the person who had been computing their tax returns for the last several years, as the administrative accountant. Not a relation of John and Gerald's (the Lee brothers already involved in cafeteria development), Henry Lee felt a little dubious; he worked for a good firm in San Antonio, and the permanence of this new venture struck him as risky enough to trigger doubts about staking his whole future in it. When Lee was offered the job, he consulted a colleague, John Lahourcade, as to whether he should accept it. Was the business, he wondered, solid enough to guarantee him a future? Lahourcade told him he should jump at the chance.

"Look at it this way," Lahourcade advised. "If there is ever another Depression in this country, at least you'll never go hungry!"

So Lee took occupancy of the small office above the Broadway store. In 1957 Bob and Charles added another room to the quarters and hired a secretary. But the only space they allowed themselves was a couch in Lee's office, which they shared the way they did the Studebaker whenever they needed it, spreading documents and plans across the cushions, plotting their next circuit-ride inspection or real estate deal for a cafeteria lot from its shallow depths, or seizing the chance for a nap in between their field trips. They were adventurers who nursed no interest in becoming deskbound executives and leaving the scout work to others—especially now that they co-owned a Cessna 210 airplane, in which George Wenglein, that accomplished U.S. Air Force pilot who had been featured in more than

Bob Luby and George Wenglein with George's Cessna, ca. 1953

one Movietone wartime newsreel, whisked them from Beaumont on the southeast Gulf Coast next to Louisiana clear across the 900 miles to El Paso in a fraction of the time the Studebaker took. Fortunately, during this time when airplanes were still comparatively cheap to buy, the Cessna didn't represent an extravagant outlay, which would have been antithetical to the partners' philosophy as well as to Harry Luby's original practices.

Eventually, though, Charles and Bob granted themselves the right to an office of their own. They had a desk installed, which they shared, sitting side by side and functioning almost as two halves of one very complete, energetic, and superpowered person. The only separate facilities they allocated to themselves were two different telephones, each with its own line, which they both employed at the same time, often cupping their palms over the receivers in the midst of conversations so they could give each other simultaneous information or ask the other's opinions. They also unofficially swapped the title of chief back and forth from year to year (although this could not be recorded on paper due to the confusions it might cause, but remained in the same realm of informal but ironclad agreement that so many of their guarantees and pledges occupied). One year Bob would act as president; the next year Charles would assume that mantle while Bob replaced him as executive vice president; then the next year they would switch back again. Soon the time came that the Luby's gang decided to go ahead and take over the entire second floor above the cafeteria of the Broadway Street building because they could now afford to dispense with tenants. The partners hired an architect to design two large, spacious, elegant offices for Bob and Charles. But the pair was so used to performing symbiotically that they couldn't stand the separation, and it wasn't long before they deserted their individual sanctuaries in favor of a combined space at the conference room table, where they could put their heads together more quickly and conveniently. The no-frills, hands-on, bootstrap approach to their projects was what they found gratifying—even exhilarating. Why else dive into this business? Well, why else indeed? Perhaps because it was eventually to prove a multiveined gold mine for everyone concerned?

Yes, everyone. Slowly it was growing clear: just as Harry Luby had conceived his first cafeteria in hopes of a possible means to early retirement, just as Earl Luby and his siblings, and lately the next generation of Mattoon Lubys—George Luby's two sons, George and Joe—had joined forces in Dallas to keep themselves comfortably affluent with a small group of jointly run stores, so Charles and Bob's operation was also busily accruing a tidy nest egg of promise for its participants. Only in their case, that nest egg was swelling into a real fortune. The fortune would only grow bigger as the cousins' vision enlarged. And the beneficiaries would be not merely a select few owners, but *all* the partners, *all* the managers, all the assistant managers, even all the employees down to the floor staff, who in the next two decades would be endowed with valuable stock. The wealth would finally percolate throughout the company, creating more millionaires per capita than any other commensurate corporation in the United States— all of it real, rather than borrowed; all of it hard property, rather than a paper mirage.

So it was that this potential gold mine now began to chafe the heart, ambitions, and resentments of one man in particular—the only family member, by blood or marriage, who had obviously never espoused Harry Luby's golden rules. And thus, a single worm from the personal side of life would finally grow sharp enough to gnaw a hole through the impeccable business world that Bob and Charles, Harry's true heirs, had created.

*Helen Lee, John Lee, Gertrude Johnston, and Charles Johnston
at the Seven Oaks Country Club*

□ □ □

In 1950, when Kenneth Weaver and J. W. Cunningham Jr., the brother of
Gertrude Johnston (and, of course, Charles's brother-in-law), became the
general manager and assistant manager, respectively, of the Harlingen Luby's on Eighth Street, they didn't know each other very well. True, J. W.
had already cut his teeth in the Love Field cafeteria at the VA facility in
Dallas. And both men were related to the Luby family through marriage,
with Ken's mother-in-law being Charles Johnston's aunt. But if they weren't
what could be labeled "friends," neither were they adversaries.

The Harlingen store, like all the others, flourished as it brought the community together over the dining tables. As the store's success increased, so of
course did Ken Weaver's bank balance. J. W. Cunningham received a very
respectable salary and, as policy then dictated, an implicit place in the line
toward a general manager's position and a store of his own. The future
looked rosy. So, sometime late in 1958, the two men chipped in with Bob,

Charles, and Opal Luby Spaulding to buy a piece of real estate for a store site in an attractive highway location with good prospects, and there prepared to build a new premises for the Harlingen Luby's No. 1—the store that was to become, at its official reinauguration, the last cafeteria opened under the old partnership formulation in Harry Luby's direct line of descent.

Approximately six months after the new location's opening in November 1959, J. W. Cunningham Jr. abruptly fled the Rio Grande Valley for Dallas, smuggling within his luggage a treasure to which he possessed debatable legal entitlement. It was not money, but an expensive roll of paper—a document that he plainly felt would insure his future wealth.

And at that moment commenced a forty-year-long war.

The motives for the theft remain to this day obscured by the mists of conflicting memory, surface appearances, and silence. The silence belongs to those J. W. left behind—principally his co-manager, Kenneth Weaver, who has disliked discussing the subject since its occurrence, and Weaver's family of descendants, the heirs to his tight-lipped stoicism. Other more vociferous speakers have argued various aspects of the episode, making excuses, providing rationales and justifications, lamenting the rancor that was engendered that day, giving version after conflicting version, of the kind people construct in order to live more easily with themselves.

Only the facts remain. They include the appropriation and its terrible repercussions, which are incontestable. They include the tangible fruits of that appropiation, which could be and were visited regularly in Dallas and commented upon by many members of the public, a concrete witness to skullduggery. And the two facts that stand out most indelibly as a result of the split are these: the initiation of Luby's Cafeterias, Inc. into a darker era of broken trust and the splintering of a long, hardworking marriage.

From the first months of its inception, the Harlingen partners' original collaboration had turned thorny. No other cafeteria experienced this problem among either partners or managers; disharmony was almost unknown, except for the one incident in El Paso. Although J. W. Jr., known as "Dub" to his intimates, was, as previously noted, a groomed product of the Love Field "boot camp," he still always struck his coworkers as surprisingly "ignorant of the business." But his connections to the organization went back much further than Love Field, to the day in 1933 when his older sister Gertrude wed Charles Johnston.

Like his sister, J. W. grew up hard-scrabble poor in the Dallas neighbor-hood of Oak Cliff during the Great Depression. His father worked as a mechanic for the Tarrant County Sheriff's Department, and was also dep-utized so that he could enforce the law if he were needed—and, in the words of Charles Johnston's daughter, he spent a lot of time hoping he *would* be needed. A large, gruff man whose presence years later would strike terror in the heart of Carol Johnston, his granddaughter, John W. Cunningham Sr. exerted a powerful dominance over his family. During childhood holiday trips to Dallas, the quaking five-year-old Carol would hide under the bed in the master bedroom in order to avoid her first con-frontation with her grandfather—an ill-advised move, since he would im-mediately head straight for the bedroom, sit on the mattress edge, remove his boots, and drop them wham! wham! onto the floor, a percussion that frightened her even more.

Cunningham's wife, the mother of his five children, had a gentle, lov-ing spirit that contravened his rough nature. She was the loquacious one, the one who welcomed grandchildren by stopping whatever task she was engaged in, pulling them onto her lap, crooning "I'm going to get me some sugar," and smacking kisses up and down their necks while they struggled and shrieked with ticklish joy. Visitors to the Oak Cliff suburban home could often hear her in the kitchen, prattling away to whatever liv-ing thing or object happened to be near—the cat, the plants, the pots and pans. Her yard hosted an endless supply of chickens, and she often boasted that no matter how many they killed to feed their guests, there would al-ways be another one left.

But the want of the Great Depression had left its mark on the family. Mrs. Cunningham had not always been able to supply the dining table during those hard years. Sometimes the chickens thinned out a little too quickly, and her children went hungry. Consequently, a strict frugality and an insatiable need for financial security were to haunt at least two of her offspring for the rest of their lives.

During the early 1930s as many members of the family as could do so worked in order to help supplement the family income. The job that the svelte and vivacious Gertrude Cunningham acquired after her high school graduation happened to be as a receptionist at her uncle's barbershop on Jefferson Street. On the particular morning that Charles Johnston strolled up to the entrance of the barbershop after picking up the barrel of pickles that had brought him to the Oak Cliff neighborhood, Gertrude had no idea that his quick trim would lead to an elopement. Or that she would now enter a family that, no matter how loyal the men remained to one another, tended to treat the women who married into it as outsiders who had to struggle for many years to win acceptance or approval.

Unfortunately, this attitude of exclusivity among the Luby clan, whether conscious and volitional or merely habitual and instinctive, would finally goad Gertrude to defend herself and her own family's foothold within the growing empire. It would pique her into choosing sides, and with woeful results. For Gertrude, when all was said and done, felt outnumbered, marginalized, and insecure as a Luby member. She felt she had little real voice in the family circle, despite her years of hard work and devoted interest, first to the Browder Street store in Dallas, and then to the San Antonio cafeterias. She felt she had no real authority over what transpired within the business. And unlike Georgia Wenglein Luby, or the other women who had married into the inner partners' circle, she felt she had contributed enough herself to earn the right to a firmer position of influence. So if she, as a woman and as Charles's wife, couldn't crack the wall cemented by Luby blood, her own gene pool should at least be granted representation and success through a male successor.

The Lubys' policy of secondary female recognition was about to ignite its first battle, and reap the first casualties.

A bombardier in the U.S. Air Force during World War II, J. W. Cunningham, like his brother-in-law and the other veterans that were busily developing this new limb of Luby's cafeterias, emerged from his military duty ready to search for a long-lasting career that would reward him and his posterity with affluence, and demolish that leftover Depression angst for good. His older sister's marriage into the Luby family provided just such an opportunity. He, too, had married. His wife, a dental hygienist named Joy from the Piney Woods of East Texas, had so far borne him two children, a boy and a girl, John W. III and Joanie. Gertrude Johnston felt only too eager to speak up for her brother and help him gain a foothold in the prosperous new venture her husband and his cousin were engineering. For Gertrude, J. W. represented her own family's interests, giving her a stronger

J. W. Cunningham with Carol Johnston

standing within the prolific Luby clan, a greater claim to her half of whatever empire and profits her husband Charles Johnston forged. To J. W, who
had had no training or higher education to fend for himself in a competi-
tive market full of servicemen returning from active duty to civilian status,
the promise of a future in Luby's must have seemed sweet indeed.

After his initial employment/training at the Love Field cafeteria, J. W.
Cunningham was soon placed as associate manager in Harlingen directly
under Kenneth Weaver as a tryout. The fact that he didn't immediately
make manager suggests that Bob and Charles already doubted his abilities,
but wished to give him every chance to improve them. Unfortunately, the
next few years failed to confirm their optimism. From the start of his induction at the Eighth Street store, J. W.'s various colleagues found his per-

sonality irritating. He was an attractive man, affable on the surface, and apparently cooperative. But his lack of a grasp on some of the simpler aspects of the business often prompted him to blunder. As associate manager he should have learned, for instance, how to buy the right amount of produce for the day from the purveyors. Yet, when it came time to order, he struggled with the weighty questions of cabbage and lettuce and had to phone for advice from his general manager even on Weaver's days off. His seeming unfamiliarity with the most basic details proved a frustration to those he worked with, and his recalcitrant attitude didn't help. A manager of many diverse employees has to remain calm, cheerful, firm, and decisively matter-of-fact; unhappily, J. W. lacked the spirit to deploy these qualities. Not many people liked him.

However, his big chance to move another rung up the financial ladder began when, after several years' labor, he first began to entertain the hope of buying a share of the partnership in the new, upgraded Harlingen store to be re-located from the old Eighth Street site to the Highway 77 bypass.

Of the five partners, Weaver, Cunningham, and Mrs. Spaulding were the only ones on site. Mrs. Spaulding, a veteran restaurateur and businesswoman, seemed a natural choice. She had been separated since the 1920s from her husband in her native Illinois and, after learning the cafeteria ropes in Dallas and then in Waco, had already been working for some time as cashier in the Eighth Street store. When the chance arose to invest as a partner in the new location, she enthusiastically jumped at it. As for Kenneth Weaver, married since the age of nineteen to Mrs. Spaulding's daughter Barbara, the progression was an obvious one. He had followed the attractive Barbara all the way from Mattoon to Texas while still a teenager, laboring in a Dallas warehouse to make ends meet so he could stay near her. Then, after their marriage, during his wartime military stint as an airman stationed at Connally Air Force Base in Waco, he had served the government by day and worked in the Waco cafeteria by night, alongside his mother-in-law. Such commitment to a life in the business spoke for itself. Thus, his stake in the partnership ranked second only to Bob Luby's and Charles Johnston's. In contrast, J. W. Cunningham's share comprised the smallest percentage.

Unfortunately, his "annoyance" threshold was quite a bit lower.

□ □ □

It took nearly ten years to ferment a brew of dislike among the Valley crew potent enough to leach through the Luby's rule of amicability. In the observation of one person who was present throughout this period, "By working hard and following directions, a person could get to associate manager level and do very well. You could even look like a superstar. [But] a general manager provides direction every day. He makes a gazillion new decisions every day, small changes, large changes, depending on the needs of the moment. Some people, you can say, 'Well, that guy's got it.' He can lead, while others are better at just following. J. W. Cunningham wasn't even a good follower."

Nonetheless, J. W. and Gertrude finally appeared to get what they wanted when he handed over his part of the stake to build and operate the sleek new Harlingen store. How he came up with the money remains to this day uncertain. It's possible that Gertrude herself gave it to him in secret. Or he may have borrowed it from someone else.

But he was destined to work in the store only a very short time.

However the other collaborators felt about him, it was evident that J. W. nursed a measure of spite. And he evidently had a strategy for escape, financial independence, and freedom from his tutelage and responsibilities in Harlingen prepared as well. The problems among him, Ken Weaver, and Mrs. Spaulding reached unpleasant proportions, possibly goaded by J. W.'s abrasive behavior. When the friction became intolerable, Bob Luby and Charles Johnston intervened.

The time had come to reach a decision. They didn't wish the public to step through the doors of their brand-new store into such a fractious climate. With the finality of men who own the controlling interest in a project, they issued an executive mandate: in fairness to all the parties concerned, one of the two battling comanager/partners had to go. Because he now owned property in the Rio Grande Valley, and was therefore well established there (as well as demonstrably competent at the helm of the store), and because his mother-in-law also had an interest in the partnership, it was concluded that Kenneth Weaver should stay. Within six months of the new store's opening, J. W. Cunningham needed to find a new home.

Opening of the Luby's in Harlingen, Texas. From left to right: Boyd Morrow,
Jennie Jones, Henry Jones, J. W. Cunningham, Bill Lowe, Herbert Knight,
unknown, unknown, Helen Luby Blodgett, John Lee Sr., Helen Lee,
Opal Luby Spaulding, Leon Armstrong, Rhea Wenglein, unknown,
unknown, Barbara Weaver, unknown, and Ken Weaver.

Understandings can grow into misunderstandings in many directions, depending on what is said and what is heard. To temper the sting of his ejection, Bob and Charles purportedly assured J. W. Cunningham that he would be offered another Luby's store to manage, just as soon as one became available. That way his future fiscal opportunities for the traditional 60/40 net profit split would be restored, and he could still reap the benefits of the partnership share in the Harlingen store. At least, that was J. W.'s report—and one he stuck to through the many embittered years of complaint to follow. His claim of being conveniently passed over promptly mutated into righteous anger. And in that spirit, he concocted his revenge.

The new Luby's Building on the Highway 77 bypass in Harlingen was designed by architect Tommy Thompson. Unlike the first Presa Street store in San Antonio, for which the architect, Addis Noonan, had so generously charged Bob Luby and Charles Johnston only his costs in a goodwill gesture for what he thought was a losing proposition, the Harlingen Luby's was now part of a proven successful chain. No one was going to offer cut-rate prices for first-rate work any longer. The plans cost the partners a huge amount of money in 1959. And when J. W. Cunningham finished swallowing his bitter pill and packed his bags for Dallas, secretly removed copies of the architectural blueprints for the restaurant that had been commissioned and paid for by the partnership went with him.

The news of the split cracked through the organization like a rifle shot. Such a rift between members of the management/partner corps was unprecedented. Certainly the shadow of rank dishonesty had never cast itself over the Luby's family, not even among the lower ranks of kitchen and floor staff.

Over the next few years, J. W. built his own cafeterias in Dallas—blatant competition to the Luby's stores that had fostered his business knowledge, which was considered fair enough. All's fair in the American capitalist system anyway. But he built them using the Harlingen store plans. In fact, he replicated the Harlingen No. 1 store so well, and with such precision, that a number of Dallas visitors to the Valley, when dining at Luby's, would remark to Kenneth Weaver, "Do you know, there's a cafeteria in Dallas that looks exactly like this, down to the color scheme. It's called J's Cafeteria. Is it another branch of this one?" Weaver would answer, "No, it's not," and grit his teeth to refrain from further comment. And every month, whether he liked it or not, he was duty-bound to mail a check to each of the Harlingen partners, gladly distributing the profits he had worked so hard to earn from the store to Charles Johnston and Bob Luby, but no doubt painfully aware that those same profits had helped to finance and were continuing to aid the results of J. W.'s grand departure scheme, his bid for a lucrative personal future in cafeteria culture. And even when George Wenglein assumed the painful necessity of driving to Dallas from time to time, approaching J. W. as spokesman for the rest of the partners, and offering to buy out his share of the partnership at a more than fair price, J. W. gleefully refused all such offers. He also made sure, whenever there was a partnership meeting involving the Harlingen store, to be present, a constant goad and irritant to the others, as he voiced his opinions and exercised his right to vote on decisions.

□ □ □

This participation in Luby's by her own blood family was the life preserver Gertrude Johnston had clung to. The rescinding of the right to participate would later become a bone of contention that she never let Charles forget. According to J. W. and therefore to the faithfully believing Gertrude, her dearest brother had been betrayed; he had been lied to, guaranteed a real position that had not materialized. In her view, to play false with him was to betray her.

"Why won't you stick up for your own family in the midst of all these Lubys?" she would come to rail at Charles over the next few years, forgetting (perhaps preferring to forget) that he, too, was a Luby—that his mother's maiden name was Luby, and that Opal Luby Spaulding was his aunt—and Ken Weaver the husband of his first cousin. She had always coddled her younger brother; at the same time she had controlled him, as she tended to try to control the people closest to her, by dangling gifts in front of their noses, always with strings attached. Charles was someone she couldn't control. If he resented his wife's pandering to her brother, he also indulged it.

Thus, when the disaster of J. W.'s perfidy came crashing down on the company, Gertrude was the sole person who didn't get told the full extent of the crime he had committed. Thanks to some inward reasoning of Charles's—whether from a laconic chivalry, a code of honor, a prideful sorrow that she would choose to champion her brother rather than automatically side with her husband, a desire to sidestep domestic arguments, or a distrust that she would ever consent to believe and accept the story of J. W.'s misconduct even if she heard it, we will never know—she was not told of it at all, then or later. It was her link to J. W., after all, that effectively saved him from possible charges. The Lubys had always been a close-knit clan. They stuck together; they were never going to seek punitive satisfaction from someone kin to them, even by marriage. Perhaps they decided that they wouldn't stoop so low. Perhaps they felt such action would put them on equal ground with the betrayer. As a result, the only version Gertrude possessed for the next four decades was the one-sided tale with which J. W. armed her: that he was a maltreated, underappreciated reject from the Luby inner circle, a man upon whom a gross injustice had been wreaked.

It's possible that J. W. Cunningham's primary known wrong was merely prompted by his own brand of dissatisfaction and his obstinate temper. Maybe the request that he leave Harlingen triggered a very basic human response, something like: "Kick me out, will you? Well, I'll show *you* who can run his own cafeteria chain!" Without question his sense of grievance, which colored all his victim-fumed complaints to his sister over the years to come, was strong enough to overcome whatever moral or ethical considerations might have initially impeded him. Whatever rationale he crafted to propel his unethical deed, it also created the momentum for a later, much grander act of looting and treachery: one that would finally and irreparably tear the Johnston and Cunningham families apart, and give him the chance at last to drink from the trough he had managed so adroitly to pollute. For now, however, the clash of loyalties he had inflamed would suffice to fuel a marital conflagration.

9

CUTTING THE JELL-O

□ □ □

Carol Lynn Johnston, the only child of Charles and Gertrude Johnston, was born into an organization founded and run by a host of only children. Like Bob Luby before her, her first home away from home was a cafeteria — in her case, the Presa Street store in downtown San Antonio. As an infant and toddler, Carol spent many hours playing underfoot in the Luby's kitchen while her mother cooked, prepared salads, and taught the staff how to re-create recipes.

Carol Johnston recalls her childhood experiences, her memories, and the lessons she learned growing up in such an environment:

While I was the only child of Gertrude and Charles Johnston, I had many parental figures—in fact, life was lived on the job and I received training from the best. Every smile, tear, or need was met by the attentive arms or presence of a caring adult. These adults came in all colors, sizes, ages, and abilities.

I learned my ABC's in English and in Spanish. I was tutored on table manners and professional conduct befitting a young lady—for instance, how

Left: *Charles Johnston and Carol Johnston*
Right: *Carol Johnston and Gertrude Johnston*

to behave when customers were in the cafeteria. I could recognize 10:45 a.m. and 2:00 p.m. on a wall clock or wristwatch. When the cafeteria closed at 2:00 p.m., the cooks, line servers, and floor girls brought out their radios or record players and taught me how to soul and salsa dance during their breaks.

I became the darling of the Presa Street store at about four years of age, when I broke my silence at the dinner table early one evening. The four managers, freshly dressed in their white shirts, seated along with my mother, father, and myself, gave witness to an expert's critique of my meal: "These mashed potatoes," I told them, "they're not smooth enough and they need salt and they're too cold."

The criticism that was commonplace among the adults who engaged in dining and discussing the meals or recipes served each evening was obviously quite different when presented from the mouth of a babe. The initial silence from the adults sitting with me at the table was broken by a round of smiles that graduated into nodding heads and a laugh from each of my fellow diners. Gerald Lee thanked me and told me that he would make a note of my comments and take care of the potatoes.

My father's reaction to what most would consider the natural course of events (a child imitating adults) was an initial look of surprise, followed by a second glance of joy and delight. Dad grabbed me up, hugged me, and declared proudly, "She's part of the team!"

Being part of the Luby's team came with its limitations. As I developed a sense of confidence interacting with those who kept company in the basement of the Riverside Hotel, I found that it was important to know which team players did what. The more I discovered about the company, the more I realized that knowing who you were required getting a handle on who you were not. My relationship to one of the head coaches became crystal clear. My dad could do just about anything—in fact, he could ask for just about anything and receive it.

The fact that he could have what he wanted merely by asking made me realize that I, too, must be pretty important. Testing the waters of this newfound ability to ask for what you want came at a very early age. I was pretty close to five and a half years old.

I knew who the cashiers were: Clara and Ina. They were both trained to cashier. This particular afternoon, Clara was "closing out the drawer." I also knew what I wanted. Gum! I wanted a piece of the individually wrapped chewing gum that she had sitting in a jar on the counter in front of her.

So I told her what I wanted: I told her that I wanted a piece of gum. Clara smiled at me and asked me if I had money for the gum. I told Clara that I didn't have any money. Clara told me that without the money she could not give me the gum. My surprise was obvious. I backed away from the cashier's booth, put my hands on my hips, and asked Clara the question that has echoed in my thoughts ever since: "Do you know who I am?"

Instantly my father stepped up from behind the place where he had been quietly watching the transaction between Clara and myself. His big hand lifted me by my seat from the floor, just high enough that Clara and I were eye to eye. "Tell her, Carol. Tell Clara who you are."

Every employee that was standing in the dining area stood frozen. The trays filled with dirty dishes were deserted; the noisy conversations between *those trying to pull the line, finish their jobs, and close up were hushed. At that very moment, my whole world was changed; attitudes and values that I hold as sacred and the way I treat others during my day-to-day life began to develop. Within the seconds that my father's hand held me in front of my friend Clara, I saw a different perspective on my importance. I could see the stern faces of those people who interacted with me, who danced with me or taught me the do's and don't's of being a part of a group, of serving other people and caring about the feelings of those you are working with.*

I felt so sad and ashamed. My dad asked me again, "Who are you?" My eyes welled with tears along with a lot of the other eyes staring back at me. "I'm sorry" was my answer.

I could see how disappointed my father was by my actions and how saddened the employees, my friends, were. My first attempt at being important was a miserable failure. That attempt has kept my eyes focused on the perspective that I saw in the faces of the people that I cared so much about, so many years ago, in a basement on a river in San Antonio, Texas.

□ □ □

Once Carol was enrolled in first grade, her time in the Presa Street store grew more limited. After school, she still often joined the employees during their afternoon breaks. Carol also carried out tasks of her own, along with another only child of the Luby's cadre, Elisse Jones, the daughter of pioneer Henry Jones. Together the girls rolled silverware, cut Jell-O into cubes, filled salt and pepper shakers, and arranged the letters to spell out the day's menu offerings on the felt marquees along the wall behind the counter.

Carol's childhood differed very much in this respect from that of her father's partner's only daughter, Martha Luby. Martha was a quiet, studious child who had to spend a great deal of time homebound due to illnesses. She participated little in the cafeteria life and remained at a distance from her vigorous father's enterprises.

As Carol grew, so did the company her father had helped generate. As a teenager and young woman, she was on the spot for many of the famous "dry runs" that heralded the opening of new stores, and then the openings themselves. The dry run was a dress-rehearsal system Charles and Bob developed that allowed the recently hired and trained workforce to coordinate their activities and then get through a whole day of a functioning cafeteria, testing the timing of chores and demands, smoothing out the bugs from the schedule, and generally getting everyone ready for the routine they could expect following an official opening. In particular it was a means of both baptizing the new manager into his store and accompanying him through the first steps of his responsibilities in order to show him how completely he was going to remain backed by the entire body of "head office" executives. For when it came to dry runs, everyone, including family, flew in to help.

The day would begin with the steady arrivals of executives and their wives, sometimes from cities scattered all over the state. Straight from the airport to the kitchen, old hands like Lola Luby Johnston, Gertrude Johnston, Helen Luby Blodgett, Ina Faye Knight, and Georgia Wenglein Luby, to name a few, tied on aprons and plunged in to start food preparation. Meanwhile, the men tackled the cleanup and last-minute decor problems, testing the machinery—dishwashers, walk-in refrigerators, and ranges—and going over the whole place, down to checking the bulbs in the recessed light fixtures. "When we moved to the new location in Harlingen," recalls Ken Weaver, "the day we opened George Wenglein was hanging doors and Bob Luby was running the carpet sweeper." The atmosphere of total support for the freshly christened manager, whom the pioneers desired, as Charles Johnston put it, to feel "completely caressed," was the cornerstone for the new store's success. No matter whether a dishwasher or icemaker broke down during the dry run or an employee failed to appear, he knew that he was now official Luby family, and everything would be handled. This inspired a huge amount of confidence in someone shouldering the onus of such a big production.

And it served to show how, once again, Bob and Charles's careful policy of controlled expansion depended not on capital resources, real estate, or a preconceived growth plan, but on one main factor: the availability of good managers. Because such men had trained for years before they were handed the privilege, fiscal rewards, and burdens of their own stores, they had even keener interests than usual in those stores' profitability, reacting with a soldier's immediate reflex to fluctuations in sales, food prices, employee problems, pilferage, and other marketplace issues, rather than waiting—like so many of their peers employed in other restaurants might do—for corporate mandates to be handed down. The magic formula of a big compensation package proved itself over and over again, inspiring greater initiative. The fact that the Johnston/Luby team always treated them as equals (as they did everyone under their umbrella, down to the pot washers and tea cart ladies) and listened respectfully to suggestions also made a difference. Often managers would see their ideas implemented if the team found them useful. After all, the managers were now in the field, and despite the active hands-on approach of the owners/partners/executives, new species of problems could arise at any time in a changing society. Such openness to improvements and willingness to weigh and value the recom-

Beaumont Luby's. Young Carol Johnston is at left.
Martha Luby is held by her mother, Georgia.

mendations of subordinates on the part of upper management—such a conspicuous lack of the usual tycoon alpha-type ego—nurtured loyalties and zeal all the more.

By the end of each first "dry run" day, as nightfall settled onto the town in which the new store was opening, every employee and manager knew what to do in the tricky choreography that would dictate their hours during the years ahead. Then the whole contingent—staff, executives, and their families—flung wide the doors, and fed the food that had been produced to whoever showed up to enjoy it, free of charge—a sort of civic feast to celebrate their efforts and their spirit of mutual cooperation, and to launch the baby enterprise. Many a vagrant ate well on the night before a Luby's Cafeteria official opening.

□ □ □

By 1957 the fourth San Antonio store had opened, as well as a second El Paso location, bringing the total number of stores to nine. A short time later, Carol Johnston, having spent her formative years as a Luby's staff crony and mascot, was approaching the adolescence during which the first cracks would begin to widen in her parents' marriage.

10

HADDOCK ALMONDINE

AND CHICKEN-FRIED STEAK

□ □ □

Don't worry about your starting salary. Make yourself invaluable-
—then, renegotiate.

CHARLES JOHNSTON

Throughout this period of growth in the 1950s, the Luby's business structure consisted of the intricate web of interlocking partnerships. Only the
equity that Bob Luby and Charles Johnston owned in all nine cafeterias
bound them together and provided a common denominator. As for the
other pioneers, the "band of brothers," each partner owned a share in one,
sometimes two or three, stores, but no one except the two Luby cousins
had slices of every single pie.

The problems this system engendered were beginning to mount. Bookkeeping, for one thing, was a real headache for Henry Lee, the accountant
who oversaw all the stores' finances. The stores that involved partnerships
with other branches and members of the family in earlier-established Luby's
made another questionable issue, chiefly one pertaining to Harry Luby. Bob
and Charles had already dissociated themselves from these separate entities

long before. But they all shared the Luby's Cafeteria name, and the amalgamation of these independent stores seemed very desirable to a thriving concern. So Bob Luby proposed a solution—one that most of the U.S.A., with its expanding businesses in a flourishing postwar economy, was also espousing. It helped set the stage for what has since become retail America: the now-familiar corporate chain, which these days is the standard rather than the exception when it comes to the places where we shop and eat out.

Bob sprang his idea on the other twelve partners at a surprise meeting called for November 12, 1958, in the conference room of the Menger Hotel in San Antonio. The Menger, a San Antonio landmark built in 1859, is the oldest hotel in continuous operation west of the Mississippi. It lies directly across the street from the Alamo, the heart of the Texas Republic, and has housed guests that included Robert E. Lee, Ulysses S. Grant, Theodore Roosevelt, Babe Ruth, Sarah Bernhardt, and Mae West, as well as having been celebrated as a Texas icon in films and books from *Giant* to *All the Pretty Horses*. There, in this dense atmosphere of prime historic moments, Bob proposed the formation of a central corporation in which each partner would have a combined interest in future growth.

"This corporation could devote its efforts to the development of new cafeterias," Luby told the men gathered around the table. "Through the new structure we could all cooperate toward a common goal. It's possible that within the next ten years the corporation could be operating thirty cafeterias and have a pretax profit of a million dollars a year." In 1958 a million-dollar-a-year business was a dizzyingly fat money-earner, and meant a huge enterprise. It was again revolutionary in terms of the restaurant industry, to think in terms of such large corporate profit.

But at first his chief partner, Charles Johnston, had doubts. "I liked things the way they were," he said later. Charles—the "people person," the good connector, the smoother of ruffled feelings and fine, old-fashioned order—probably wasn't sure how a corporation could continue to maintain the united spirit among employees, among other concerns. But then he quickly admitted, "I was wrong."

The plan Bob announced arrived on the cusp of the new era in American business, when consolidation in a number of retail areas—hardware, jewelry, clothing—was just beginning as a major, forceful trend, and the old family-style, mom-and-pop businesses were about to start scrambling for survival. Bob went on to point out that informal partnerships were shortly to become obsolete in a fast-growing market, and new government regulations were helping that process along. In fact, the whole world was changing just as rapidly, including international dining attitudes. The novelty Harry Luby himself had helped to invent was now invading older cultures. According to a 1958 *New York Times* article, in Paris, that bastion of traditional dining and haute cuisine—the country where, during the eighteenth century, the first restaurant had been born—American-style cafeterias were springing up all over town, representing "a revolution in French lunch habits."

So on February 4, 1959, a corporation called Cafeterias Inc. was formed. The directors were Bob Luby, Charles Johnston, Harry Luby (the patriarch of the serving line), George Wenglein, John Lee, Norwood Jones, Henry O. Jones Jr., Art Kidd, Gerald W. Lee, Henry J. Lee, Kenneth Weaver (of the Harlingen cafeteria), Boyd Morrow, William Smith, George Evans, Virgil Hill, and Asa Hubbard. The company's by-laws limited stock ownership to participants in the preceding partnerships and employees of the new corporation. In other words, from the very beginning of the corporation's life, cafeteria employees could and did own stock options—a highly unusual circumstance for business at that time.

As for the financing practices of the growth the new corporation was anticipating, certain policies were put into place. Money would be raised internally, rather than borrowed. Programs were instituted that included, for instance, the sale of ten-year debenture offerings yielding 6 percent interest to all members of the corporation, thereby guaranteeing an in-house debt-free expansion income. Luby's took care of itself, and it took care of its own. It would owe no outsiders a penny. All of Harry Luby's principles were to be honored, including the premise that one's business grew only when one's previous endeavors had earned enough money to afford and support that expansion.

Over the ten years that followed, eighteen new stores opened their doors. This number fell short of the projected thirty by a mere three cafeterias, but the very next year, 1970, would see two more cafeterias added to the roster. And after that, the list steadily swelled by at least one to two new locations each year, until finally, in 1987, the one hundredth store opened in Round Rock, Texas. By then, Luby's had long breached the state borders to establish stores in New Mexico, Oklahoma, and Arizona.

But those stores still waited as promises for the future on that November day when Bob shared his thoughts and ideas with the group of men who were about to become not only fortune-earners but fortune-makers for others. And plenty of challenges, crises, and triumphs, including hurricanes, internal family strife, and wild success, lay in store before the second decade would end.

The corporate staff began to grow just as soon as Bob's proposal was voted on and approved. The newly structured roster of jobs was filled by seasoned, handpicked individuals from within the company who knew every nook and cranny of the business, from grease traps to books. Bob Luby was formally named president. Charles Johnston was made executive vice president. George Wenglein became vice president in charge of installations, personnel, and organization of new units; Norwood Jones, vice president in charge of financing and leasing; John Lee, vice president in charge of food and service; George Evans, vice president in charge of unit operations. Art Kidd was placed in charge of advertising, and Henry Lee became vice president, secretary, and assistant treasurer. Most of the new officers had ac-

McAllen Luby's, 1962

Interior of the McAllen Luby's, 1962

cepted substantial pay cuts in leaving their management positions at lucrative cafeterias in order to fill these corporate positions, in the belief that if the corporation proved successful, everyone involved would benefit.

And they did.

□ □ □

When Bob and Charles first banded together to serve American palates, their iron-clad pledge that they would never open a Luby's Cafeteria in a town or city where a store already existed under that same name was subjected to no challenges. It was not until 1961, when Houston got selected as the site of the Manned Spacecraft Center for the newly launched NASA space program, that the city's flourishing chemical and petroleum-refining industries' job forces and economic base got an added boost, suddenly making it the premier market in the Southwest. Of course, Houston already had a Luby's, owned by Harry Luby's cousins. True to their word, Bob and Charles wouldn't open a store under the corporate title. But with so much potential business in far-flung locations, there seemed room enough to start more cafeterias there without promoting competition with relatives. So it was decided in 1965 to open the first Houston corporate store under a brand-new name: Romana's Cafeteria. The name was suggested by a Luby's executive's wife, in honor of a plaza in San Antonio. Interestingly enough, few customers in Houston ever realized that when they dined at a Romana's, they were actually eating Luby's classic dishes. Everyone, including the previously established Luby's owners, felt satisfied. And according to Bob Luby, "Getting into Houston was a real turning point in the company."

The first store was a tremendous success, and two more soon opened, in 1967 and 1969. The directors' instincts in penetrating that market were right on the money, and Bob Luby's prediction became truer than even he could have guessed. Cafeteria dining obviously suited the Houston lifestyle very well because, through the ensuing years, the popularity of Luby's was to get endorsed by its golden expansion record. As of December 2004, Houston boasted no fewer than twenty-nine Luby's branches—not counting a number of others in suburbs and bedroom communities outside the city limits.

But meanwhile, in the midst of all these rich triumphs, the worm in the apple of Luby's immaculate integrity was biding its time.

1 1

THE WORM GNAWS DEEPER

☐ ☐ ☐

On the ladder of life, be careful of who you step on as you're going up.
You might just run into them on your way down.
CHARLES JOHNSTON

It was in 1959, when J. W. Cunningham Jr. left his position as assistant manager at the Harlingen cafeteria in a huff with the partners' architectural plans in his possession, that home life first began to grow very difficult for the most famously considerate man in the Luby's organization, Charles Johnston. From the moment of J. W.'s departure from Harlingen, Charles found himself in a novel predicament. He had been married since the early 1930s to Gertrude—more than twenty-six years had passed since that day in Oak Cliff when they had found one another over a pickle barrel and fallen in love. During those years they had worked hard together, raised their daughter Carol together, enjoyed their vacations together with the rest of the Luby clan up in Colorado, square-danced together, shared every aspect of joy and hardship that marriage can bring. But now Gertrude was

Gertrude and Charles Johnston square dancing

J. W. Cunningham, his wife Joy, and their three children (clockwise from top left), John, Joan, and Jay

very upset. In fact, she was so upset she was willing to turn her home into a torment cell. She couldn't contain her outrage, and her recriminations went on and on.

Didn't Charles remember, for instance, that her brother was a family man with two children and a pregnant wife when he made the decision to move J. W. on to another assistant management post? And how could Charles be so unfair as to have kept J. W. in suspense about the future general manager's position he truly deserved? How could he allow Bob to do so? After all, she knew the *real* story; J. W. had already told her how it had been he himself who had offered to transfer from the Harlingen store in order to heal the friction caused by his rift with Ken Weaver. According to him, he was the noble party who then was left out in the cold, without another berth. Hence his defection from Luby's, and the establishment of his own cafeterias in Dallas. He had had no choice. What else could he do, with a pregnant wife and two children? In her opinion, it looked as if Charles had just been waiting for J. W. to *offer* to transfer, and then he had cut off J. W.'s life support by simply never finding him another Luby's to manage. So why was Charles abandoning her side of the family with such determination? Why hadn't he looked after J. W., the way the Luby pioneers always looked after their own so conscientiously?

By the time J. W. had built his own new Dallas cafeteria, Gertrude's irritation had turned into an open sore. Through the coming years it continued to fester, driving Gertrude to ever-more furious reproaches that gave her husband no rest. J. W. had eventually built *five* cafeterias, and they were now doing so well under his good management that Gertrude couldn't understand why in the world the Luby's contingent had ever thought J. W. was not excellent manager material. J's Cafeterias, in fact, made a real success story. Wasn't that enough evidence in itself that Bob and Charles had been wrong? Besides, Charles had let her, Gertrude, down. Charles had betrayed their marriage; Charles valued his business more than he did her wishes; Charles was slighting her. Charles was willing to sin against her family. Any time there was a chance for an argument, she whipped the subject of J. W.'s ejection into a tornado of conflict. Objects got hurled against walls. Quarrels escalated into full-scale battles, with Gertrude bearing relentlessly down on her spouse. Screams and tears erupted.

But the louder the screams became, the further Charles withdrew from Gertrude emotionally. Finally the time came when Charles couldn't stand it anymore. J. W.'s wrongdoing had strained the marital tensions to the breaking point. Abruptly one day, he announced to his wife that he was leaving her. He wanted a separation.

Gertrude couldn't believe it. She simply couldn't accept that her husband would not only leave uncorrected the gross injustice he had aided and abetted but also would leave his marriage of more than two decades without a backward glance. She especially couldn't imagine that there was no more motive for his desertion than the simple desire for harmony. She wanted to believe another woman was involved. Was he having an affair with his secretary? Was he in love with someone he had met in the course of his cafeteria rounds? But there was no evidence, nor would there ever be, that such a woman existed. When Charles walked out, he did so with peremptory finality, leaving behind his clothes still hanging in the closet, his possessions, pictures, everything, severing all ties completely and turning his back as best he could on the pain that the Harlingen situation had generated. His only vocal excuse was that his doctor had told him he couldn't absorb any more stress. His health was at stake.

Yet when he left, he still hadn't told Gertrude the facts behind her brother's defection. His instincts and principles, so typical of his old-fashioned generation, so gallant in their concepts, dictated that he "protect" the women in his life. He had protected his wife from many things through the years. He would go on protecting his daughter from many others as long as he lived. So despite all her venom, trained on him, he shielded Gertrude from the worst suspicion in the whole snare of troubles: that J. W. had committed a wrong against the Luby's organization—that J. W. was a thief.

And he never told her later either.

On some level, Charles probably comprehended that to tell Gertrude the truth would be a futile exercise. She would never believe him or take him at his word. She would demand proof. And the only way to truly, indisputably provide that proof was for the Luby's organization to press charges against J. W. and accuse him of felony theft. And if that happened, and J. W. was convicted and sent to prison, it would not only destroy Gertrude; it would rip the corporation apart. Thus, there was an even greater reason than family protection that Luby's did not either try to have J. W. arrested or denounce him publicly, or even privately (except among the ones most directly affected), as a crook.

But these omissions would cost Gertrude dearly. The untold truth would exact its toll in several ways: through misplaced trust, in the loss of hard cash, and eventually, in harm to her very health and well-being. And it would cost those she loved almost just as much, shredding the fabric of her own family, turning member against member. It would even come down through the years to entangle her and Charles's only grandchild in a spiderweb of deceit, larceny, and courtroom clashes.

But that still lay four decades in the future.

□ □ □

It took four years for the mild-mannered Luby's executive vice president and cofounder to reach his crest of exasperation. When he did, in 1963, his daughter Carol was still a teenager. She was busy getting an education, working hard, and seeking a normal degree of happiness after a happy childhood of home solidarity.

The disintegration of that home's foundations came as a huge blow. Suddenly Carol found herself in an impossible position. She, the only child, was the one who would keep attempting in the years ahead to bridge the chasm that now separated her mother and father. Over and over she fought, and failed, to heal the bitterness between them. In fact, the sole result of her efforts was that she, too, soon found herself alienated from each parent in a new way. She was asked, by her mother in particular, to convey messages, to take sides, to report on Charles's private life, to spy, to soothe and comfort and advise—and especially, to help keep the hope burning in Gertrude's heart that somehow Charles would eventually change his mind and come home. When Carol refused to perform these tasks, she received the brunt of her mother's suspicions and accusations. Meanwhile, Gertrude never stopped lamenting her plight. Nor did she cease to vent her undying indignation about the brother left out in the cold. She blamed a big raft of individuals for what had happened: she blamed Charles's doctor; she blamed his secretary; she blamed Carol's great-aunt, Mrs. Opal Luby Spaulding. In short, she blamed everyone but herself and J. W. Cunningham Jr.

And throughout all this, it never even occurred to her to question the likenesses between the Luby's stores and the cafeterias J. W. had built and opened in Dallas.

As for Carol's father, he refused, from the moment he left home to his last days on earth, ever to discuss any aspect or detail of what had happened. Consequently, Carol's visits with Charles grew strained. Now she was truly an outsider, looking for any basis of conversation that wouldn't tip over the edge into tension. Her father, the "people person" in the Luby's hierarchy, was plainly uncomfortable talking about his living situation. Unlike his workaday life, he had no room here in which to use his wonderful skills as a peacemaker. There was seemingly no way to smooth the ruffled feathers of the two women in his life, so he didn't try. Because he disliked any references to the rupture, there wasn't much he and his daughter could safely talk about. Instead, Charles and Carol played a lot of gin rummy, and let the companionable silence that can attend a card game become the new core of their relationship. They also spent a great deal of time together dining out at big restaurants, a pastime they both enjoyed, and one that was safe from the potential bombs of intimate confessions.

So, thanks to Charles's closed-mouthed policy, Carol possessed no notion or warning insight into what kind of bad behavior of which her uncle J. W. was capable. All she had was her mother's version of events. And all she could witness directly was her mother's humiliation at having been "left," what an ordeal of embarrassment Gertrude went through now every time she entered one of the cafeterias—acutely aware, of course, that everyone inside, down to the tea-ladies and cashiers, knew her husband had cried "Enough!" and had slammed the door behind him.

But the other thing that Charles especially didn't share with Carol at the time was what the knife thrust of the Harlingen episode had done to his lifelong connection with his cousin, Bob Luby, and therefore to the Luby's structure itself.

Because of the position his brother-in-law had jammed him into, Charles Johnston's loyalties were now suspect. Gertrude's loud objections didn't help. Thus, over the four years after the Harlingen debacle, his relations with Bob grew more circumspect. A new caution tainted their former easy communion. Due to the fact that *Charles's wife's brother* was the culprit, no one from the Luby's head office would even consider legal prosecution—particularly not Bob Luby himself. Nor would George Wenglein, nor Ken Weaver, nor Mrs. Opal Luby Spaulding—all of them related in one way or another to both Charles and Bob. Nor would anyone else involved in the Harlingen store partnership. No matter what he had done, J. W. was family, just as were the others whom he had hurt. And Luby's took care of family. That was Harry's way. It was unthinkable to press charges against someone bound to you through blood or marriage. It went against the whole Luby code. So there remained only one option, given such an impasse. The whole subject, bitter as it was, had to be dropped from all conversation. It must never be brought up again. There was no point in dredging through the acrimony and pain. Nothing would ever get resolved through discussion; instead everyone would just continue to simmer in their anger and reinforce their sense of betrayal by dwelling on it. Losses had to be cut. Mature men needed to move on. The atmosphere had been spoiled with a smell like rotting meat by mere association with such a bad episode. Luby's Cafeterias had never had anything to feel shame about before. So the subject became taboo. Even the two founders, the cousins who had loved and respected each other since their youths, tacitly agreed that the sanest course was to avoid any mention of it. But this meant that they, too, were left dangling in the limbo created by J. W.'s action. They couldn't clear the air; neither could they redeclare their faith in one another.

And so, for perhaps the first time in his life, Charles found himself ringed with a certain kind of isolation.

□ □ □

After a while his widowed mother, Lola Luby Johnston, came to live with Charles and keep house for him so that he wouldn't be completely alone. She cooked him dinners using her famous recipes—it was said that Lola could make cardboard taste as good as a gourmet meal—and remained in Charles's home for thirteen years, until her death in 1978. After that,

Charles's aunt Helen Luby Blodgett took her place. Family looks after its own, especially if you're a Luby.

But there was one Luby descendant who didn't get taken care of in the circle, in the way that she had been brought up to count upon. For she was caught between the proverbial rock and hard place. Month by month, the abyss continued to deepen between Carol Johnston and *her* only immediate family. The week Charles left Gertrude, Gertrude phoned Carol at her apartment in Dallas late one night, in hysterics, pleading with Carol to quit her job, move back to San Antonio, and live with her. The job in question was one Carol had only recently acquired: working in a public relations program for the executive director of the Oak Cliff (Dallas) Chamber of Commerce. What's more, she had just rented her very first apartment.

Over the next week or more, Gertrude called Carol several times a day, repeating the request, and telling her daughter that she would offer her "early retirement" if Carol would just come back home. After consulting her boss and her uncle J. W. Cunningham, who both made the strong recommendation that Carol decline the offer, at least for the time being, as it would both sandbag Carol's present life and perhaps hinder her mother's creation of a new life for herself, Carol replied to Gertrude that she felt to stop working would be a bad career choice.

But Carol's refusal disappointed and infuriated Gertrude. And after a short while, Carol became aware that her parents' trust in her had diminished. Often she felt that perhaps her father suspected her of reporting his activities to her mother, just as she felt her mother probably thought the same thing: that she was informing her father regularly of her mother's business. For many years to come, there was no dialogue at all among them, except on the most formal terms. J. W. Cunningham's perfidy had spawned a monster indeed, one that was unfortunately nourished by the idiosyncrasies of his adult victims.

But the crowning irony in the division between Charles and Gertrude was that neither of them wanted a divorce. Just as J. W.'s wrong had triggered a limbo inside the Luby's organization, so their troubled union was kept in a state of suspended animation, rather than resolved in a legal way so that they might both go ahead with their lives. In Gertrude's case, it was because she still hoped that the marriage had a chance of renewal. About a year after Charles left her, she asked Carol's opinion as to whether or not she should file to make the marriage's end permanent. In her reply, Carol made what she would later come to view as a mistake: she told her mother she believed that if her father should ever think about returning, it would be easier for him to come home if he was still married. Whether Gertrude found this convenient to believe or not, it is true that for the next twenty-six years, the clothes Charles had walked away from went on hanging in the same back bedroom closet, untouched and undisturbed, as if he was going to walk back into the house any minute. Gertrude never let go; she never cut the tie that might free her to pursue another kind of happiness.

Charles's reasons for hanging on to the legality of the marriage were clearly more business-oriented. If he and Gertrude were to divorce, the community property laws of Texas would require that his major share in Luby's Cafeterias, Inc. would have to be divided in half. The results to his estate, to his influence and position, to his voice in the company, and to the company's health itself would be disastrous.

So the two of them, each stuck in his or her dilemma, were therefore doomed to live alone and remain alone for good. It was a pitiful outcome to what had been a long and constructive partnership.

□ □ □

The only person in Gertrude's life during these long years who presented himself in the role of loving sympathizer and helpful adviser was her brother, J. W. Cunningham Jr. Upon "Dub," Gertrude could always rely. He cared about her loneliness. He commiserated with her on the terrible way her husband had had the gall to first shaft *him* and then walk out on her. His story as an honest, martyred fellow played on and on through the years like a broken record in the two siblings' visits. Because the fiction both condemned Charles's mistreatment and vindicated J. W. and Gertrude, it supported their self-righteous stances while reinforcing Gertrude's solitude. Indeed, "Dub" wanted to be his sister's hero; he wanted to ride in on his white charger and rescue her from her misery. Or so he chose to appear. And perhaps he sincerely believed that version of himself.

But soon after the split-up, he also began to volunteer often and eagerly to relieve her ignorance and confusions as to how to invest all the money that Charles had settled on her. He had more than one suggestion to make, and each involved a great new idea.

The problem was Gertrude had no such confusions, much less ignorance. She had been living in the business world for a much longer time than her younger brother. After all, she had been in on the founding of the present Luby's organization; she had helped to run a Dallas cafeteria years before J. W. reached adulthood. When it came to managing money, she was anything but a fool. And the conservative wisdom of her investments, the direct product of having come to maturity during the Great Depression, meant that her portfolio was filled with blue-chip stocks and tax-exempt bonds and that she wasn't about to take any risks.

But she did appreciate his concern. And she did value his devotion, and they did share a Dallas accountant. And slowly, through the years to come, that appreciation, coupled with her loneliness and broken hopes, would lead to her undoing.

12

SCALLOPED SQUASH

AND SPINACH PUDDING

□ □ □

By the year 1969 Cafeterias Inc. was zooming like a steady comet through the business firmament. The first out-of-Texas store had been opened in 1966 in Las Cruces, New Mexico—a particularly fateful crossing of frontiers, as the future would reveal, with consequences beyond anyone's most morbid imagination, and implications adverse to the values Luby's represented. A new seed of corruption and evil had been planted in that bare New Mexico desert space—one that wouldn't sprout into its fullest growth for twenty-five years. The store, however, was a great success. Other locations were flourishing as well, and more were being added.

But even more important at the time: the biggest barrier of the past had just been cleared away, and the outcome was to everyone's advantage: the company had finally reached an agreement with the various partners in the nine Luby's that were still privately owned and founded prior to incorporation. These included the last holdouts owned by Harry Luby's many cousins, strewn in various cities across Texas. In essence, the agreement stipulated that the corporation would manage the stores for fifteen years, with the option to purchase them at the end of that period at a price commensurate with "as is" market value.

Through this decision, the original owners profited hugely, both by switching from a solitary mom-and-pop type of operation that was now able to depend on an efficient corporate system and by the full affiliation with the corporate name. Meanwhile, the corporation also profited, of course. For at last the umbrella that Bob and Charles had designed sheltered almost all the outstanding cafeterias under its shade, even if it didn't yet own them all. Romana's Cafeterias in Houston and the Dallas/Fort Worth area naturally remained Romana's, because Don Luby, Earl Luby, Dan Luby, the brothers George and Joe Luby, and other family members still technically owned the old Luby's, which remained Luby's. So faith was kept. The sole exception to the agreement was the cafeteria in Wichita Falls, since the owner there preferred to keep running his cafeteria by himself. For this reason, Cafeterias Inc. didn't establish a store there, as there was no room or market for competition and the executives wished to keep their word about nudging in on previously claimed family territory.

But the corporation now ran a total of twenty-six stores, seventeen of which it owned outright, and every single one of them fell into line with the continuing corporate managerial profit-sharing policies—60 percent net profit for the company, 40 percent for the store managers—as well as generous compensation packages with stock advantages for all employees. As a result, Cafeterias Inc. didn't tend to have much personnel turnover.

The head office also continued to respond to all customer complaints, no matter how far-flung and seemingly trivial. Comment cards were supplied at all locations, with prepaid postage and a direct address to the office in San Antonio, and customers were encouraged to write down their requests and gripes. Consistent quality was every manager's goal, but sometimes he found himself so busy handling day-to-day schedules, purveyors' irregularities, and other issues that he didn't necessarily catch a momentary failure in the taste or texture of a dish offered to the public. By now Luby's had so many devoted regulars, each with his or her own preferences, that the likelihood of a stringy piece of beef or undercooked vegetable sneaking past their notice and protest was very slim. So if a store garnished a total of three successive complaints pertaining to the same topic, an officer—usually Norwood Jones, Henry Jones, or in later years, Herbert Knight— would spring a surprise visit, similar to the one the partners had made to the El Paso store when dissension had broken out there, and pinpoint the problem. This high-visibility vigilance paid off. What the manager of a particular store might find acceptable or even excellent, somebody passing down the line had not. The executives wouldn't rest until the clientele was satisfied, and the customers knew it.

And they rewarded it.

This banner year of 1969 also saw the hiring of the first "nonfood" executive to enter the Luby's inner circle. Such a move signaled a big departure from former policy, and would greatly influence the company's financial decisions, for good or ill, in the years to come. The new executive was an accountant named John Lahourcade. Lahourcade was a man with expertise in a field other than the physical needs of the food industry, and for this reason he seemed a necessary addition to the head office. He had critical knowledge needed in order to help install the next stage of Luby's growth: he understood stock market procedure. His sons were brokers. He had worked in high-end corporate accounting for years, at the firm of Bielstein, Lahourcade and Lewis. He could advise in areas in which the rest of the executive team had no experience. It was Lahourcade who, only a short time later, was to bring in another new name to the Luby's roster, a man who would start as an internal auditor there, get quickly promoted in the accounting department, and work for the next eighteen years, during which he would eventually get groomed for the head position in the company: president and CEO. That earnest young man with a profound respect for Luby's beautiful record of integrity was named John Edward Curtis Jr.

Simultaneously, some of the pioneers now began to retire from the corporate office to fill places on the board of directors. The first to take this step was Henry Lee, the first administrative employee ever hired, who retired from his vice presidency in 1970. The same year, total sales surpassed the $18 million mark, and an employee profit-sharing plan was introduced. The year after that, the founders themselves emulated Henry Lee. Bob Luby and Charles Johnston, both of them sixty-one years old, vacated their posts as chief executives and assumed seats on the board, with Luby as chairman.

Luby's board of directors, 1973

"I had run the company with Charles since the beginning," Luby said later. "We knew there were going to be big changes ahead. We had anticipated a public stock offering for several years. Before we started selling stock to the public, I wanted to be darn sure the company could operate without me as president. So Charles and I stepped down earlier than we had to."

This kind of responsible approach to "going public" was synonymous with the integrity that glued the Luby's organization together. What would be the point in staking the general public's stock-purchasing money on a business that couldn't hold its own once the captains left the helm? The inner circle might get a great deal richer, but its members had no intention of sucking funds from a trusting investor merely in order to reinforce a ship that might later founder. They had no wish to cement their own private fortunes before the vessel veered off course or even started springing a few leaks.

The "band of brothers"—the sixteen founding directors who had for so many years golfed, danced, played poker, and shared family vacations at Estes Park, Colorado—remained close friends. Only Charles Johnston found himself perhaps living on the social periphery of the group. He was

Square dance group, New Year's Eve, 1957

no longer one-half of a married couple—he was the odd man out. And Cafeterias Inc. liked married couples; it encouraged happy, stable marriages and families. Charles's separation from Gertrude and its consequences had left scars that still affected the dynamics of his other relationships. People were amiable and admiring, he was ringed with great respect, but things weren't the same. And they never would be again.

But to all appearances, at least inside the Luby's boardroom, they seemed as normal as they had throughout the last quarter century, running with the smooth, well-oiled, and congenial attitude that had served them so well through whatever issues they faced. John Lahourcade later said of his first sense of the group, "One of the things that impressed me most about this organization was that I never heard anyone raise his voice." Management disagreements were rare, and always were settled without confrontations. Perhaps this was because the feeling of fellowship and equality was so great at Luby's that no egotistical prima donnas would have survived there.

A good example of this mechanism was an incident that occurred a few years later, when, in the new age of logos and branding, it was at last decided to pick a sign that would become common to all stores, unify the image, and insure brand-name recognition. When the board was shown a new logo design that might go up on the signs outside the cafeterias, it was John Lahourcade himself who provided the voice of dissent. He complained about—of all things—an apostrophe. This mark, the fat piece of yellow punctuation that hangs wedged nowadays between the *y* and the *s* in the red-painted *Luby's* name like a splotch of mustard, was something Lahourcade just didn't like. When he said so, Bob Luby just smiled. "Well, John, you think you could learn to like it?" he asked gently.

The meeting adjourned immediately afterward, in unanimous accord. It had lasted all of five minutes.

□ □ □

The first public common stock offering from Cafeterias Inc. took place on January 24, 1973. One day after the stock was introduced under the listing CAFE, another Texan's inadvertent influence nearly scuttled the entire enterprise. For it was that day that the U.S. government declared as a day of national mourning for former president Lyndon Johnson, who had died suddenly of a heart attack on January 22, only hours before the cease-fire ending U.S. involvement in Vietnam would be announced. Therefore, on the twenty-fifth, in observance of the mourning, all trading was temporarily suspended. The very next day, the market collapsed, diving to perilous lows and sending the Dow Jones average into its deepest plunge in eighteen months. If Luby's had delayed its offering by so much as a week, the venture would have proven impossible.

Which might not have been such a bad thing after all. For on that fateful January 24, Luby's entered a new era, as a very different body of decision makers started charting its future course. That group of people consisted of the new stockholders from all over the country who had noted a promising avenue of investment, but who had never eaten a single meal inside the Luby's Cafeteria doors.

13

YEAST ROLLS, BISCUITS,

AND TWO KINDS OF CORNBREAD

☐ ☐ ☐

Over the next two years the board of directors watched performance of their stock as anxiously as parents monitoring the first steps of a toddler. Despite the opening market turmoil, the stock had in five days climbed from $14 to $16 per share, so the baby's future strides looked promising. But the board realized that such a triumphant debut couldn't last, and in fact it didn't. For within that twenty-four-month period, CAFE shares declined bit by bit to finally reach bottom prices.

Thus, the onus of earnings growth and quarterly reports gradually began to take its stealthy toll on the company's former optimism and humanist mentality. It wasn't the cafeterias' actual operations that prompted the stock's descent. It was the overall market conditions. Such a contradiction is interesting, in light of just how oppositional the two pictures of Luby's looked on paper. For Bob and Charles had been right in their assessment of whether the Luby's ship could stay afloat and keep on course without both of them still manning the operational helm. The ship could, and did—buoyed by rising sales and profits. At the end of the first year after going public, profits were up 19 percent, and up 20 percent at the end of the second year.

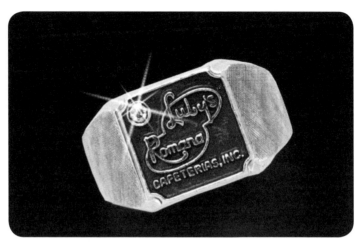

The gold Luby's/Romana ring

Such growth generated revenues of $22.5 million. Now everybody in the inner ring of pioneers truly *was* making a fortune. And despite the current plunge in share worth, so would be all Luby's stockholders, including staff—if they just waited patiently until the slump was over.

Two more large urban cafeteria openings in Houston took place during this two-year period, along with the rise in revenues. And there was no reason to think that the ship was in any trouble or would slow down, no matter what happened in the market. It seemed everyone in Texas and New Mexico wanted to slide their trays down Luby's lines. Even the gasoline crisis caused by the Arab oil embargo launched in October 1973 (in which OPEC's Arab member nations declared a refusal to ship petroleum to any country that had supported Israel during the Arab-Israeli war, triggering a major international oil shortage) helped inflate Luby's business. While other restaurants across the United States were suffering, the Luby's customer base actually increased. This was due to several factors: the lower prices, the high-quality food, and the convenient location of the new suburban branches only a short drive from many homes, which meant people didn't have to spend much on gas to reach them. And, thanks to the OPEC crunch, the resultant new Texas petroleum boom now crowned the state as the technological center for the worldwide pursuit of energy reserves, confirming a huge market for good eateries.

By 1975 Luby's sales had improved another 33 percent, and net income had climbed by 47 percent. By 1977 the business boom encompassed the whole state. Late in the year *Newsweek* ran a cover story entitled "Texas: The Superstate," which named it "the economic heart of the American Sun Belt," and pointed out that were Texas an independent country, it would have a gross national product ranked "ninth in the free world—

Recipe for cornbread and a list of other breads served at Luby's

```
                    Large Dishpan of Cornbread

  2 cups of baking powder
  ? cooksp. salt
  1 1/2 dozen of egg yolks
  1 cups of sugar
  7 sifters of meal
  3 1/2 sifters of flour
  1 gallon of buttermilk
  1 gallon of sweet milk (More if needed)
  1/2 gallon of melted lard


                    Cornbread

  6 sifters Cornmeal
  2 sifters flour
  1 good handful salt
  1 cup sugar
  2 cups baking powder
  2 dozen eggs
  2 T (heaping) soda
  1 gallon buttermilk
  1 gallon sweet milk
  About 1/2 gal. melted shortening

        Cream eggs, sugar, salt, soda and add meal
  and flour and baking powder together alternately
  with the milks.  Add shortening after the above
  mixture is well mixed.

                    Smaller Amount
  2 1/2 sifters cornmeal
  1 1/2 sifters flour
  1 1/2 dozen egg yolks
   T (heaping) baking powder
   T     "     soda
   qts. buttermilk
                    (Cond.)
```

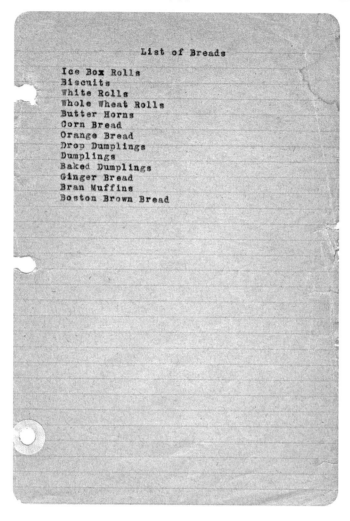

List of Breads

Ice Box Rolls
Biscuits
White Rolls
Whole Wheat Rolls
Butter Horns
Corn Bread
Orange Bread
Drop Dumplings
Dumplings
Baked Dumplings
Ginger Bread
Bran Muffins
Boston Brown Bread

ahead of Brazil, Australia, and Sweden." That same year, both the *Wall Street Journal* and *Forbes Magazine* touted Cafeterias Inc.'s sterling return on equity—"frankly 12 percent higher than McDonald's"—and its stock performance, which not only had recovered from the first two-year slump but had doubled in price in five years.

Bob and Charles's corporate ship was sailing through wide seas now.

□ □ □

Back in 1973, Luby's built its first large-scale corporate headquarters. That same year, the company also brought another long-fostered idea to fruition. It opened an official management training school.

In doing this, Luby's was following the precedent of one of its competitors—the very one mentioned in the business journals that had compared the values of their stocks. It was emulating McDonald's and the training facility that company had founded in 1961, Hamburger University. If McDonald's institution had been the first of its kind in the general industry, Luby's wasn't going to be far behind. Thus it was that Luby's as usual continued on the path of a rapidly modernizing America. The training school meant that no longer would managers rise through an apprenticeship at a local cafeteria. The change represented the recognition that not all general managers were able, due to their own time constraints, or lack of teacherly talents, to maintain a quality of training consistent enough to help the apprentices eventually meet the criteria for the management of their own stores. During the old days of football player preference—when Bob and Charles had been gung-ho for hiring the athletes who could "think on their feet" and combine the physical prowess and quick, simultaneous problem-solving skills required by the manager's job, while still maintaining the ability to make good decisions in a state of deep fatigue—the training had taken several years of gradual promotion based on acquired mastery of those skills, *plus* all the hands-on familiarity with the various tasks in the kitchen and on the floor. Now, instead, the young men and women trainees came from a dozen different colleges, and the prerequisites included two vital conditions: a college degree and a *complete lack of any* kind of prior restaurant experience. Training itself would take three months. The point of a virginal background in the food industry was simple. It was summed up by Davis Simpson, the first director of management training, and the man who designed the school's program and curriculum. "People who have worked for other restaurants or who graduate from restaurant management programs often have their own ideas about how to do things," he said. "We'd rather teach them our way." The cafeteria business, so different from other food enterprises in its necessity to cook large amounts of food at once that would stay savory and appetizing under heat and light for longer periods than the plate-by-plate preparation methods used in à la carte or fast-food restaurants, had to be run like a well-oiled machine that gauged every quantity, quality, and duration with precision. And students had to learn how to do that. By the end of their stints, the trainees knew everything they would ever need to know, from how to butcher a side of beef to how to bus tables, refresh coffee cups, mop a floor correctly, keep balance sheets, and negotiate with employees to how to mix, bake, and cut a perfectly presented, impeccable slice of lemon meringue pie. By graduation, the candidates should be prepared for an associate manager's position, then to train for another four to seven years in an actual cafeteria, enduring sixty-five-hour workweeks, before receiving the fat fiscal rewards of a full managerial position with its six-figure income: the American Dream, as it had come to be understood by then.

And a good thing, too. The managers who had been on deck since the 1950s and 1960s were now stepping into the executive positions vacated by the pioneers. And the pioneers themselves weren't the only ones who were aging. The list of personnel who had been with Luby's since Bob and Charles first opened the Presa Street cafeteria in 1947 was also beginning to grow long in the tooth. By now many of the floor staff and kitchen employees had worked several decades for the company. In 1977 Annie Musgrove, who had been such a loyal and first-rate cook at the Presa Street store, and who had regularly hidden leftovers behind her famous pot full of water on the shelf above her kitchen workstation, was honored with a thirty-year service award. Several other serious long-timers were also recognized, including a dishwasher who had worked at the Broadway store in San Antonio, the second store Bob and Charles had established. By now he was busy putting his children through college on his dishwasher's wages, and he and his colleagues, owners of Luby's stock and beneficiaries of the profit-sharing plans, could boast healthy portfolios. Many of them no doubt presumed that these financial arrangements would be their old-age economic cushion. The *Webster's Dictionary* definition of the verb *presume* is "to take for granted"; unfortunately, that phrase almost always suggests someone is making a big mistake.

However, there was one graduate of the Luby's management training center, a young Houstonian named Pappas, who was learning powerful tools to use in the restaurant business, including Luby's principles of earning loyalty and respect, and as a result would one day become vital enough to the life and future of the whole organization to reverse the disasters that resulted from those mistakes.

□ □ □

During these years, more Luby's stores than ever were opening across the American landscape. Between the time in February 1973, when the Houston cafeteria No. 5 was inaugurated (under the name of Romana's) and May 13, 1987, when the one hundredth Luby's opened in Round Rock, the corporation started up no fewer than seventy-five new locations, including several in Harry Luby's second-oldest territory: Oklahoma. These startups, of course, cost a lot of money. The trick lay in how to finance them without depleting the profitable coffers of the company.

For a brief time in the 1970s, Cafeterias Inc. relied on borrowing from financial institutions to support its never-flagging growth spurt. It had been an experimental measure, one that seemed dictated by conventional business wisdom. But interest rates were soaring during that time, the stock market took a tumble, and Luby's debt increased from $2.5 million in 1973—just before the first public offering—to $6.9 million in 1978, casting a shadow over the company's books. An alternative strategy had to be devised that was more commensurate with the original Luby philosophy. So, in addition to a new 300,000-share stock offering (the first had put 250,000 shares into play) that wound up raising more than $6 million for land acquisition and cafeteria building construction, Bob and his comrades conceived the means of generating internal funding that precluded taking out any more loans at all: selling debentures to their employees and executives. As a result, from 1978 until the early 1990s, Luby's never borrowed another cent—a phenomenal achievement in the corporate business world. And a very wise one. It also seemed only fitting that in 1978, with the company restored once more to the complete self-reliance that had been part and parcel of Harry Luby's philosophy from the inception of the first New England Dairy Lunch in 1911, Harry Luby died.

Harry Luby, Bob Luby, and Julia Luby

He had been a quiet but steady exemplar for many decades, an invisible man who had founded something much bigger than a new trend in dining or a cafeteria chain. He was old at the end: ninety-one, to be precise. For fifty-two of those years, he had resided with Julia in retirement, always within close proximity to their only child—in San Francisco, in Dallas, and in San Antonio. His life had been long enough to see the results of both his innovative ideas and his moral business principles manifested on a grand scale, while he hovered deep in the background shadows, a mere observer. All the fire and drive for innovation he had possessed as a youth had passed to his son when Bob came of age, and in Bob they had concentrated into a heightened and amplified bundle of charismatic ambition. Thereafter, Harry had been content to be merely contented.

But his big heart and his sweeping policy of benevolence were the stones thrown into the lake that continued to spread their ripples outward, on and on.

□ □ □

Throughout the late 1970s and the entire 1980s, the company remained absolutely debt-free. What's more, by 1981 annual revenues surpassed the

$100 million mark for the first time, coming in at a total of $110.2 million. One unit alone exceeded $3 million in yearly sales. And it was all gravy— for the company expansion coffers, and for everyone involved on any level with the organization.

So in 1981 there were now fifty-nine cafeterias in operation, with loyal third-generation customers who had grown up inside Luby's—including, significantly, the Luby's in Las Cruces, New Mexico. In an age of dying downtown centers and vanished town squares, Luby's customers regarded their local cafeteria as a replacement for those sites—in other words, as a community meeting place. There they could mingle with their friends and neighbors from table to table. There they knew the names of the long-time counter servers, and friendly greetings and inquiries after family members often got exchanged when they passed down the lines. A new generation of customers with young families were also growing up in Luby's. Such a clientele—and it was numerous—frequently held special events, even weddings, within Luby's walls. Entire church congregations in many small towns and cities would converge through the doors and swell the lines at noon on Sunday after worship services finished. It had always been a common sight to see three or four generations of one family dining together at Luby's on any given day of the week. Now, when families traveled together, they counted Luby's as the place to stop in and get a dependable meal. There were even some who would consider eating nowhere else, and when one town didn't have a Luby's when they were on the road, they would travel to the next rather than stop at a more convenient café.

□ □ □

In 1981 Cafeterias Inc. got a rechristening. The name was changed to Luby's Cafeterias, Inc. At the same time, it also moved to yet another, more majestic corporate headquarters, inscribed with the name "The Luby's Building." This was a curved office shaped like a slice of pie, located on Loop 410, a major San Antonio traffic artery. It was truly a far cry from the front seat of the Studebaker, the original business office that Bob Luby and Charles Johnston had first occupied.

But the very day the company moved in, Charles suffered a stroke. It was to prove the first of several. For the next eight years, Charles was confined to a wheelchair. His courageous struggles to recover his strength and mobility and to defy the debilitating effects of the handicap incited admiration throughout his circle of friends and acquaintances. He was now alone, without the support of his wife or his mother. His aunt Helen Luby Blodgett, who had moved in with him years earlier, was herself growing older and more infirm, so he needed to hire a nurse to care for him. Also, he was still semi-estranged from his daughter Carol due to the continuing bitter wounds of his marital separation and the relational stalemate they had set into place; their relationship, although loving and affectionate, nonetheless remained on a more formal footing. By now, Carol had married, borne a single child (a son, Charles Scott, named after his grandfather), divorced, and then remarried, and was living in Vail, Colorado. So her own life was fully occupied with her husband, motherhood, and her career as an interior designer. Fifteen years had passed since Charles's marriage had shattered, and although no divorce had ever been sought, Charles still considered it an unofficially finished union. Therefore, he steadily refused all of Gertrude's offers of assistance, conferred through the medium of second parties, preferring to rely on professionals. As for Gertrude herself, it is possible that she might have thought this was the opportunity she had been waiting for so long to mend the broken union. But whether she did or not, Charles most certainly did not. He adamantly clung to his singleness.

After several trial employees that didn't work out, Charles finally settled on a young male nurse named Rick Gozaydin, who could help him with the physical challenges of his affliction. They became fast friends. Even from the confines of his wheelchair Charles still maintained his involvement with Luby's, holding on to his directorship and attending almost every board meeting, attending the opening of every new cafeteria, regularly visiting stores already in operation, keeping up with the latest in restaurant and food-service concepts, developing recipes, and planning all the menus for special corporate events, such as the annual managers' meeting and the office Christmas party. His keen eye for choice cafeteria real estate sites and projected suburban demographics continued to work in Luby's favor. Good food would remain his overriding interest to the last. But most of all, he stayed a hands-on presence and influence as he had always been—a true field man, a "people person," and a benign overseer to his and Bob's endeavor.

□ □ □

So now America's changing economy and culture not only informed the decisions Luby's was making about its operations; it also, through the influence of stock-market considerations, propelled the company on a roller-coaster cycle that would carry it forward to a seeming triumph, then toward the tipping point, then to an ultimate collapse.

But we're getting ahead of the story.

14

CHERRY COBBLER

AND COCONUT CREAM PIE

□ □ □

If you're not getting your facts from the horse's mouth, you're probably dealing with the other end.

CHARLES JOHNSTON

It has been a long time now since the idea of virtue—of goodness itself, either as a resource or as an asset—made up an intrinsic element in American business thinking. Despite America's Puritan roots, *goodness* continues to be an undervalued ingredient, at best, in the recipe for almost any business endeavor. In this, the birthplace of the free enterprise system, virtue is considered somewhat quaint; its very irrelevance is an indication of the general "me first" mentality of our contemporary culture. And in this linear history, as the upcoming decade of the 1990s soon would show, ethical behavior was not going to occupy a prized place in American corporate guidelines either.

But the slogan that Luby's Cafeterias, Inc. adopted as its flag was not born of crass jingoism; it was not the mere brainchild of a cynical advertising copy writer. It rang utterly sincere, because its words remained embedded in the fairness, sense of public service, and dedication to employees and to excellence upon which Harry Luby had first insisted. When Luby's proclaimed to the world that it supplied "Good Food from Good People," the company meant it literally. Goodness was as essential a prerequisite to the end product as table salt.

"I started out as a pot washer on Main Avenue in 1954," said Leslie

Recipes for various pies and a list of pies served at Luby's

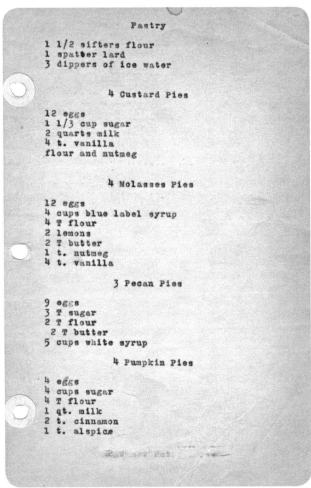

```
                    Pastry

        1 1/2 sifters flour
        1 spatter lard
        3 dippers of ice water


                4 Custard Pies

        12 eggs
        1 1/3 cup sugar
        2 quarts milk
        4 t. vanilla
        flour and nutmeg


                4 Molasses Pies

        12 eggs
        4 cups blue label syrup
        4 T flour
        2 lemons
        2 T butter
        1 t. nutmeg
        4 t. vanilla

                3 Pecan Pies

        9 eggs
        3 T sugar
        2 T flour
         2 T butter
        5 cups white syrup

                4 Pumpkin Pies

        4 eggs
        4 cups sugar
        4 T flour
        1 qt. milk
        2 t. cinnamon
        1 t. allspice
```

Sanders of Houston, a kitchen supervisor and by 1987 a thirty-three-year veteran employee. "When my wife was sick for a year, the managers gave me time off, sent flowers, and asked about her condition."

Other such stories abound. Said Minnie Bowers of Austin, Texas, a longtime elderly customer of Luby's who was blind, "I live adjacent to a Luby's. Each morning an employee stops by to take me to the cafeteria for coffee and a muffin. I have a circle of friends and acquaintances who join

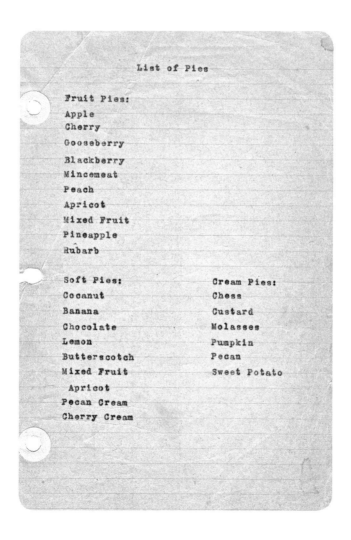

List of Pies

Fruit Pies:
Apple
Cherry
Gooseberry
Blackberry
Mincemeat
Peach
Apricot
Mixed Fruit
Pineapple
Rubarb

Soft Pies: Cream Pies:
Cocanut   Chess
Banana   Custard
Chocolate   Molasses
Lemon   Pumpkin
Butterscotch   Pecan
Mixed Fruit   Sweet Potato
Apricot
Pecan Cream
Cherry Cream

CHERRY COBBLER AND COCONUT CREAM PIE

me there. Once, when my picture appeared in the Austin paper, people would recognize me in Luby's and say hello. I counted over a hundred! When I'm ill or the weather's particularly bad and I can't leave home, Luby's sends my lunch over and they check on me. One of their employees even spent the night one time. The kindness of the managers . . . and the employees makes me feel I have another family. My Luby's gives me a wider window on the world."

In September 1961 Hurricane Carla, one of the most damaging hurricanes in recorded history ever to hit the coast of the Gulf of Mexico, scoured the Texas coast, wiping out millions of dollars' worth of property in scores of communities and killing 43 people. During the storm, the two managers of the Corpus Christi Luby's stayed put in their cafeteria. At daybreak they were joined by their assistant manager, and together the three started cleaning up the mess: broken windows, water damage, and a wrecked sign. Electrical power was gone; the city lay in wreckage. But soon the store became the outpost for the National Guard and other emergency agencies called in to help with the disaster. The gas-fired stoves in the kitchen permitted the managers to begin serving coffee and food to the police, guardsmen, neighbors, and the homeless—anyone who came in from the street. "We didn't charge anything but we made a lot of friends," recalled Bill Lowe, who was one of the managers. Because the store shared an electrical grid with a nearby hospital, its power was restored only thirty hours after the storm passed over. Then the managers called in employees and their spouses, so that Luby's became the first Corpus Christi restaurant to reopen. "The radio stations heard we were open, and after they announced it, we were swamped with customers until nine o'clock that night," Lowe said later. A large number of Corpus Christi residents might have had to go hungry if it had not been for the bounty, hard work, and fierce devotion of the Luby's crew.

Or, as Herbert Knight put it, "Many lives have been touched and enriched because of our company's philosophy of both sharing and caring."

But now, would the changing conditions of the American market and the pressures of "going public" slowly begin to erode and undermine the selflessness that had always so typified Luby's practices?

□ □ □

Back in 1969, while attending a six-week course in Advanced Management Development at the University of Hawaii, Bob Luby met Dr. Walter J. Salmon. For reasons no one could have fully anticipated at the time, it was to prove a historic occasion. Salmon, a professor who since 1956 had taught at the Harvard Business School, was currently serving on several corporate boards and was intrigued by the success of Luby's Cafeterias, Inc. and its decentralized system of management. In his conversations with Bob Luby he expressed an interest in studying the procedures that had helped make the company the shining example it had become. Would it be possible for him to be placed into a position that would allow him to do this?

The following year, George Wenglein also attended the same course and met Dr. Salmon. The year after that, Norwood Jones in his turn participated in the course and was introduced to and tutored by Salmon. Once Jones returned to San Antonio, the three Luby's men—Jones, Bob Luby, and George Wenglein—conferred about the wisdom of nominating and inducting Salmon onto their board of directors, both to give him the opportunity he wanted, and to benefit from his presence there.

Only two men, up to now, had ever been involved with Luby's decision-making processes who were not already themselves veterans of the kitchens and the cafeterias: John Lahourcade and Henry Lee. Of the two, Lee was possibly much more cognizant of the mechanisms behind the restaurant business, having worked for years in an office directly above the kitchens and dining room of the Broadway Street store. The pioneers had always felt that hands-on experience and the intimate understanding it brought was essential to any influential position in the company. Nonetheless, it was concluded among the executives who had gotten to know a little of Salmon that he would make a very good addition to the board. For one thing, he was at the forefront of Harvard Business School theory, policy, and practice, and could perhaps offer insights and expertise on the ways in which modern business was evolving. For another, he was regarded as a professional mentor in consumer marketing and retail distribution. For yet another, he had plenty of prestige and an impressive résumé and credentials in both the academic and business worlds, so he would no doubt present an appetizing addition to future stockholders. But most of all, Walter Salmon represented something Luby's didn't have prior to his advent: the new age of corporate thinking, the latest technology of corporate structure. He was a member of and a contributor to that most highly regarded Olympus of the business world—the Harvard Graduate School of Business—which, along with the Wharton Business School, would mold and indeed dominate the attitudes of American commerce for the next thirty years.

Throughout the ensuing decade, more or less, Salmon quietly occupied a seat on the board of Luby's Cafeterias, Inc., deferring to Bob Luby's judgment in all matters, and doing what he had set out to do: studying the internal mechanics and principles of the company and observing the reasons why Luby's, a business run so differently from the retail empires and manufacturing companies with which he was more familiar, was such a winner. And how could Salmon have done anything else? The proof was in the pudding—or, in Luby's case, the icebox pie. In a company where everything worked so well, and worked in the favor of not only stockholders but also company personnel and customers, there could be nothing very dramatic to alter. In the course of their association, Salmon and Bob Luby became good friends. Thus, Salmon was already a fixture on the board when rumors of takeovers began to surface.

In its April 16–22, 1979, issue, the periodical *Financial Trend* published an article revealing the fact that already a number of people had approached Luby's with the desire to buy out the company and assume control of the juicy, lucrative plum hanging on Texas's corporate tree. The article was headlined "Staying 'Home-Made'" and subtitled "Buyout Offers Lure Cafeterias Inc., but Management Says Nothing Cooking." The title seemed more than glibly appropriate, as everyone then on the board or in the head executive office except Lahourcade and Salmon had from the very beginning submerged their hands in soapy dishwater, whipped cream, beef, fish, and chicken blood, cream and clear gravies, all kinds of batters, salad dressings, watermelon juice, and hot Jell-O mix. No matter the culinary-related fluid or solid: nobody knew more about cooking than the "band of brothers," the Luby's boys.

Bob Luby's response to the takeover invitations was genial but firm, as usual. He observed that, so far, there had been no hostile bids. "The approaches have all been friendly because they want our goodwill," he told *Financial Times* in an interview. "Anybody can buy pots and pans, but we know how to run cafeterias." Walter Salmon contributed his commentary to Bob Luby as well: "If it were ever known that this company was willing to agree to a merger, you'd have a line all the way out the door." Of course, lines all the way out the door were by this time a commonplace sight during the noon hour at any Luby's one might name.

Walter Salmon was also there when a looming economic trend, the oil glut of the 1980s, began to change the business climate in the Southwest, profoundly affecting the recent prosperity there. And he was, of course, still firmly in position on February 22, 1982, the red-letter day on which Luby's Cafeterias, Inc. finally entered the big leagues by setting up shop in an entirely different place—a listing on the New York Stock Exchange.

The new listing went onto the Big Board under the initials LUB. The same year, Bob Luby stepped down from his position as chairman of the board, while Charles Johnston simultaneously stepped down as vice chairman. Luby's primary stated goal, that "we could work reasonable hours with multiple management, pay the best wages in town, and offer the best food and service at a good price" had been honorably achieved, from Bob's first infantile glimpse of his father's prototypical Springfield cafeteria to the day LUB stock commenced trading.

Hard times always cost markets for luxury goods their customer bases, as was recently seen in the economic crunch of the early 2000s. But because of Harry Luby's original inspired edict—to make good food available at lower prices to a wide variety and class of clientele—the prosperity of Luby's remained undiminished. The company continued to post record sales throughout the early 1980s, and added six new stores—all built with internally generated funding.

Until the NYSE entry, Walter Salmon, Bob's latest protégé in the cafeteria business, had stood respectfully aside while Bob continued to guide the company with the tried-and-true policies that had promulgated such wealth and hearty unity. But with the advent of George Wenglein as board chairman and the promotion of John Lahourcade from president in 1982 to CEO in 1983, the different trend in advancement was slowly and subtly being laid. Salmon, and the rest of the board of directors began to offer their acumen more readily for the sake of Luby's continuing financial health.

□ □ □

Because of the debt-avoidance policy, Luby's, unlike its competitors and the myriad other corporations then wrestling with enormous debt service in a weak economy, was able to pay its loans and finance expansion purely from cash flow. By 1986, however, even Luby's was beginning to feel the pinch caused by the oil glut, in the form of a 2 percent reduction in customer counts at established stores. But that didn't stop the company from posting a 15 percent increase in sales and a 13 percent gain in net income.

John Lahourcade commented on the reason why. "We've not been nearly as badly affected by the Texas oil slump as many other restaurant companies," he said. "When customer counts are off, it's disturbing to us, but it's not something that gives us nightmares. The reason is because we know we don't owe anybody any money, so our profits are not devastated by a small loss in sales."

In fact, in the national restaurant picture throughout the 1980s Luby's profitability was second only to McDonald's. Even in 1988 the company was still maintaining a debt-to-equity ratio of about 4 percent, astonishingly low for the restaurant industry as a whole. And what comparatively small long-term debt they did still have was a relic left over from the seventies, all of it mortgage-based. In 1985 Standard and Poor's added Luby's to their Fortune 500 list—one of only five restaurant businesses to be named. In 1986 Luby's Cafeterias, Inc. was praised in Ronald Paul and James Taylor's book *101 Best Performing Companies in America*, which included organizations demonstrating an exceptional ten-year history of productivity, expansion and growth, efficiency, shareholder returns, and job creation. Because Luby's managers (and of course its pioneer board members) traditionally knew the art of running cafeterias down to every stove burner, grease trap, iced tea glass, chicken-fried steak, leftover dish, and flour sack, they were expert in avoiding food waste, trimming labor costs, and adjusting food purchasing and labor scheduling to meet the exigencies of the slowed economy. Therefore they retained profitability in the face of reduced sales.

Nine new cafeterias were opened in 1986, and between 1986 and 1988 the company built several more in Arizona, Florida, and Arkansas, enhancing the out-of-state expansion already accomplished in Oklahoma and New Mexico, where two more cities were added: Albuquerque and Santa Fe. Also in 1988, net income amounted to 10.2 percent of revenues. And in 1987 the one hundredth store opened in Round Rock, Texas. Charles Johnston, cradled within his wheelchair, and accompanied by his faithful private nurse and companion, Rick Gozaydin, attended that opening.

It was to be his last.

□ □ □

Shortly after Charles had his first stroke, Gertrude Johnston asked a lawyer to contact her daughter, Carol, who was at that time staying at Gertrude's house, and let her know that Gertrude, as Charles's still-legal wife, intended to have a guardianship placed upon Charles. The question the attorney put to Carol was: would Carol be willing to testify to her father's incompetence?

Carol's reply to this query came swiftly, "Not only no, but hell no! There is nothing wrong with my father."

First appearances might have suggested incompetence. But Carol knew that although at that moment Charles was challenged by his handicap, he was ultimately not mentally incompetent at all. His left side was affected, which meant that he could no longer write very well. He had always been a fairly quiet man, but because his speech was impaired due to the slackening of the muscles on the left side of his face, he was even quieter than usual. Neither could he any longer whistle a tune absent-mindedly while mulling on an idea or walking from room to room around the house (a trait that Carol had found endearing); but then, he couldn't walk at all, so that was moot. But once he began to recover from the stroke, he started learning to do these things all over again, and the determination he brought to the task proved just how completely he had retained all his faculties.

Her mother, Carol felt, must be trying to get the guardianship enacted in order to gain control of her father's money. But Carol suspected that this was not her mother's own idea. It seemed highly uncharacteristic of Gertrude's usual way of thinking. Was Gertrude being influenced by someone's voice, murmuring in her ear? There was no way of knowing for sure. But neither did Carol believe that her very conservative mother really understood what her move for an incompetence declaration meant to her estranged husband. Fortunately, Gertrude never could implement her plan, and shortly after the attempt, Charles was once more able to demonstrate just how competent he really was—to the tune of actively keeping his directorship and continuing to work hard for Luby's. Nonetheless, Carol's conviction, then and now, was that the betrayal broke Charles's heart.

In 1986 Carol Johnston finally moved home to San Antonio. The previous year, when she divorced her second husband, she had become once more thoroughly alienated from her mother. It seemed that Gertrude's method of venting the hurt she felt on her daughter's behalf, and her disturbance over the marriage's termination, was to accuse Carol's ex-husband of having borrowed unreturned money from her. Perhaps Carol's marital failures reminded her too searingly of her own humiliating separation; perhaps not. But this apparently baseless allegation caused conflict and division between mother and daughter to such a degree that the door of communication slammed shut. But the next year, 1986, was the year Carol chose to finally restore her relationship with her father, and to reopen the flow of frank discussion that had been dammed into muteness ever since her parents' split. In this, she succeeded. That was when Charles finally told Carol a little something about the nature of the rift over J. W. Cunningham that had risked his health with its stress and ultimately razed his marriage.

Meanwhile, back in the boardroom at Luby's Cafeterias, Inc., Charles remained busy. All through the years, whenever the accountants had wanted to put management on salary to save the company more money, rather than keep in place the 60/40 net profit incentive, Charles would remind them of the simple fact of Luby's philosophy with a one-liner: "Pigs get fat, hogs get slaughtered." In other words, don't be too greedy or you'll lose everything.

Another piece of advice that Charles was famous for was something he also passed on to his daughter: "When the fourth accountant or nonfood

Gertrude and Charles Johnston at daughter Carol's wedding

person gets appointed to the board, bail out!"—that is, sell your Luby's stock. For that, he felt, would be the beginning of the end.

George Luby was Charles and Bob's cousin based in Dallas—the man who had worked in his Uncle Earl Luby's cafeterias since his freshman year in high school in the early 1930s. Later, with his brother Joe, George spent decades running the Browder Street, Loma Alto, and Inwood branches of Luby's cafeterias, partnering first with Earl, and then, after a nasty schism destroyed their trust, solely with Joe. He represented the third branch in the Luby's tree that Harry had planted way back in 1911. Now that Luby's Cafeterias Inc. had taken over the running of all outstanding stores, George had sold his shares, closed his independent cafeterias, and pursued another, very different career in retail menswear—in haberdashery, in fact, the very field that Harry had given up on early in the century to start his first dream restaurant.

According to George Luby, there was a morbid joke Bob always used to make to Charles. "Wouldn't it be hell," Bob would quip, "if one of us wound up choking on a bite of food and dying?"

Considering the enormous amount of food tasting and recipe testing they both carried on over the course of their long lives, the joke held more than an unlikely irony. But such a pratfall was not to be Charles's fate. After more than eight full years in his wheelchair, he collapsed on January 13, 1989, and was rushed to the emergency room of Northeast Baptist Hospital. The problem was his heart. A repair that had been made to his aorta in 1960, during the most stressful time of his marital conflicts after the Cunningham episode in Harlingen, had now ruptured.

Immediately after telephoning her friend Wende Wilkes to please pick up Scott from school, Carol hurried to her father's side in the hospital ER. When Wende reached the hospital with Scott in tow, she noticed that a few people from Luby's were present. Wende Wilkes remembers:

> Over the next couple of hours, more and more Luby's people began arriving. They lined up in the hallways. We took up two entire rooms. Gertrude then arrived and the doctors consulted with her. She would not make a decision regarding [Charles's] care, leaving it to Carol. Carol asked the doctor what he would do if that were his father. He gave her the outcome. Mr. Johnston would die without the surgery [needed to once more repair his aorta]. He would probably not survive the surgery, and if he did, it was highly likely he would be a vegetable.
>
> Carol made the decision to not have him undergo surgery and risk becoming a vegetable. The doctor told her and everyone there that hearing was the last sense to go, and if they wanted to say good-bye, now was the time. I think every Luby's person went through that room in Emergency, where Charles Johnston lay, and said their good-byes. I do not know if Gertrude did, but I did, and so did Scott.

Carol Johnston recalls how, four or five hours after she got to the hospital, she was advised by the doctor there to okay the removal of her father's life support system; if his central nervous system was capable of maintaining his breathing, and if the surgeons could repair the rupture damage, he

Charles and Carol Johnston

would have a good, healthy quality of life. Otherwise, he would live the vegetative existence Wende Wilkes mentions.

Once life support was removed, Carol sat at her father's bedside and held his hand. "Keep talking to him," the doctor suggested. "I assure you, he can hear you." All the while she did this, Carol was aware of her mother, hovering in the emergency room's shadows, wordless and isolated, a distant, helpless witness to the last moments of her estranged husband's life.

Thirty minutes later, Charles was gone.

□ □ □

Charles Johnston left an estate worth $30 million at the time of his death. In addition to a few specific bequests to friends and family, he left his home to his aunt, Helen Luby Blodgett, as she was still residing with him at the time of his death, and the remainder of his estate to his daughter, Carol, and his grandson, Charles Scott. Gertrude was left with her share of their community property, but nothing of Charles's. A provision in the will also stated that any person who filed a will contest would be disinherited completely.

But the circumstance of not receiving any benefit from her husband's will stung Gertrude to almost unendurable anger. After the funeral, she repeatedly instructed Carol to contest Charles's will—for her sake, for the fairness she felt had been denied to her during his life. When Carol refused, she erected a barrier of hostility that would take the next ten years to dismantle. Meanwhile, her relations with her brother J. W. Cunningham began to grow more confidential, and over the next few years, frugal Gertrude came to rely on his financial advice more and more. This was a situation that would have, no doubt, goaded Charles to distraction. For in his mind he was, after all, the one who had made the money in the first place, and kept the secret about her brother.

At last, the moment came to pass that Charles had staved off for so long: his majority ownership of Luby's stock was now halved, his wife finally gaining control over her community share and his daughter and grandson benefiting from his share. All three were reduced to wealthy but comparatively minor ownerships. Charles's many decades of work and his part in the regency over a solid cafeteria empire were over.

15

DEVILED EGGS

AND STUFFED JALAPEÑOS

□ □ □

During the years of 1990 through 1992, Luby's Cafeterias, Inc. continued its accelerating expansion program. New cafeterias were launched in Louisiana, Tennessee, Missouri, and Kansas, marking the company presence in a total of ten states. In the November 12, 1990, issue of *Forbes Magazine*, Luby's held the number 93 spot on that year's "200 Best Small Companies in America" list. In an independent survey conducted by the journal *Restaurants and Institutions* (February 1990), Luby's led all competition as America's first choice in cafeteria dining.

The Luby's mastery, now affecting an ever-widening wedge of U.S. demographics, made the stock an even more tempting bet to investors and continued to promise the many employees who owned shares a cushy retirement. Certainly their prospects seemed more solid than those of any of their peers working for other corporate restaurants. Word-of-mouth approval had filtered down through three generations of local residents and out-of-state travelers, and brand recognition was now assured. People knew that wherever they went, they could count on Luby's for a good-tasting, nourishing, and affordable hot meal, a comfortable atmosphere, consistent service, with friendly greetings from the staff. Indeed, the sense of reliable homelike repetition in an otherwise foreign city was one of the aspects of Luby's that set it apart from its slicker franchised competitors. No matter how the menu might vary from region to region, customers always stepped into an ambiance of familiarity that depended more on format and long-established personnel than on uniform decor.

Recipe for deviled eggs

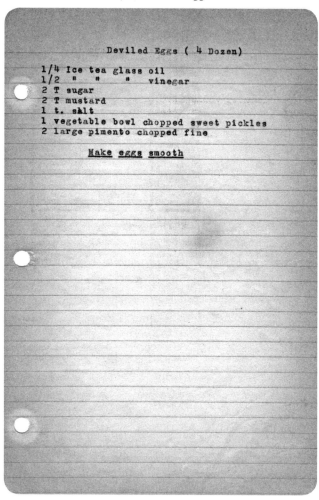

```
            Deviled Eggs ( 4 Dozen)

   1/4 Ice tea glass oil
   1/2  "    "     "   vinegar
   2 T sugar
   2 T mustard
   1 t. salt
   1 vegetable bowl chopped sweet pickles
   2 large pimento chopped fine

      Make eggs smooth
```

But on a crisp, sunny noon hour in mid-October 1991, a totally unexpected factor suddenly and horribly brought the staid corporate name to the attention of a much broader audience. By day's end it lay scorched upon the national consciousness, and one of Luby's most thriving stores was out of business.

Spree killings, like cafeterias, are a peculiarly American innovation. The first major landmark in this murder category, in which a solitary individual takes up arms against his fellow citizens and randomly continues to shoot them dead until either police or suicide stops him, is generally regarded to be the case of Charles Whitman, the gunman who climbed to the top of the 27-story University of Texas Tower on August 1, 1966, and sniped from its observation deck. Whitman's final fatality score that day was fourteen, a number that has seldom been surpassed in mass shootings since.

His spree, however, was antedated by another spectacularly grim spate of carnage, on September 6, 1949, when a twenty-eight-year-old man named Howard Unruh took a twelve-minute stroll through the streets of his hometown of Camden, New Jersey, with a German Luger in his hand, killing everyone he encountered. The death toll included a barber, a toddler getting a haircut, a shoemaker, and three members of one family sitting in a car at a red light. By the time he was captured, he had murdered thirteen people.

The next rage-inspired killing spree that could be said to resemble Whitman's and Unruh's was that of Robert Smith, eighteen years old, a scrawny high school student who, only three months after the Whitman calamity, walked into a Mesa, Arizona, beauty college and shot four women and a three-year-old girl. As he told his police apprehenders after his arrest, he did it because "I wanted to make a name for myself. I wanted people to know who I was."

From then on, the pace of mass shootings increased at an alarming rate. Whitman, it seems, had set a fashion and signaled a permission among the disaffected and disturbed. On an average of every two years throughout the 1960s and 1970s, someone armed himself for a public slaughter. What's more, the summer months seemed to trigger such behavior more often than other times—especially in states with hot climates, like Texas and California, and various other spots in the Southwest. The scenarios predicted in Jules Feiffer's award-winning play and screenplay *Little Murders*, written on the brink of the new trend in random shootings, were coming true with horrendous accuracy.

The 1980s ushered in an era of even greater frequency in mass murder, with rampages occurring yearly, sometimes three and four times in one twelve-month interval. Workplace shootings became the norm with the advent of Leo Held, a Pennsylvania paper mill employee angry with his superiors and carpool members, who in October 1967 wreaked fatal vengeance on six people prior to receiving the wound from police that would end his life. In August 1984 the post office worker Patrick Sherrill aired his grievances by slaying fourteen co-workers in Edmond, Oklahoma—the original incidence of "going postal." Since then, the newly coined phrase has become commonplace, achieving such a normalized currency across the world that two computer video games bear it as a name and invite their players to repeat the activities and state of mind that inspired it (with a tagline promising that the game is "only as violent as you are"). The games are so unusually brutal that until recently they were not only blacklisted in the United States, but banned in ten other countries as well.

The first mass shooting at a food industry site took place in San Ysidro, California, in July 1984. James Huberty, a recently unemployed security guard, marched into a McDonald's near his home and opened fire with three weapons, including a submachine gun, killing twenty before a police sniper removed him with a single well-placed shot. It could be regarded as an accidental irony that only seven years before, Forbes Magazine had commented on how Luby's return on equity was "frankly 12 percent higher than McDonald's," thus bracketing the two companies' business performances in the same division and coupling their names. It would be another seven years before their only other common association would boil to the surface, at which time McDonald's would rush to Luby's aid, offering the advice and support that Luby's solicited from them before resorting to Luby's own humanistic approach to their problem. Meanwhile, the practice of mass shootings had, it may be estimated, now begun to climb toward its "tipping point."

The year 1991 began quietly and without incident. This hiatus from mass murder continued through the late winter, spring, summer, and early fall. Only one multiple-death spree had occurred in the United States by the date of October 15, as opposed to three by that time the year before, in 1990. It took place on October 10 in Ridgewood, New Jersey. The perpetrator was another disgruntled postal worker, and the lower-than-usual body count of four included his ex-supervisor.

But that mid-October day, the Tuesday following the New Jersey killings, happened to be an especially dark day for one lone man in Belton, Texas.

Georges (George) Pierre Hennard was a handsome, well-built fellow whose looks might have been very attractive to women. His thick, dark hair lay across a high forehead in a tousled sweep above his dark eyes; his features were symmetrical and classically modeled; his cleft chin emphasized the lean jaw line and strong cheekbones on either side of a shapely mouth. Only his constant expression flawed the presentation that otherwise would suggest the type of social acceptance that usually accompanies an attractive appearance.

Hennard had been born of affluent middle-class parents. His father, Georges Marcel Hennard, was an orthopedic surgeon. His mother, Gloria Jeanne Hennard, was a housewife with a reputation for being high-strung. They had three children, of whom Georges Pierre was the eldest.

If truly "all happy families are alike," then the unique ways in which the Hennard family was unhappy eventually propelled a far greater reaction than Tolstoy ever envisioned when he wrote the famous opening of his novel *Anna Karenina*. At the commencement of the middle years of his life, Hennard's solitude looked almost complete. His rejection of and ejection from the family circle had created a canker that festered without relief inside him.

The large red-brick colonial-style home in which George lived had belonged to Gloria Jeanne Hennard since she had divorced George's father in 1983. But as she was now residing in Henderson, Nevada, she left her son to tend to the house and keep it in immaculate condition. She had just listed the house for sale. Perhaps this gave rise to George's rancorous feelings and insecurity. For she and George, also known as Joe or Jo-Jo, argued often and stormily.

This was not a new circumstance. George and his two younger siblings,

Alan Robert and Desiree, had grown up on military posts across the country while their father, Dr. Hennard, worked in various army hospitals. In George's case, the peripatetic lifestyle led to a fracturing of community consciousness, enhancing his sense of isolation and aloofness. His parents' neglect didn't help. While living at White Sands Missile Range Army Base, and still in elementary school in Las Cruces, New Mexico—home to the first out-of-Texas Luby's Cafeteria, Inc. store, opened in 1966—he was regarded by his schoolmates as outgoing, "cool," a good-looking boy everyone looked up to. But one year later, all that changed. George's father, who had a reputation for toughness, confronted him physically during a fight. From what Lou Catoggio, one of George's classmates, has said, the results were disastrous.

"Joe came to school the next day looking like he'd been mauled," Catoggio recalled. "It looked like his old man had taken a butcher knife and cut his hair. He was never the same after that. He was completely introverted."

Another White Sands/Las Cruces neighbor enlarges this picture with his high school memories of Hennard. "You never saw him with girls. He never hung around with anybody," said Paul Crowe. "His parents never did care and were hardly ever around."

After high school graduation in 1974, Hennard joined the navy and three years later signed up for the merchant marine, working chiefly in the Gulf of Mexico until 1981, when he set out on the first of thirty-seven overseas voyages. His family had moved to Belton in 1980 when his father was stationed at Fort Hood Army Base in Killeen, Texas. After an arrest for marijuana possession in Texas in 1981, George's troubles worsened, as did his temper. In May 1982 his seaman's papers got suspended when he engaged in a racial quarrel with a shipmate. Jamie Dunlap, who shared an apartment with Hennard for a short time that year in Temple, a few miles from the family home in Belton, said later, "He hated blacks, Hispanics, gays." Gloria Jeanne Hennard, by many reports a very domineering woman as well as a testy one, seemed to stir George's ire to an alarming degree. A seaman who bunked with him in 1982 recalled that he often talked about killing her, and drew caricatures of her, depicting her as a snake. "He said women were snakes," Jamie Dunlap, his Temple housemate, added. "He always had derogatory remarks about women, especially after fights with his mother."

This illuminating comment, which suggests the depths of disaffection to which George Hennard and his mother had plunged, does not reveal what he felt about the community at large. It would take several public declarations made from a site in the community's heart to clarify that opinion: that in some agonized place inside his twisted mind, he held the population of Belton, Killeen, and Bell County itself responsible for the problems afflicting his family.

After his parents' 1983 divorce in Belton, and his seaman's license reinstatement, Hennard traveled around the world for a few more years. Then in 1989 his license was once again revoked due to marijuana possession aboard a cargo ship. He began drifting from job to job, working construction in Killeen and South Dakota, and living part-time with his mother in Henderson, Nevada, while waiting to hear the results of his reinstatement appeal.

During a February–March 1991 stint in Henderson, he legally purchased two semiautomatic pistols: a Ruger P89 and a Glock 17. Upon his return to Texas, his behavior grew more and more bizarre. During the summer of 1991 he was reported to the police for harassing two young sisters who lived on his street by sending them a rambling five-page letter containing this weirdly frightening threat: "Please give me the satisfaction of someday laughing in the face of all those mostly white treacherous female vipers . . . who tried to destroy me and my family." He invited the sisters to assist this triumph by suggesting, "You think the three of us could get together someday?" No charges were brought against him.

In September, while he was still employed at a cement company, Hennard asked a co-worker a question: What should he do if he killed someone? The co-worker replied that he should kill himself. Shortly after this conversation, Hennard attempted on two different occasions to sell his guns. He found no buyers. Perhaps this effort indicates a momentary respite from the brooding that had lately submerged him. Perhaps his conscience, or some humane impulse, was flickering to life, and this was his way of trying to fan it.

But apparently the occasion of his thirty-fifth birthday, which he spent alone and cantankerous, impelled George Hennard into a fiercer state than before. His paranoia coalesced. His congested resentments and angers bloomed. There was, in his perverted reasoning, an outlet for these terrible forces, a target that deserved his attentions.

During the early days of October he had taken his guns to a Killeen shooting range and practiced with them. On his birthday, a day recognized by our American culture as one in which families conventionally fete the arrival of one of their own, he made his decision and prepared for action. The community that had earned the blame for rending his unhappy family asunder would receive its reward.

And where to go to best effect this justice? What gathering place—familiar to him since childhood, since his years in the town of Las Cruces that was the locale of his primal humiliation—symbolized both family and community? What concrete link connected that dusty, sandy desert landscape to this green Central Texas army town? With perhaps unconscious manic logic, Hennard picked the meeting place he knew would hold the greatest number of victims, the largest cross-section of the community, at the hour when they would be concentrated most heavily. And even better was the fact that this place served several communities as a gathering spot—both Killeen and Belton residents liked to go there. After all, his purpose could best be accomplished in a locus for the experiences he surely must have felt to be out of his reach: fellowship, conviviality, and a shared family meal.

On October 15, 1991, George Hennard celebrated his thirty-fifth birthday by eating a cheeseburger and fries for dinner. He drove to a small grill outside of Killeen alone and ate alone. While there he vented his explosive fury about his circumstances and grievances by roaring at the grill's TV screen. The evening news was highlighting coverage of Clarence Thomas's Supreme Court appointment confirmation hearings. According to the grill's manager, Bill Stringer, "When an interview with Anita Hill came on, he just went off. He started screaming, 'You dumb bitch! You bastards opened the door for all the women!'" The theme of women's betrayal, which would feature so strongly in his utterances the following day, seemed to be gathering force within his psyche. How much the Thomas-Hill hearings influenced the tide of his anger must remain forever conjectural, but by the next morning, that anger had overturned all other considerations. His identity as a loner and female-hater was completed.

There were other signs over the months leading up to his birthday, however, that could have been clearly read by Hennard's observers, had anyone been in a position to see them collectively. The most telling presented itself only one and a half weeks before October 15. At that time, Hennard quit his current job at a cement company in nearby Copperas Cove, abruptly marching into the office and announcing his termination while picking up his last paycheck. During the same visit he wondered aloud what would happen if he killed someone. "He got to talking about some of the people in Belton and certain women that had given him problems," his co-worker Bubba Hawkins said later. "And he kept saying, 'Wait and see, watch and see.'" Until the night of his birthday feast, that was the last known occasion when a witness heard him express his state of mind. Although he spoke briefly with his mother long-distance over the phone on his birthday before going out for his cheeseburger and TV rant, his words are unrecorded.

□ □ □

The year of 1991 was a distinguished year for Luby's, commemorating the anniversary of a full eighty years of existence. Exactly eight decades had passed since Harry Luby founded his first cafeteria, and there was no reason to think the company wouldn't enjoy another eighty years to come. No one could have guessed what lay in store that would change the company's profile in a matter of moments.

Just before dawn on the morning of October 16, George Hennard followed his usual routine of driving to a certain convenience store in Belton and buying the same breakfast he bought every morning. His regular selection of a sausage-and-biscuit sandwich, orange juice, and doughnuts, along with a newspaper, was customarily made with a surly, hostile frown. An aura of sullen withdrawal hung over him like a cloud, and when he broke his silence, it was usually to say something unpleasant. Once he had even remarked out of the blue to the female counter clerks, "I want you to tell everybody if they don't quit messing around my house something awful is going to happen." This aggressive non sequitur had naturally made the women nervous; they dreaded his daily business and wished he would take it somewhere else. But on this particular early morning after his birthday, his demeanor was quite different, quite changed. He seemed calm, even friendly, for the first time that Mary Mead, the cashier who rang up his purchases, could remember.

Nobody knows what Hennard did after leaving the Leon Heights Drive-In convenience store. All the eyewitness evidence suggests the possibility that he went somewhere, perhaps his home, and rehearsed for the scene he would conduct a few hours later, but this is mere speculation. Whatever his movements, the only thing known for certain is that about 12:20 p.m., seven hours after his breakfast-time appearance, during the height of the noon rush, he drove his blue 1987 Ford Ranger pickup truck straight through the plate glass window of the Killeen Luby's Cafeteria, seventeen miles from Belton. Amid the sounds of shattering glass, the front of the truck smashed into an elderly man who happened to be in the way. As diners rose hastily from their tables and collected around the man to render assistance, Hennard emerged from the pickup's cab. One woman, the recently retired Barbara Nite, who had joined seven of her ex-workmates from the Fort Hood dental clinic for a chatty lunchtime get-together, had just been admiring her friend Kitty Davis's snapshots of her baby grandson when the glass exploded. At first she thought that the vehicle lumbering to a halt right beside her table was a runaway car that might burst into flames at any moment. She leaped up to bolt to safety. But then Kitty Davis murmured a warning, "He's got a gun. Get down."

Instantly Barbara Nite dropped to the floor and crawled under a roller-footed chair. Above her, chaos ruled. In each hand Hennard hoisted the pistols he had bought in Nevada. His shirt and pants pockets bulged with 9 mm semiautomatic clips. Sunglasses hid his eyes. A lit cigarette dangled carelessly from his lips. With a chill, casual efficiency, he methodically began to shoot every person in sight, starting with the man struggling to rise from the spot where the truck had felled him, and then moving on down the serving line as if his victims had been conveniently arranged as his own personal shooting gallery targets—or an array of cafeteria dishes. Aiming mainly for the head or chest, he killed one after another, sometimes passing up several people before stopping on a fresh victim. Screams rang through the building, punctuated by the pop of the guns. Against the cacophony Hennard cried, "All women of Killeen and Belton are vipers!

See what you've done to me and my family!" Then he added, "This is what Belton did to me! Is it worth it? This is payback day!"

Shortly he left the line and reached the table beneath which Nite and her friend Davis crouched. Shots plowed through the table-top; plates, cups, saucers, and cutlery went flying. He aimed the guns under the table and shot off more rounds. A bullet drilled through Nite's foot, kept going, and shredded Davis's thumb. As she stifled her scream to keep from drawing Hennard's further attention, Nite clutched the five-dollar bill and her meal check for $2.68 in her hand and thought, inanely, over and over, "Well, with this mess, how am I going to get up to the cashier and pay?" Then the realization finally penetrated through her shock: the staff as well as the patrons were all shot up, and there was no one left to pay.

Immediately the rest of the diners dove for cover under the chairs and tables as Hennard began to slowly circle the room, singling out more victims. Scowling at one woman, he said, "You bitch," then shot her dead. To another, shrinking under a bench near the serving line, he accused: "Hiding from me, bitch?" Then he shot her too. Only moments after he had selected a salad for his tray and was debating which meat entrée to choose, the Reverend Shannon McMullen found himself wounded in the leg and scuttling under the same bench. From that shelter he watched Hennard walk from the middle of the cafeteria floor toward a woman cowering against the far wall. The bench then obscured McMullen's view of Hennard's face. But he could clearly see the killer's arm extend, the pistol take aim and fire, and the hole appear in the woman's head as she slumped lifeless to the floor, while Hennard slowly turned back to the main dining room.

He orbited the room several times, shooting as he traveled and stopping only to reload. One of the points he revisited was the table of Barbara Nite and Kitty Davis; this time, while Nite lay very still and played dead, he shot Davis in the back three times. Returning to some victims he had merely wounded during his first rotation, he paused, shot them again, made sure they were now dead, and continued on his journey. In his only semblance of mercy, he pointed a pistol at a blood-spattered woman who had just seen her mother shot dead and said, "You with the baby, get out." The woman scooped up her four-year-old daughter and ran to safety. A number of people escaped his wrath by running through the kitchen door; one kitchen staff member hid in the industrial dishwasher.

Gradually the screaming ceased. An eerie silence fell. By now all the patrons had begun to helplessly wait their turn. Hennard still excoriated the crowd: "Take that, bitch! This is what Bell County did to me!" Sam Wink, an attendance officer for the Killeen Independent School District, heard Hennard snap in his third fifteen-round clip. "He was about twelve feet from me," Wink said. "When he turned, our eyes met for a second. They were mean. There was a smirk on his face, as if he was thinking, 'I've been waiting for this for a long time.' He was very intense, well prepared, almost as if he had practiced at home. And even though he was yelling, he was very calm. The contrast between the fire in his eyes and the calm on his face was unbelievable."

Wink wasn't the only horrified observer to notice Hennard's composure. A chiropractor named Dr. Shawn Isdale, who had come to Luby's to lunch with his wife, infant daughter, and parents, watched the killer approach Steve Ernst, a friend of Isdale's who was hiding under a table, and shoot him in the abdomen, all the while displaying a facial expression that was "completely relaxed, no emotion at all," even when Ernst yelled "Oh, God," and rolled over, grasping his stomach. Hennard then shot Ernst's wife, Judy, in the arm; the bullet went clean through and killed Venice Ellen Henehan, Ernst's seventy-year-old mother-in-law. Another survivor recalled Hennard's look of pleasure during the whole ordeal. "He was smiling," the man said, "kind of a grin, like a smirk."

The balance of fear finally shifted when, during a brief lull in the shootings, a twenty-eight-year-old, six-foot six-inch tall auto mechanic named Tommy Vaughn saw Hennard advancing toward him and realized he was next. Suddenly the paralysis that had gripped him for the last few minutes broke. Vaughn had remained huddled on the floor beside a window while the massacre continued. Now he picked up a table and hurled it at the window. The table bounced off; the glass held intact. So Vaughn mustered the full power of his three-hundred-pound body and charged the glass, using himself as a ram to smash it and then throwing himself through. Once outside he rolled onto the concrete below. In this instant he had created an escape aperture for dozens of people who then shoved, pushed, and knocked each other down as they scrambled to get through it.

Only one person had challenged Hennard early in his lethal onslaught.

Al Gratia, seventy-one, seated with his wife, Ursula, and chiropractor daughter Suzanna, rose to confront him and immediately was gunned down. Suzanna managed to flee, thinking her mother was with her, and cursing the fact that her own handgun, which she believed could have stopped the killer, was stowed worthlessly out of reach in her car in the parking lot in accordance with the state weapons laws "and all I had was a butter knife," she said later. Ursula Gratia crawled to her husband, raised her head, looked up at Hennard, bowed her head once more, and was shot in the skull at point-blank range. The profound impact the Gratias' particular deaths would eventually have on legislation for the entire state of Texas would in turn spark a nationwide furor of debate.

After ten interminable minutes of systematic close-range marksmanship, George Hennard found himself facing three police officers who had slipped into the building. They shot him four times but failed to kill him. So once more Hennard took matters into his own hands, stumbled backward to the alcove beside the cafeteria restrooms, put a bullet through his right eye with the Ruger, and dropped dead to the floor.

Partway through the carnage, the associate manager of Luby's, who had fled from the kitchen through the back door with several members of the kitchen staff, placed a call to the company's head office in San Antonio. In the boardroom a directors' meeting was in full session. Because all the secretaries, the switchboard operator, and the office staff were out to lunch, Herbert Knight, now the vice president in charge of area management, happened to answer the call. He was the first to hear the manager say, "We've got a problem here in Killeen."

The associate manager went on to describe what was happening. Immediately Knight informed the men in the boardroom, and then rushed down to his car with another vice president, Jimmy Wolliver. Although neither man knew yet the severity of the situation, they both jumped in and drove the 150 miles to Killeen. Meanwhile, Ralph "Pete" Erben, the current company president and a board member, hurried with a couple of other directors to the airport, chartered a plane, and flew to Fort Hood. He was already on the spot when Knight arrived. Together they surveyed the corpses still lying on the cafeteria floor, the crowds gathered outside the building beyond the police cordon, and the ambulances with their tally of twenty-three wounded being rushed to the hospital. The death count, including Hennard himself and the last wounded woman, Kitty Davis, who died three days later, stood at twenty-four.

It was, and is to this day, the largest mass killing in U.S. history, superseding the Columbine High School massacre in April 1999 by ten and the Atlanta investment brokerage killings in July 1999 by eleven. Only the 1984 McDonald's shooting in San Ysidro—the sole other U.S. restaurant shooting to date—comes close, with a toll of twenty-one dead. Killeen suffered a terrible communal loss. As it turns out, the Luby's mortality rate proved twice as high as even that of Fort Hood, the biggest and most densely populated army installation in the country, during the entire Persian Gulf War earlier in 1991.

Herbert Knight prefers not to recall the aftermath of the bloody scene that sunlit October day. Like many of the survivors and emergency personnel who dealt with the casualties, he has struggled to obliterate the mental images. John Marr, who one year later became the Killeen Luby's assistant manager, would for a long time after the remodeled building was reopened see a mental picture whenever he looked at a certain area of the dining room: "There was a woman at a table up there, still sitting, dead." But Knight had many tasks to see to, accounting for all the employees, reassuring them they would have no loss of income, and making immediate and long-term counseling available to them should they choose to use it. One woman survivor, to Knight's relief, was found hiding in the walk-in freezer; she was quickly treated for hypothermia. But for the whole night of October 16 Knight couldn't locate a missing nineteen-year-old food preparer named Mark Matthews. Not until the next day, when he had spent more than twenty hours in his hiding place, did Matthews emerge from the industrial dishwasher, where he had been curled up in a narrow space, stiff with fear and loss of movement.

Galvanized by Ralph Erben, the public relations firm that worked in tandem with Luby's advertising department started to organize local overnight accommodations for the many relatives of the victims, arranging for intensive psychological counseling for survivors, and helping to advise the company on a policy of action in the tragedy's aftermath. Immediately Luby's donated $100,000 to finance this assistance. The company also es-

tablished a fund for the victims' families. Erben himself broke the corporate habits of all other previous disasters—plane crashes, mass shootings et
al.—by remaining on the spot and available for two straight days to talk
directly with surviving victims and the relatives of the dead, counseling,
praying with them, and holding meetings with community leaders to find
out how he and Luby's could help everyone come to terms with the atrocity. He then continued to return frequently to Killeen, remaining in touch
with the victims' families for a long time afterward. Bob Luby made a public statement to the press, quoted in the *Houston Chronicle*, that in his
opinion, the store would have to close for good.

As one of the wounded victims, the Reverend Kirby Lack of Copperas
Cove, later summed up about Luby's handling of the catastrophe, "They
were wonderful. Pete [Erben] came here himself and visited with me often. And they kept in contact with people for some time."

The U.S. Army, having anticipated heavy casualties in the Persian Gulf
War, had earlier brought in a phalanx of counselors to assist with grief
therapy for families of military personnel. Now some of these professionals
who had remained in the area rushed to the aid of the devastated citizens.
But Luby's Cafeterias, Inc. regarded its role of responsibility very seriously.
When a reporter approached President Erben at the scene of the blood-
bath, he noted aloud Erben's emotional state. "You're displaying tears in
your eyes," the reporter said. "Is that because of all the money this will cost
you?" Erben, instead of replying with the expected list of estimated lost
revenues or even projecting one mentally to himself, gave a different answer—one characteristic of the historic Luby's philosophy: "No," he said,
"I care about the people."

Luby's then proceeded to provide long-term counseling and accommo-
dation to the victims and their families.

In the years since the Killeen tragedy, Luby's has often been utilized as
a model of corporate crisis management in business schools throughout
the United States and abroad. More than 150 employees, customers, and
emergency services personnel were directly involved in the incident in
one form or another. Robert Kelley, a paramedic with the Killeen Fire
Department, describes the kind of haunting disturbance that preyed on
many of these people for years afterward. His regular nightmares affected

his sleep, and one picture especially, of a man with a gaping chest wound sitting in the aisle when Kelley arrived on the scene, tormented him. "He is still with me—the memory of him sitting there with his hands reaching out to me," Kelley said later. The majority of the people involved participated in a study performed shortly after the massacre by researchers from the Washington University School of Medicine, who published their findings in the January 1994 issue of the *American Journal of Psychiatry*. Their article noted that almost a third of the survivors suffered from a condition similar to post-traumatic stress disorder. Virtually all of those interviewed by the research team exhibited at least a few symptoms of the disorder, including "intrusive recollections," "emotional numbing," and hyperanxiety, according to Carol North, the psychiatrist who conducted the study. Of the studies conducted on the emotional aftermaths of several recent disasters, the researchers concluded that, along with a 1987 USAF jet crash into an Indianapolis hotel lobby, the Luby's shootings had the most acute and severe effects on the survivors. Luby's proactive offer of long-term assistance to the victims had one special, indeed remarkable, side effect: despite the overly litigious climate of late-twentieth-century America, only one lawsuit was filed against the corporation, and that suit was withdrawn before it ever reached the courts.

But the invisible effect on the corporation, which, directly and tangibly at least, cannot justifiably be linked to the 1991 massacre, was nonetheless soon manifesting itself. An appalling aspect of American society had just been enacted within the same space where so many other more gracious and benign aspects had been demonstrated throughout the eighty years preceding the Killeen horror. Once more Luby's was reflecting the nation's culture with a startling microcosmic precision. For ten hellish minutes chaos had ruled, leaving in its wake a field of dead. Could chaos possibly spill over into the other sectors of the company?

Judging from the wild direction it started taking in response to market pressures very soon afterward, and from the ambitious, careening departure from former policies of integrity that now seemed to infect its board of directors, Luby's Cafeterias, Inc. could perhaps be said to have suffered a form of post-traumatic stress all its own.

─── 16 ───

HOT COFFEE, ICED TEA,

PINK LEMONADE,

OR JUST PLAIN WATER

□ □ □

*Those people who put all their eggs in one basket have the dubious task
of staying awake to guard the coop.*

CHARLES JOHNSTON

At the beginning of 1992, Luby's Cafeterias, Inc. was still mourning the
victims of the Killeen massacre. The company was also still haunted by
the mystery now to stay locked forever by death in George Hennard's
brain: Why, of all places, Luby's? This remained a question no one at the
time could apparently answer. Many people, including a number of officials in law enforcement agencies, didn't even try. Certainly nobody in the
Luby's organization gambled on any strong guesses. Bewilderment among
all the personnel, as among the press and the forensic experts, continued
as the dominant response, after raw grief.

Monetarily, Luby's was still standing tall. The company had just weath-
ered the horrific tragedy and come out the other side of it with honor, demonstrating genuine compassion, pragmatic responsibility, and classic Luby's

empathy, rather than a mere cold regard for the bottom line. It could also boast that it had increased cash dividends to stockholders by 8 percent, from $11.9 million in fiscal 1990 to $12.9 million in 1991. The company's net income held steady, *in spite of* the miasma of shock, death, and gloom that hung over the cafeteria locations. Sales in 1991 were $328.2 million, an increase of 5 percent from the previous year. Operations generated approximately $50 million in cash. Shareholders' equity passed the $200 million

Recipes for coffee, lemonade, fruit punch, and limeade

```
                    Coffee

   1 pound coffe makes 2 1/2 gallons

                   Iced Tea

   1/2 cup tea to the gallon
   Put 1/2 cup tea in 1/2 gallon boiling water
   let set 5 minutes.  Stir and pour this in 1/2
   gallon cold water.  This makes clear tea.

                  Lemonade

   8 lemons and
   4 oranges to one gallon
   1 cup sugar

                 Fruit Punch

   Use juices from canned fruit for fruit punch
```

Limeade (1 gal)
15 limes
½ cup sugar (Simple syrup)
Pour into glass ½ squeesed lime
rind, ½ marishino cherry garnish
with orange slice

mark. Even more significantly, the company's long-term debt at year's end was under $2 million, or below 1 percent of shareholders' equity.

The old, mortgage-based debt left over from the brief foray into fiscal experimentation in the early 1970s had, by 1991, actually been lowered. By the following year it would be paid off completely. Added to all those figures, investment of $35.4 million in land, new buildings, leasehold improvements, and equipment—for which every single expenditure was accomplished through internally generated funds—painted the final varnish on the portrait of success. And it had been achieved through the steady standards set forth by Harry Luby's wisdom.

But all good things must come to an end, they say—even though this aphorism might not yet apply to the fundamental offering of "Good Food from Good People." Bob Luby still functioned as a vigorous member of the board of directors, and still enjoyed excellent health. His directorship, however, was due to expire in 1995, when he would be eighty-five. His awe-inspiring influence had begun to wane, and soon would vanish altogether. So it was in the early to mid-1990s that the board, chaired now by John Lahourcade, began to hearken, according to certain retired board members, chiefly to the advice of Walter Salmon, plus a few other pecuniary experts. That advice: start taking out large revolving loans from outside financial institutions in order to pay for expansion.

The experts' reasoning went something like this: Luby's was a publicly traded company; as such, it owed certain obligations to people beyond the ring of directors, executives, employees, and patrons. The pressures from stock analysts to show good returns on investment—ever-increasing, *big* returns—were growing more urgent. They must be heeded; they must be satisfied. The only way to realize this would be to build more and more cafeterias, to plant the company presence in yet more states. It was, in essence, the modern American capitalist way. It represented the philosophy of the entire later-twentieth-century commercial scene: bigger was better, especially in these days of huge corporate machines and prolific financial rewards.

But Luby's also had an obligation to its stockholders to be fair. After all, fairness had always been a major theme in the company's considerations. And it *wasn't* being fair, Salmon, Lahourcade, and their colleagues argued, if it was using the stockholders' own money in order to forward this necessary growth. Borrowing outside funds would make the return on equity look better.

According to these financial minds, the old-fashioned notion of spending only what nestled in your own pocket had become obsolete. Almost every successful corporation was endorsing such practices now, and admitting their necessity, echoing the accepted viewpoint taught in the nation's most important and influential business schools. Priorities had changed; they *had* to change to keep up with the times. These days the people in charge at Luby's were not so much in the business of serving a splendid array of appetizing food. The company was looking beyond that kind of cornucopia. The abundance it was more truly in the business of providing was a vaster profit.

It was now up to Luby's Cafeterias, Inc. to make not just the employees and executives, not just the managers, but *every* person who invested in the enterprise a fortune.

□ □ □

One far-reaching outcome of the 1991 Killeen massacre turned out to be the effect it had on existing and future gun legislation, both in Texas and nationally. The repercussions of that fatal autumn day went on and on in various directions. The most concrete result lay in this specific arena: should ordinary citizens be permitted to walk the streets with guns hidden in their bags or pockets?

During the early nineties, while Luby's and the rest of the country were reeling from Hennard's atrocity, the same laws relating to the carrying of a concealed weapon on the licensed and registered owner's person that had been on the Texas state books for more than a century were still in force. To carry a concealed weapon was prohibited, and therefore an offense leading to potential arrest. No doubt the pioneer mentality had been behind first the allowing and then the disallowing of the sporting of a "piece." But the advent of the twentieth century had primed the state for a more civil approach to daily life, and at that time the potential danger posed by a handy gun outweighed the convenience that it offered.

After the Killeen massacre, both in the state of Texas and in other states where the National Rifle Association promotes its agenda, the campaign to change the existing concealed-weapon laws, in place since 1871, began to gather momentum. At the forefront of the campaign was the chiropractor Dr. Suzanna Gratia Hupp, a survivor of George Hennard's deadly assault. It was she who had been crouching behind an upturned table at the Killeen Luby's, and there witnessed the murder of both her parents. After their deaths, her outrage at her own helplessness and that of the other victims waxed white-hot. Hupp began to tour the United States, speaking fervently in favor of "concealed-carry" legislation and what she saw as a restoration of the entitlement specified in the Second Amendment of the Constitution: the right of citizens to bear arms. She testified before numerous state legislative bodies, recounting her Luby's experience and repeating that if one person in the cafeteria that October day had had a weapon in his or her immediate possession, George Hennard could have been stopped. Thus, many lives might possibly have been saved. She described her positioning on the cafeteria floor, with the table top as a makeshift shield and described the opportunities she had had to take good, careful aim and shoot Hennard before he could have noticed what she was doing. She recounted her own father's heroism, when he leaped up unarmed, approached Hennard, and tried to stop the carnage with his bare hands, getting a bullet in the head for his attempt. Hupp's public appearances extended to television, where she was featured on *48 Hours*, *ABC World News Tonight* with Peter Jennings, the *CBS Evening News* with Dan Rather, and other programs. In addition, she received a great deal of printed press attention, and was quoted in *U.S. News and World Report*, the *Wall Street Journal*, *Time*, *Texas Monthly*, and *People*.

A new public persona that identified her as "the poster girl for the NRA" assured Hupp of an enthusiastic following among gun aficionados and those who felt that every individual should have the right to defend him- or herself against attack by use of a firearm. And the result of her efforts was the expedited passage of the Texas concealed-carry law, signed into effect in 1995 by then-governor George W. Bush.

And it seems that hordes of Texans felt just as passionately as Hupp did. Once the law got passed, the flood of applicants rushing to get their concealed-carry licenses swelled to such great numbers that the Texas Department of Public Safety issued letters requesting them to please exercise patience, as the heavy volume was drastically lengthening the processing time. People proved to be patient, and the DPS eventually plowed through the backlog of background checks and necessary paperwork. As of May 2004 there were 240,816 people in the state of Texas licensed to carry concealed handguns, with many more waiting to receive approval.

In 1996 Dr. Suzanna Gratia Hupp ran for State Representative on the Republican ticket and won a seat in the Texas Legislature. The National Rifle Association recognized her by awarding her the Sybil Luddington Women's Freedom Award. In 1998 NRA president Charleton Heston honored Hupp as the first Texan to be awarded a National Rifle Association lifetime membership. She is currently regarded worldwide as one of the leading advocates for an individual's right to carry a concealed weapon.

Largely because of what happened on the Killeen Luby's premises that fateful day in 1991, Texans once more had the legal permission, after more than one hundred years of proscription, to protect themselves from deadly weapons by carrying deadly weapons. The debate over the wisdom and moral rightness of the State of Texas's decision still rages to this day.

□ □ □

At the same time that Dr. Hupp was getting elected to the state legislature, Luby's Cafeterias was plunging into a brand-new phase of business enterprise. For it was during January 1996 that Chairman of the Board John Lahourcade retired to a directorship and the role of consultant to management, and Ralph "Pete" Erben, the Baylor University football star who had come to serve so long and faithfully as the protégé of the original pioneers, took his place in the chairman's seat. In July Luby's announced plans to acquire twenty facilities and locations previously belonging to Triangle FoodService, formerly known as Wyatt's Cafeterias, Luby's now-defunct chief competitor. Fifteen of these units were reopened under the Luby's name the next October. In addition, the company entered a joint venture arrangement with Waterstreet, Inc., a seafood restaurant company operating five units in Corpus Christi, San Antonio, and Fort Worth. According to the wording of the Luby's annual report for 1996, the objective of this alliance was to provide growth and profitability into the future and enhance shareholder value. What it really meant was that Luby's Cafeterias, Inc. was no longer merely a network of cafeterias. It was branching out into other restaurant businesses.

Also at the January 1996 annual board meeting, a new president and chief operating officer was elected by the board to replace Ralph Erben. Erben, who had been president and COO since 1988, was scheduled to step down from his position, and take up the reins of the board, later in the year. The newly elected president who would then assume executive command was himself a longtime employee of Luby's—one who, like John Lahourcade, had never worked in a cafeteria, but who had proven his diligence and loyalty over eighteen years' worth of stewardship in the Luby's accounting department. Erben and Lahourcade both felt great confidence in his abilities. They esteemed his strong sense of responsibility, which could be perceived as an admiring reflection of the integrity represented by Bob Luby and Charles Johnston; held strong hopes for his future contributions to the company; and looked upon him as their own protégé. Erben in particular had been grooming him for some time now to ascend to the pinnacle of the presidency.

His name was John E. Curtis Jr.

□ □ □

It is important, at this juncture, to note that up until this period of the mid-1990s, the ethics of Luby's Cafeterias, Inc. had remained impeccable. No real flaws existed either in the personal integrity of its executive leadership or in the integrity of the business as a whole. Even back in 1959, when the Harlingen crisis involving J. W. Cunningham—the theft of the blueprints that also robbed the Luby's structure of its innocence and disrupted its harmony—had shaken the company's inner circle, the course had remained true. This breach, back then, had seemed to be painful but recuperative, a minor blemish that could be transcended by holding steady to established ideals. Any shift in moral energy it might have introduced could be easily overcome. And it was overcome, for a great many years into the future.

Yet, in the private lives of two of the main players, Charles and Gertrude

Johnston, the breach served to open a door onto further darkness. And that darkness affected the corporation, subtly or not, as well as the individuals trapped in its shadow.

An important aspect of this loss of innocence, and the point that universalizes it as a paradigm for other cycles of turmoil and harmony, is the very aforementioned shift in moral energy. When enough change has occurred, enough of the diverted energy has accreted, people's outlooks change too. Now, in the 1990s, as in 1959, the people at the helm of Luby's neither failed to uphold their ideal principles nor fell short of correct ethical behavior. They didn't cheat or lie. Through all the change and the disastrous business mistakes to come, they committed no fraud or deception, posted no fake earnings statements, and made none of the other blunders so familiar in the late 1990s and the new millennium among corporations such as Enron, WorldCom, Tyco, and others. (As of this writing in September 2005, there are currently no fewer than forty-two American companies under investigation and/or convicted of serious corporate wrongdoing by the SEC and the criminal justice system, according to a list posted by Citizen Works: The Corporate Scandal Sheet.)

And the decisions the Luby's executives started making in the mid-1990s never crossed the line into criminal conduct. Those decisions were all taken in good faith, which only the corrective lens of hindsight would reveal to be misplaced. The Luby's board and executive officers were still as earnest and well-meaning, still as honest and conscientious, as their predecessors, the pioneers. Yet, the rest of the corporate world had begun setting precedents, such as overpayment of executives, reductions of employee benefits, and skimping on quality of products, if not service, that would eventually sway the Luby's leadership from Harry Luby's, Bob Luby's, and Charles Johnston's initial high standards.

Another factor also played into the decision-making picture. The ratio of old-line hands-on cafeteria veterans had gradually been reconfigured; there were now more "nonfood" people on the board than there were food people. In 1988 the conditions for Charles Johnston's dictum had already come to pass: "When the fourth accountant or nonfood person gets appointed to the board, bail out!" At that time, the nonfood people reached the number four. Then Charles Johnston died. By 1996, the year after Bob

Luby officially vanished for good from the premises of the Luby Building, all the most recent additions to the board of directors, men *and* women, were nonfood or outsider electees. Those board members outnumbered the food people by a majority of seven to three.

And the wake of their mistakes would ultimately wreak economic havoc just as drastic as that caused by some of the companies guilty of fraud and criminal misconduct they had felt the need to emulate.

It would be tedious to the reader for this book to tabulate here the ebb and flow of escalating short-term and long-term revolving debt that Luby's began to incur from year to year, starting in 1993 with a quickly repaid loan of $5 million. Suffice it to say that by 1996, the company that had opened its 100th restaurant nine years before now operated 200 self-built stores in eleven states: Texas, Arkansas, New Mexico, Oklahoma, Tennessee, Arizona, Mississippi, Florida, Louisiana, Missouri, and Kansas, with four more scheduled, plus the twenty extra just acquired that year through the buying of the moribund Wyatt's Cafeterias chain, bringing the total to 224—with still more stores in the planning stages. The worst problem about the decision to buy Wyatt's lay not in the huge debt incurred. It lay in the defiance of a precept almost biblical in its weight and magnitude, a precept so deeply established and respected under Bob Luby's and Charles Johnston's regimes that to go against it had been unthinkable. That precept was: Do not expand until managers have been adequately trained who can fill the positions in the new stores. But the purchase of Wyatt's caught Luby's short. Their competent management was now spread so thin that they were actually doing the unthinkable: they were bumping Number Two men and women (associate managers) up to the Number One general manager position before they were ready.

Only a tried-and-true, dyed-in-the-wool cafeteria "food" man would have recognized and understood, with horror, just how catastrophic such a move might be. Unfortunately, the one food person still in charge, Pete Erben, was as caught up in the whirlwind and blind to the impending catastrophe as all those who didn't know any better.

As Brad Lomax, the owner of Waterstreet, Inc., with whom Luby's had just consolidated, quipped to George Wenglein in 1996, "Well, Mr. Erben opened the 200th Luby's this year. Maybe he'll open the 300th next year."

The growth and expansion was by now perceived as almost out of control. And the amount of money the company owed by this time, not counting mounting interest, was $57 million, with a line of credit to a four-bank syndicate for $100 million.

It was a long road from Springfield, Missouri, in 1911.

And despite the tragic violence of 1991, more blood would yet be spilled. In fact, the most significant bloodshed—the violent act directly connected to what was going on in the intimacy of the boardroom, the murder that would strike at the heart of the corporate headquarters itself—was just about to occur. Luby's real public exposure, and the company's subsequent chaos, would then ensue.

CONDIMENTS ON THE SIDE

□ □ □

Once your organization makes a decision and a direction is chosen, treat it as your own. Never, never spend time looking for blame if it doesn't work. You'll be the only person blamed if you do.

CHARLES JOHNSTON

John Curtis, having stepped into the presidency and chief operating officer's job at Luby's Cafeterias, Inc. less than three months before, was about to attend his first board of directors' meeting in Phoenix and was expressing anxiety about it. "Don't worry, John," said Pete Erben to Curtis. "If you've got a problem, just tell them, 'I inherited it.' Blame everything wrong on me. And think how good you'll look next year."

But Curtis, it seems, took Charles Johnston's adage stated above far more deeply to heart than he did Pete Erben's encouraging words of solace. And the consequence of this embracement was quickly to lead Luby's to a more ominous turning point than any other it had faced in its entire history so far.

□ □ □

According to a number of people interviewed for this book, Pete Erben, the last old cafeteria hand to captain the helm at Luby's, was asked by the board of directors to resign his chief executive position in 1996 because he protested the nonfood board members' complaints that Luby's was overpaying its management.

The very basis of the former "old guard" or pioneer regime's philosophy—that wonderful compensation package of 40 percent net profits guaranteed to every manager who had charge of his or her own store—was now not only considered obsolete, it was regarded as a liability. It seemed especially a liability in view of Luby's present mid-1990s financial commitments: the large debt burden it had taken on, the rapid expansion rate, and the necessity of keeping the stock analysts and stockholders happy. Although increased sales and earnings per share were up for the twenty-eighth year in a row, conditions had changed. Lifestyles had changed. Public tastes had changed. Markets, too, were changing; in established stores, traffic and sales were declining. Younger people weren't eating at cafeterias as often as they used to, but were instead taking their patronage to the new family restaurant chains springing up all over the country. Certainly they still flocked to the newly opened stores in districts that had not yet featured a Luby's. But the novelty value didn't necessarily recruit lasting customers. For the first time since 1992, Luby's same-store customer count trend dropped into negative numbers.

A vicious circle had formed in Luby's business operations, and the company was, in effect, chasing its tail to keep up with the circle's demands. The CPAs and financial experts who now ran the organization simply could not understand the concept of giving so much of the profits to management. They were appalled at the apparently reckless precedent Luby's had set. For them, Charles Johnston's old explanation of this policy didn't make a grain of sense. "The advantage of giving management a large percentage of a store's profits should be obvious," Charles had said. "You don't have to wake the person up, dress them, and then show up to do their job." This autonomy and entrepreneurship among managers had always been the key to Luby's outstanding success. "If your business requires long hours and strict rules, be prepared to pay your management big money, or get a real thrill out of retraining!" Charles had also warned. But because none of the new board members had ever worked in a cafeteria, they had little idea what a manager's day really implied, and why this incentive loomed as so significant in the company's fortune-making potential.

So Erben's seemingly stubborn championing of the old rule pushed the board members beyond the limits of their patience. But sadly, Erben had also incurred the resentment of what was left of the very same "old guard" he represented, when he had resisted *their* opposition to the buying of the twenty Wyatt's Cafeterias units. Most of the cafeteria veterans still present at headquarters—Tommy Griggs and Vernon Schrader, to name two—felt such a purchase to be unwise. It seemed reckless in light of the board's proposed managerial-reward cutbacks, and financially unsound. It involved a debt leveraging the company had never incurred before. Not enough managers were ready to step in and fill the places the new stores would immediately require. Debt leveraging to acquire more stores without the incentives in place not only to hire new managers but to retain the experienced managers necessary to carry out the on-the-job training spelled disaster.

At the same time that he was strongly objecting to the direction in which the board was intent on taking the company, great friction existed between Erben and his old cronies. But since they no longer occupied positions on the board of directors, they did not fully understand the pressures placed on the current directors to expand, nor did they understand the courage Erben exhibited in fighting for the managers. The only pioneer still left in a directorship was George Wenglein, a lone food man voice in the boardroom.

"During Erben's tenure as president and COO, the company grew from 127 to 224 cafeterias, and annual sales increased from $283 million to more than $450 million," John Lahourcade was to remark later, after Erben's departure. "He provided leadership through a period of great growth, and we are indebted to him for his dedication to the company." But obviously such a performance was not, in and of itself, enough.

Although Erben himself had groomed John Curtis for the position of

Bill Robson, George Wenglein, John Lahourcade, Pete Erben,
and John Curtis, 1994

president and CEO, it was an irony that Curtis knew the board was going to ask Erben to resign before Erben himself knew of the demand for his resignation. The president who had actively seen Luby's through the aftermath of the horrifying Killeen massacre carnage—the man who had been first on the spot the moment the police opened their cordon, who had stood among the dead and personally counseled as many of the victims and their families as he could, who had reassured the employees that they would get paid regular wages until the company could rebuild the cafeteria and get it back into shape to reopen, who had been so shaken by the shocking experience that to this day he still weeps openly at its memory—that man remained in the dark about his ejection, while his successor had to bear the grim burden of private knowledge as to his mentor's fate and future.

For a deeply religious man such as John Curtis, this irony must have grated his conscience. But perhaps not as much as the first tasks he had to perform as soon as he assumed his new responsibilities: that of closing two stores, and releasing the employees to fend for themselves. At a time when a total of 13,000 workers entrusted their labor and good faith to Luby's, and the company had to pay their wages and benefits as well as meet its fresh fiscal obligations, this action might have simply seemed like tough but sound business sense. But such a step, in the long, beneficent history of Luby's employment practices and care for the well-being of its personnel, was unprecedented.

And John Curtis knew it.

□ □ □

As has been observed in the opening chapter of this story, John Curtis took his new duties very seriously.

He had always been impressed by the honesty, business integrity, and dedication to employees and clientele with which Charles Johnston and Bob Luby had run the company. And apparently he was very glad to be associated with such excellent procedures. There is no doubt that he profoundly admired the company's two entrepreneurial founders. To work for Luby's truly meant to work for good people. This seemed to have been, even more than it might be for many average Americans, a crucial issue for John Curtis, whose religious convictions dominated his attitude and his life. His attendance at his church, the Tree of Life Fellowship in New Braunfels, Texas, was constant. Even after he and his family moved back from New Braunfels to San Antonio, it continued to be regular almost to the point of infallibility. For ten years he had served on the church's advisory board. Prayer was an integral feature of his daily routine, and often he and Kathi, his wife of twenty-eight years, prayed together before going to bed at night. In addition, his respect for the minister of his church, the Rev. Don Duncan, blossomed into a friendship so close that Duncan became Curtis's main confidant outside of the Luby's Building, after his wife. Although Curtis was someone who didn't open up freely to many people, he opened up to Duncan. The two men, who were the same age and had each fathered three children, talked often and candidly about many issues in their lives. Their families socialized together as well.

But then, six months before the fateful day of March 13, 1997, Don Duncan suffered a sudden, massive heart attack and died.

From what Kathi Curtis later told *The San Antonio Express-News*, John Curtis apparently felt overwhelmed with grief at Duncan's death. He must have also felt suddenly lonelier, having lost his pastor. Duncan's widow, the Rev. Karen Duncan, who took over her husband's duties as minister, recalled the depth of Curtis's mourning. "John just cried and cried for days. He missed him [Don Duncan] a lot. I think it was because Don was more than a friend to John. He was his pastor, his spiritual advisor, so John confided in him. Don prayed for John whenever he had a big decision to make."

And sure enough, very soon after Duncan's death Curtis was thrust into a veritable maelstrom of big decisions. In the midst of that unexpected isolation, he was asked to assume the top person's responsibilities and obligations for a company in a major stage of transition—one that was trying to uphold its time-honored customs of uprightness while adopting new and very different methods of conducting business. Such a position might make anyone but the saltiest maverick tycoon nervous. Certainly an accountant, whose training is as absolutely antithetical to risk-taking behavior as any professional's in the world, was entitled to feel a little anxious. And Curtis had been acting as Luby's chief financial officer from 1988 until his 1997 appointment as chief executive officer. So he knew precisely, down to the last penny, where Luby's assets and obligations lay, and what they were destined to cover.

But the other task that had fallen onto John Curtis's shoulders the moment his induction into the Luby's presidency was completed was even more gargantuan and perhaps more galling than the two-store closure he had to execute. For Curtis had been assigned the chore of integrating the former Wyatt's Cafeterias into Luby's operations. This meant that, no matter how hard Pete Erben tried to soothe him and take on the blame, it was Curtis who would be answerable if the ill-prepared managers failed, and those stores failed along with them. And the very action of those managers' premature promotions ran so contrary to Bob Luby and Charles Johnston's well-tested approach that its failure could almost be guaranteed.

Add to that an accountant's nightmare—the huge burden of newly accrued debt that, before long, as Curtis very well knew, would start accelerating, or, as Pete Erben put it, "coming up to the bloom"—and one begins to see a man who had already seen the handwriting on the wall. And it was all coming to pass under his watch.

If such a man also felt even a slim sense of moral and practical responsibility for his charge, the weight could have seemed crippling. For the likes of John Curtis, it must have appeared as monstrous as the iceberg that the SS *Titanic* struck.

□ □ □

There is no doubt that John Curtis was what is known in modern parlance as "a nice guy." He had always been that way. Former classmates who attended kindergarten through high school with him have attested to his genuine good nature, his reliability, and his stability. They remember him as friendly, happy, and solid—the kind of fellow who was dependable and unaffected—the kind who would choose well, live well, and never do anything that didn't smack of strong common sense. An undramatic, undemonstrative sort of person. A quiet person. The last person they could think of who would commit suicide.

Kathi Curtis, who fell in love with him in their Wilshire Elementary School sixth-grade classroom, at the age of twelve, and waited from then on for him to grow up so she could marry him, discovered in John Curtis the partner of her dreams. He had been a boy who "was, of course, adorable," she said. "He was such a good-looking kid. But as we grew up, one of the things I found he had was a morality in him—a reverence for life. I did not see that in a lot of young men. This was the sixties—a radical time. I really did keep my eye on him throughout his high school years."

After high school they grew closer. John Curtis first attended Texas A&M and was admitted to its military corps. But "he hated it," said Kathi later, and he transferred to Texas Tech University. He and Kathi were married the spring of his senior year. Their marriage continued in true happiness and harmony for the next twenty-eight years. To all obvious purposes, it seemed that each had chosen the other well.

But there came a point when, as John Curtis slipped more deeply into the state of anxiety that apparently overwhelmed him with his promotion, he evidently no longer felt confidence in Kathi's empathy for his situation. As devoted as she was, as much as she wished to be his loving helpmeet, he clearly discerned a certain unbridgeable gulf between them—in one area, at least. "John was an extremely quiet man—very reserved, very private," Kathi Curtis has described her husband. "He kept a lot inside—never talked badly about people—always a leader, but a very humble, quiet man." And in the most significant document placed in their kitchen for her detection on that fatal night of March 13, 1997, written in a pain he had never confided, he told her, "You can't understand." As Kathi Curtis was later to comment about the contents of that poignant note, "He was right. I couldn't understand the pressures he was feeling. I had never worked."

According to those who knew him well at Luby's, including David Daviss (who became chairman of the board after Erben abruptly resigned), Curtis was self-contained, thoughtful, and analytical, "not conniving or political. He really gave the impression of being laid-back and very much in control," Daviss added. "Everyone liked him. There was nothing not to like."

"I don't know if there are adequate superlatives to describe him as a man," Pete Erben told the Associated Press later. "Very bright, very conscientious . . . a real sense of dignity."

But once he stepped into the empty shoes of Luby's president and CEO, John Curtis's even keel and outer calm began to desert him on the inside. He started to grow uncharacteristically troubled. Soon he could no longer sleep well at night. And before much longer—before he had even been President for two months—he found he could no longer sleep at all.

The day before his initiatory board of directors' meeting in Phoenix, Curtis shared a private word with John Lahourcade. Although Curtis always presented an upbeat public attitude about his new position, Lahourcade felt that Curtis was looking edgier and more depressed than he had ever seen him before. The sleeplessness and despondency over letting Bob Luby and Charles Johnston's dicta down had gathered within Curtis until they could no longer be transcended. A few days earlier, Curtis had expressed to Pete Erben his disappointment that during his first quarter as chief executive, the company's earnings would come in below those of a year ago. But Erben had reminded him that both the Wall Street analysts and the company had been expecting a slight decline, owing to the Wyatt's acquisition. Now Lahourcade took Curtis aside and offered his support.

"Do you feel you're up to this, John?" he asked. "You seem anxious."

"I'm fine," Curtis replied.

"Just remember that I'm here if you need anything. If there's anything bothering you, you can feel free to tell me."

"Thank you, but I'm fine. Everything will be fine," said Curtis. "Don't worry."

Lahourcade still felt uneasy at Curtis's plain discomfort. "Is it the financials for the Phoenix expansion?" he pursued. "Are you worried about those? How do they look?"

"I haven't quite finished them. They're not ready yet. But I'll be done with them tonight," Curtis promised. "They'll be okay."

Lahourcade knew very well what a trustworthy man Curtis was. So, reassured, he went on his way and prepared himself for the trip.

The Southwest Airlines flight out to Phoenix was scheduled for early the next morning. The San Antonio team of directors and their new president all had seats on the same plane. The game plan was that they would congregate in the departure lounge; then they would fly out and meet up with the directors coming from other cities when they reached Arizona.

Once the troop of directors arrived at San Antonio International Airport and got called for boarding, a few noted Curtis's prolonged absence. They felt puzzled, and somewhat concerned. But after a little discussion, and one or two hasty phone calls with no results, they went ahead, boarded the flight, and readied for takeoff.

Little did they know that the airline ticket John Curtis's secretary had purchased and prepared for him was still lying untouched in his office desk drawer in the Luby's Building, where he had deliberately left it the night before.

It was when they paused for a stopover in El Paso and made another call to company headquarters that they heard the news. This was when they discovered to their shock just how much the stress John Curtis had been toiling under, the symptoms of which he had so successfully suppressed, had exacted its toll. It was also when they learned exactly what the full fruits of their mistakes looked like. For in the small, still hours of the morning of March 13, just five or so hours before the directors landed for their layover in El Paso, John Edward Curtis Jr. had committed the unthinkable: he had slipped out into the darkness, dressed only in his pajamas and a pair of sweatpants, driven to the Motel 6 on Loop 410 that he had checked into at 10:30 the previous night, unlocked the door to Room 214, and there commenced to stab himself nineteen times in an act of emblematic self-sacrifice that, consciously or not, echoed the ongoing self-inflicted death of the company he had served so sincerely for eighteen years. His first few stabs fell experimentally: wrist slits, abdominal incisions, flesh punctures. But gradually his blows grew more and more forceful, until he had cut himself fourteen times. Then at last he flailed the kitchen knife he was wielding into the most vulnerable parts of his body, his neck, administering at least three mortal wounds, bringing the count to a total of five critical ones. With the final slash, he cut his own throat.

□ □ □

No one can ever know just what went on in John Curtis's mind before he took the drastic measures that he must have believed would halt his torment forever. No one can ever guess to what greater or lesser degree the imagery of his fundamentalist Christian faith might have haunted him, or how deeply the concept of sacrifice guided his choices. As one Luby's family friend and observer, Wende Wilkes, has commented, "I can't imagine how desolate and alone he must have felt, as if Christ had deserted him, and that was why he had punished himself. Christianity does not embrace suicide as an honorable endeavor, and so in this last act he even abandoned the tenets of his faith."

The speculations of his family, his friends and colleagues, the forensic experts and medical experts and psychiatrists and journalists are all, in the end, moot. For the one thing everyone who really knew him agree upon unanimously is this: his action ran completely counter to who he seemed to be.

"This was something way out of character," his son Daniel J. Curtis told the *New York Times*. "It was unexpected to all."

"We were completely shocked when we heard the news at our reunion. He was the last person you'd expect to do such a thing," one of his classmates from junior high, McArthur High School, and Texas Tech University said. "That was why at first we thought it *couldn't* be suicide, it *had* to be murder. Only who would ever want to kill him, and why? John was the

All-American kid. I never saw him mad, never saw him cross with anyone. To me, his life, marriage, and career looked like the perfect situation."

His beautiful blonde wife, Kathi Curtis, summed it up for the Associated Press a few days after his funeral. "He loved me well, and his children. He was a good man, a godly man." She would later declare, a year after his death, "This was so outside his character. It was the most shocking thing in the world. It's almost as if this was a different person," repeating the information that he was a born-again Christian, an elder at Tree of Life, a faithful husband, and a devoted father who loved nothing better than being with his children. The dynamic of love, indeed, permeated his home and his existence, which were exemplary.

"I had anticipated everything about John, all our married life," Kathi said. "I have no explanation for it. I don't know if I was just naïve. I am shocked at myself that I did not see." But she then went on, "I think John in some way punished himself, and he had nothing to punish himself for."

Dr. Ann Blake Tracy, a Salt Lake City–based independent researcher who, for eight years prior to Curtis's death, had been studying violent behavior and its potential link to certain antidepressants and other drugs, thought it possible that Curtis's actions may have been related to Serevent, an asthma inhalant that had then been on the market for three years, which he was taking twice a day—and which was the only foreign substance found in his body when the toxicology examination was concluded. In its clinical trial data, Serevent's manufacturer, Glaxo Wellcome, lists headaches, tremors, mild anxiety, and nervousness among Serevent's possible neurological reactions. In 1998 Tracy maintained that certain antidepressants and asthma medications can be dangerous in some people. She thought that Curtis's inhalant might have caused an REM (rapid eye movement) sleep disorder and an abnormality in his level of serotonin, the brain's so-called coping chemical. Dr. John Chiles, chief of psychiatric health services for the University Health System in San Antonio, agreed that abnormal serotonin levels had been linked with repetitive impulsive behavior, suicides, and violent suicide attempts.

But to lay the blame for the extreme punitive steps John Curtis took against himself on a drug that, although currently in 2005 in the legal spotlight for its critical and possibly life-threatening side effects, has never been proven to actually cause depression is to avoid the crux of meaning that John Curtis's life and death might contain. For the connection between his sense of guilt over the company's impending fate and his suicide is inescapable. And it is hard to peer closely at Curtis's lethal conduct and fail to notice how ritualized his suicide appears—the first tentative cuts, the gathering momentum into frenzy—and how this one seemed to be manifesting, or "acting out," the business determinations that Luby's decision makers had also taken in recent years, and their self-immolating effects on the company.

Pete Erben had this to say to the one hundred workers at Luby's company headquarters, when they collected together to talk and pray in the immediate days following the grim revelations of the blood-soaked Motel 6 room. His words to them were quoted in the *New York Times*: "We obviously created more pressure than what we realized. It is horrible to feel that maybe I led him [Curtis] to where his life seemed intolerable."

But John Lahourcade contributed his own thoughts to the *San Antonio Express-News*: "I'm not only shocked, but I find it inconceivable," he stated, adding, "There is nothing that would explain it as far as the company is concerned. Nothing untoward occurred."

One may suspect, however, that John Curtis at least, by his very action, did not agree.

□ □ □

In the first three days following John Curtis's suicide, several significant things happened as a result of the announcement of the terrible news. The first was the inevitable reaction on Wall Street: on Friday, the day after the suicide was revealed, Luby's stock fell to a 52-week low. But David Leibowitz, an analyst at Burnham Securities in New York, was confident the company had the internal wherewithal to emerge intact from the tragedy, based on its handling of the Killeen massacre. "The corporate structure is very much in place," he told the *San Antonio Express-News*. "This is an organization of the highest integrity, and if any company is capable of getting through what they've experienced, it's Luby's." A few days later, nearly a week after the announcement of Curtis's death hit the media, the stock in fact began to rebound.

But spirits were boiling up to a more conflicted heat in the Luby's Building. For Pete Erben, who had volunteered to resume his duties as president and CEO once the vacancy was known, found his offer rebuffed by the board of directors, on which he now sat as chairman. Their argument was that the SEC had already been informed of his retirement, and the decision couldn't be retracted. So enraged was Erben by what he regarded as this flagrant shunning of his services that he instantly resigned from his position as chairman of the board as well, and retired from Luby's Cafeterias, Inc. and public life for good.

The board then went on to name Lahourcade, who was taking Erben's place as chairman, to become CEO. But Lahourcade declined, giving as his reason his desire to devote more time to the search for a new CEO. So David B. Daviss, the director who had headed the audit committee of Luby's board for the past thirteen years, assumed the interim title until a new CEO could be found.

Thus, the very last food person except for George Wenglein departed the premises, leaving the CEO position to a certified public accountant who had previously worked as chief financial officer for Church's Fried Chicken and chief operating officer of La Quinta Inns.

And the candidate that the Luby's board finally, after a five-month search, chose to succeed John Curtis to the presidency turned out to be nearly as pernicious, nearly as prone to ill-considered expenditures, no less destructive to the company's long tradition of integrity and benevolence, and no less driven by his own vision of late-twentieth-century corporate entitlements than many of the corporate CEOs whose names have now become bywords of scandal and criminality.

18

DIRTY DISHES

□ □ □

If you treat your fellow employee as a partner, you won't have to pull the plow alone.

CHARLES JOHNSTON

In September 1997, after a "very deliberate and thorough" five-month search, the Luby's board of directors announced the results of their quest for a new president and CEO to replace John Edward Curtis Jr. The name of their appointee was Barry J. C. Parker, a Dallas resident who, to judge from his photographs, bore more than a passing resemblance to Dick Clark of *American Bandstand* fame, and who held a master's degree from the Wharton School of Business. He was fifty years old—almost exactly the same age John Curtis would have been had he lived. The company itself was now also celebrating fifty years of operations, having been founded by Bob Luby, Charles Johnston, and their band of pioneers in the year of Parker's birth. And for the first time ever, it was bringing in a complete outsider, a stranger, to act as its chief.

George Wenglein joked at the time to a fellow board member that they had been searching for the equivalent of Jesus Christ to step in and "save" the company, and if Parker's middle initials were any indication, they had found their man. And indeed, the company was by now in dire need of a rescuer. Admittedly, the market had changed irrevocably, and the company's efforts to keep up with new trends by introducing a "Food to Go" system was helping a little. But between the higher newly set minimum wage it was having to pay workers (which prompted an increase of $4.5 million in overall store operating costs), and the closing of four more stores during the executive search period alone necessitated by their "underperformance" (thereby canceling out some of the expansion created by twenty-nine new store openings plus the fifteen Wyatt's reopenings), it was fairly clear that Luby's was in trouble.

But Parker's credentials seemed appropriate to the current nonfood board of directors. His résumé included two past positions as a retail executive. Although he had never had anything at all to do with the foodservice industry, the board felt that his sheer presidential qualities, polished during his eleven-year tenure as CEO of a large retail clothing outlet company called The County Seat, were just what the doctor ordered. He understood retail selling through long experience, they reasoned. That savvy was a gift he could bring to the table at Luby's, which desperately needed, they felt, to further emphasize and reform its sales methods and customer appeal. And Parker understood the exigencies of growth and expansion. While running The County Seat, he had engineered a strategic plan that took the company from 276 units to more than 750 stores in forty-eight states.

That Parker had also resigned from The County Seat in July 1996, following a net loss of $97 million on revenue of $619.2 million, and that right after his resignation, The County Seat had filed for Chapter 11 bankruptcy protection were not seen as bad signs at Luby's. Parker had merely been a victim, according to David Daviss, who was now stepping down from his interim presidency and succeeding John Lahourcade to resume his duties as chairman of the board. The blame for The County Seat's problems could be squarely laid on an investor group that gained an interest in the company as the result of a 1989 leveraged buyout.

"Everybody has always, in a very predictable fashion, marched up the corporate ladder [at Luby's]," Daviss explained. "With Barry, I think a look from the outside will be very healthy. I think this is basically a cafeteria company, but that isn't to say that we might not find other ways to deliver fresh, scratch-cooked food to customers." Daviss added, "We looked carefully at County Seat and are satisfied that it was not a reflection on Barry's ability or integrity."

The fact that the previous Luby's president and CEO had perished by his own hand rather than shuffle the blame of failures under his aegis onto other shoulders seems to have escaped the satisfied board's notice. Charles Johnston's maxim of treating one's organization's decisions as one's own, and "never spend[ing] time looking for blame if it doesn't work" obviously wasn't a sentiment close to Barry Parker's heart.

But Parker, in addition to his retail record, also apparently stepped into his position on October 1, 1997, with every intention of fulfilling the newly espoused business philosophies of the nineties—those taught and recommended by his alma mater and by Harvard Business School. The humane, philanthropic approach to employee consideration and compensation was now passé, irrelevant to a smartly run operation. He defined his mission in this way: "not necessarily to make wholesale changes, because this is a very successful company with a terrific corporate culture. But I do think every company needs to redefine itself every few years and continue to evolve."

And it wouldn't be long at all before he made the meaning of those words patently clear.

□ □ □

Once Parker took over the Luby's reins, he wasted no time in implementing the changes he deemed necessary to comply with this philosophy. In a two-year period, all the mandates Bob Luby and Charles Johnston had nailed into place disintegrated. Store maintenance budgets were slashed. The fresh food made "all from scratch" to be served in the cafeterias was replaced with cheap, preservative-laden premade ingredients and frozen dishes. Many of the old recipes customers had loved for fifty years got jettisoned in favor of the menus that Parker selected. And, most disastrously of all, the board's complaint of managers' overpayment (which Erben had deflected and opposed so often) was now supported and urged by Walter Salmon, with cuts arranged by Parker.

The end of an era had truly arrived. In 1999, managers' compensation packages—the jewel in the crown of Luby's gilded history—were dismantled. No longer would the famous 60/40 split in net profits exist. Instead, the managers were put on salaries, in what the administrators called "a payment adjustment." And the salaries fell far short, not only of managers' original expectations of the 60/40 split, but of the earnings they had been generating for themselves, and therefore for the company, during the time in which they had run their stores. Even the trainees just coming up for placement who had been promised the Luby's reward package as incentive for all their years of hard work felt disappointed and deserted. The veteran managers who had already trusted in the traditional compensation package grew alienated to such an extent that a number of them left the company's employ. As a result of the pay cut that in many cases amounted to half the manager's income, some of them lost their homes, lost their good credit ratings, and got their cars repossessed; some of them had marriages that failed under the stress of the new economic hardship. The cost to morale and to longtime Luby's expertise and efficiency was catastrophic. It didn't take long before the executives, who had so ignored Charles Johnston's dictum about treating their fellow employees as partners, found themselves in truth pulling the plow alone.

Meanwhile, the perks that some of the new, up-and-coming executives at headquarters were enjoying put the remaining managers who were trying to stay loyal to the company in the face of its betrayals under further strain. For it was accepted procedure that if one of these men or women was throwing a party, he or she could come into any convenient Luby's and commandeer a catering menu full of delicacies and entrées, absolutely free of charge. More than once, certain of the executives marched into a store at the last minute, informed the general manager that he or she was shortly to be entertaining a group with cocktails and food, and exhausted the restaurant's entire supply of shrimp or other goodies during peak dining hours. Their sense of entitlement, it seems, became as conscienceless, as arrogant, and as ravenous as that of the highfliers like Jeff

Skilling, Kenneth Lay, and Rebecca Marks, who were at that same time flaunting their wealth and gutting Enron.

So it seems an especially ironic twist of fate that it fell to Barry Parker, as president and CEO, on August 13, 1998, to announce to the world the death of Bob Luby.

□ □ □

Bob, who was eighty-eight years old that summer, was spending the hot months with his third wife, Kathleen, up in Colorado Springs, Colorado, where they owned a condominium. He had outlived his old friend, comrade, and cousin Charles Johnston by nine years. He had also outlived his first wife, Georgia Wenglein Luby, who had died of cancer when their daughter Martha was still a girl, as well as his second wife, who had also fallen victim to cancer. Now he was free of the onerous Luby's schedule—free at last for a leisurely retirement—to indulge his passions for travel, fine dining, and visiting friends, and no longer to spend his days tasting Luby's dishes and overseeing the restaurant routines. During the final conscious moments of Bob's life, however, it so happened that he was enjoying a meal at the exclusive Garden of the Gods Country Club outside of Colorado Springs. In the midst of eating a bite of food, he choked and passed out. He was rushed to the local hospital, but his heart couldn't stand the strain. He died a short time later, without surviving to see the calamity that would overtake the empire he and Charles had founded so idealistically, and with such hardworking, youthful, collaborative optimism.

□ □ □

By 1999 the customer base of Luby's had started falling rapidly, both as a result of the new policies of cut-rate food and cut-rate service Parker was activating and the new competition offered by family-oriented fast-food restaurants. Meanwhile, Parker was receiving an unprecedentedly large payment package for his services.

According to a keen Luby's observer who had journalistic opportunities to interview him, Parker possessed a "heads will roll," "get the hell out," adversarial personality. The reporter added that he seemed to have borrowed his business approach from the *Dynasty* television series of the 1980s. Apparently this attitude extended to employees, managers, and press alike. Another observer found him to be "slick and smug, the worst guy they could have hired." Certainly one of the managers who defected from the company under Parker's domination and went on to start his own cafeterias considered him an obnoxious presence, deleterious to Luby's entire tradition, and vowed to "get that SOB" through creating the competition necessary to fill the void left when the old Luby's cooking methods got abandoned and its prices simultaneously rose. Attracting older customers was that manager's particular goal, and he has since been quite successful, providing the kind of service, friendly atmosphere, and food quality that such clientele had been used to receiving at Luby's, and getting lucrative results—proving, he says, that the old-fashioned cafeteria concept run the old-fashioned way is far from dead.

Throughout the first two years of his employment, Parker continued his "redefining" process for Luby's. Part of that plan was apparently his salary, which had been $330,000 when he started in the fiscal year of 1998 (with an additional bonus of $132,000 and stock options worth $170,000), but which by 1999 was raised to $375,000 (with an additional bonus of $93,500 and stock options worth $106,000)—a severe departure from the old pioneers' notions that "you share the wealth and share the profits" with employees and management. Several examples of his early executive decisions stand out as prime examples of his misplaced thrift and policy alterations. For instance: when he first took office, a parking lot outside a San Antonio cafeteria needed renewal. The general manager of the store in question had found a contractor who would install proper drainage and the best materials for a total cost of $20,000, following Bob Luby and Charles Johnston's tenet that "if it's done well, it will last." Parker scrapped the plan and had the lot seal-coated for $7,000, without filling the potholes. During the next heavy rain the lot was destroyed, flushing the money down the city drains along with its debris. By this time Parker had also revamped and standardized the menu, and was claiming to managers about ingredients and processes—claiming that the prepared foods they were now receiving by shipments from purveyors had been made exactly the same way as of old, using the same recipes they had always served, but made by a new, centralized source. This included, for instance, items like prebreaded fish, which required the use of raw eggs. Managers knew the FDA will not permit shipment of raw eggs, which meant a substitute was part of the contents, and the phrase "food cooked from scratch" was thus a misrepresentation. The same was true of raw bread; the frozen dough balls Parker provided needed five times the amount of yeast to rise than the previous, "homemade" versions, and were almost inedible. Parker also started hiring untrained, unskilled part-time labor to diminish wage costs during the heaviest dining times of the day. By cutting staff tasks through his use of preprepared foods (as well as halving staff wages), Parker demolished more than just the Luby's promise to serve nothing but the freshest, most excellent dishes to its customers. The ballet of the kitchen, that careful dance choreographed so many years before by the two founders from their literal lifetimes' worth of experience in cafeterias, now collapsed into a shambles. When even one task was removed from the roster of a multi-tasked employee (such as the "scratch food" cook), a hole was left in that person's routine and he or she wound up with idle time to fill.

Another step Parker took was to change the name of the corporation. In a professed desire to reshape how the public perceived the company's image, he discarded the word "Cafeterias" from the letterhead and stock listing and shortened the title to Luby's Inc.—in a sense, officially erasing the entire premise on which Bob Luby and Charles Johnston had founded their enterprise. Luby's was just another restaurant chain, in a world teeming with restaurant chains. In the opinion of at least one former manager, the change in concept hastened the decline to an avalanche's speed.

And statistics suggest that he was correct in his conclusion. During Parker's tenure as Luby's CEO, the company's share price fell nearly 75 percent, from a high of $21.25 shortly after he took over to $5.44 within a three-year period. The abolition of the 40 percent compensation package for seasoned managers and its replacement with salaried compensation was so unpopular that after so many veteran managers left Luby's employ altogether—an almost unheard-of proceeding—there were few managers to succeed them. And whereas previously there had been thousands of applicants clamoring for acceptance into the few hundred positions available in the Luby's Management Training School (including not only college graduates with the degrees mandatory for admission, but some with master's degrees as well), recruitment now grew difficult. Rick Gozaydin, the former private duty nurse of Charles Johnston who, after fours years at Charles's side, had then entered the training program, graduated number one in his class. He went on to become a general manager himself in Tennessee. Gozaydin now says, "Once the compensation policies changed, we knew it was over. The carrot was gone, and all we had to look forward to was a job."

Or, in the wistful words of a manager who had been hired during Parker's regime, "Working seventy-five or eighty hours a week on my salary is hard. But I'd be willing to work one hundred twenty hours a week on the old incentive plan."

The efficiency of the individual stores had already begun to suffer. The price of the time-honored Luann Platter—the classic Luby's offering that included a meat entrée, two vegetables, and a choice of breads—had shot up. That rise plus the declining quality of the food discouraged new consumers as well as repelling older ones. More stores were being closed—a total of ten by the end of 1999. But Parker was planning, building, and opening yet other stores called "Super Luby's" across the state of Texas and elsewhere. Despite the grandiose implications of their name, these were a great deal smaller in size than the older cafeterias, with more intimate atmospheres, and with "All You Can Eat" counters to lure "family" customers. Most tellingly, the long-term debt burden that Luby's now had to service, a whopping $80 million, was crushing the company profits. The American business hubris of the nineties was now in full sway.

But Parker had plenty of excuses for the abysmal decline in earnings, and other scapegoats to indict in order to account for his failure. It was the changing market trends, he told the stockholders. It was the economy (booming for the last eight years). It was the times; the whole restaurant industry was suffering. Some people weren't willing to work as hard as was necessary to make the turnaround that would bring back the company's prosperity.

Late in 1999, conditions were reaching a crisis point at Luby's corporate headquarters. The cushy retirement funds that so many Luby's employees, pioneer families, managers et al. had depended on for their old age were evaporating. The stock had plunged too low. For years these loyalists had refused to diversify their portfolios, placing their faith in the company that had supported them. They resisted the temptation, even as the stock price began to sink, to "back-stab" Luby's by selling out. Now the former multi-millionaires, or their widows and heirs, saw their fortunes shrink. Retirement plans shrank almost 74 percent in three years, an appallingly sharp drop in such a short time. Pot washers, cooks, cashiers, and tea-ladies faced utter indigence. Everything Bob Luby and Charles Johnston had envisioned for their employees' benefits now crumbled. The managers who had joined Luby's under the 60/40 percent split policy and now worked for the basic low-ceiling salary Parker had set were still expected to work twelve- and fourteen-hour days. Managers quit in droves in search of better employment—which was more than the thirty- and thirty-five-year lower-echelon workers could do.

It is interesting to note here that Kim Clark, dean of the Harvard Business School, recently said in a televised interview with Charlie Rose that, as a result of the behavior of its own graduates over the last fifteen years (such as Jeff Skilling, the notorious president and CEO of Enron, class of 1979), Harvard is changing its curriculum to introduce a new approach, with courses such as "Leadership, Values, and Corporate Accountability" that address ethical decisions made within corporations that will benefit employees as well as stockholders. The Wharton School, Barry Parker's alma mater, was also mentioned as exemplifying the Harvard Business School philosophy under need of amendment.

Despite the seriousness of the corporation's ailing health, the Luby's board of directors renewed Parker's contract in July 2000, while simultaneously retaining a restaurant consulting firm to examine Luby's and pinpoint the areas that needed revamping. The firm's first recommendation was that Parker be removed. So his resignation, requested immediately, was accepted in September. His "golden parachute," a full preceding year's salary of $473,540 plus a debt retirement of $127,000 owed by him to the company, was similar, although on a smaller scale, to the kind of generous self-awarded emolument many corporate executives were receiving during this stage of U.S. business. In October, after reporting a fourth-quarter net loss of $8.5 million and a 68 percent plunge in profitability, Luby's suspended its quarterly dividend and announced the departure of Laura Bishop, the chief financial officer who had so optimistically endorsed Parker's initial hiring.

The second recommendation of the consulting firm was that Luby's close fifteen more of its cafeterias.

But superseding the news of these changes was the groundswell of a major stockholders' revolt.

☐ ☐ ☐

It began in September 2000, the same month that saw Parker's resignation and the announcement of the fifteen store closures. Getting rid of Parker wasn't enough. The stockholders were angry. In fact, they were furious. They felt misled, they felt that Barry Parker had taken the company in which they had invested their money down a long, dark corridor of ruinous decisions, and the board of directors had aided and abetted him. They were disgusted with the board for behaving with such obtuse blindness by upholding Parker's rehiring. And they wanted to do something about it.

The stockholders' protests had been gaining strength and thrust throughout Barry Parker's tenure. A return to the old tried-and-true practices was necessary, they argued, to restore Luby's equilibrium and increase its sales. The company needed to move away from outsourcing its food production and start making everything from scratch on site again. It needed, even more, to give more flexibility back to the managers, and reward them accordingly. The relations between managers and corporate officers were, by this time, frayed almost beyond repair.

Most of all, Luby's needed to get rid of Parker. And yet the board of directors had had the imprudent effrontery to renew his contract, even in the face of his terrible record.

But the abrupt removal of Parker after the restaurant consultants' report came in, and the restoration of some managerial autonomy, did little to assuage the shareholders' ire. By early October a surprising number of them had leaped to the barricades, for one reason only: the Internet. Through a Yahoo! message board, they had communicated and assembled great numbers who were in agreement long before Parker's ouster. Now, for the first time in U.S. history, the solicitation of support for a proxy shareholders' fight was getting focused in Internet chat rooms, and a battle that historically had cost shareholders of other companies millions of dollars to mount was this time to be achieved for only $15,000. Their goal was to replace four board members whose terms were expiring, plus a fifth who was expected to resign, with their own representatives, during the next annual stockholders' meeting on January 12, 2001. One of the nominees was Elisse Jones Freeman—the daughter of Henry Jones, the cofounder/pioneer famous for his strict operations, observations, and tactics. Having grown up in Luby's alongside Carol Johnston, and in childhood helped with the early kitchen chores (cutting Jell-O, rolling silverware, and so on), she was a lifelong expert in what it took to run an effective cafeteria.

Three of the other dissident nominees were a former Luby's manager, a Tyler, Texas, investment manager, and a California lawyer and arbitrator for the National Association of Securities Dealers. In their opinion, the new leader Luby's needed to replace Parker was someone who had come up through the ranks.

So, with mutiny declared, the group calling itself the Committee of Concerned Luby's Shareholders filed a document with the Securities and Exchange Commission. In it, they told the SEC that "Luby's needs new blood at the most senior level. Shareholders need their own 'watchdogs' to mind the store and to make sure that their concerns are heard."

The proxy fighters began to gain national attention and interest, especially after they continued to file more SEC documents—a total of ten from mid-October. By January the group had pared its number of nominees down to three. Their fierce determination to gain a voice in the fate of the company promised an ugly battle.

When the day dawned for the meeting, more than five hundred stockholders streamed into the meeting room at the Omni Hotel in San Antonio. Soon the room grew so packed after every seat was filled that participants stood four deep against the walls and spilled out into the hallway, crowding at the doors and straining to hear the speakers. The stockholders' angry feelings burned higher when they discovered that the board had hired armed security guards to help keep order among the massed congregation. Luby's, with its tragic history of death by a madman's firearms, was the last place one would expect to find such preventative measures taken. The tacit insinuation the guards' guns represented—that the dissident shareholders were possibly out of control, bloodthirsty rebels harboring violent tendencies—seemed a shocking and despicable insult. After all, there was not only a widespread cross-section of the general public with a legitimate stake in the company sitting in the room; there were also disaffected family members, descendants of pioneers, and a few of the original pioneers themselves. And none of them felt happy. The board had gone too far.

They had gone too far in all directions, it seemed. For stockholder Helen Lee, the widow of founding Luby's executive John Lee, was one of the incensed attendees of the meeting. Unlike many of the other shareholders with only nominal amounts of stock, Helen Lee owned 200,000 shares, and felt furious at the way the board had handled the company's recent problems.

"I'd smack them in the mouth if I could," she said. "My husband always said you have to give people quality food at a reasonable price. Then you'll have a full cafeteria at all times." This simple formula was the very thing, of course, that Parker had most effectively razed.

But in the end that day, explosive tempers and denunciations notwithstanding, the proxy fighters lost their bids for the board seats, and their war. The board was reinstated by a vote of more than two to one, with about 75 percent of shareholders voting. Though the dissident group lost its fight, it did receive an outpouring of moral support. When Chairman David Daviss cut some speakers off before they could finish making their point, the people in the room booed. Likewise, they applauded critical questions. And when Daviss explained to the crowd that the company had scheduled a limited time for the meeting, and had already gone over, investor L. L. Davis retorted that executives were obligated to hear shareholders out. "You're the hired help, frankly," Davis added to the board chairman.

The outcome might have discouraged some participants, but others left the Omni bloodied yet unbowed, vowing a relentless continuation of their tactics. "If you think this year's meeting was contested, next year's meeting will be contested even more," warned Guy Adams, one of the chief insurgents, who ran a Los Angeles–based financial firm. "The clock has started, and people are going to have to see some visible results."

"The most important thing they need to do is get an outstanding CEO," commented Tom Palmer, the dissident investment consultant from Tyler who had helped lead the revolt and who had campaigned for one of the board seats. And Les Greenberg, the California lawyer who had also lost his bid for a seat, hinted that the group was not going to go away. The mere $15,000 that they had just spent to launch and carry on their proxy fight had required more than $200,000 spent by Luby's to counteract. "So it's easy for us to come back," he said. "We'll just add one phrase: 'We told you so.'"

However, a far more unexpected intervention than a future stockholders' coup was now lurking in the wings, waiting to slip into the Luby's Building. It would prove as effective a deus ex machina as any divine intercession in a Greek play. In fact, you might say it was nothing less than a superb and surprising piece of honest-to-goodness theater.

19

OVER, FORK OVER

□ □ □

Every dime I ever made came directly or indirectly from my generosity.
CHARLES JOHNSTON

The same worm of corruption that had been gnawing away at the heart of Luby's glossy apple for forty long years—ever since Harlingen, 1959—had now finally reached the surface. And only a few months before the stockholders' revolt first began to brew, all the rotten meat of the apple finally burst into its ripest decay.

□ □ □

On February 14, 1999, eighty-six-year-old Gertrude Johnston—known to her friends as Trudy, and widow of Luby's cofounder Charles Johnston—suffered a fall while alone in her house. Once she came to her senses sufficiently to overcome her stubbornness and realize the extent of her helplessness and the seriousness of her predicament, Gertrude's reflex was to phone her daughter, Carol. But her demand was somewhat strange. "Carol," she said in a message on her answering machine, "you have to come to the house and help me. I need to get inside. I have phone calls to make tomorrow."

When Carol heard the message, she felt baffled. Throughout the years before Charles's death in 1989, the two had been so wary of one another that attempts at communication had usually presented a prickly challenge. Hurt pride, mistrust, the provisions of Charles Johnston's will, and the awkward position Carol's parents' separation had imposed upon her had left daughter and mother at odds with one another. But in the ten years since—once Gertrude had finally accepted that Carol was not going to challenge Charles's last will and testament—they had tried to reconcile, and their interactions had turned friendlier and more loving. Now Gertrude sought help from the most natural source by leaving a message on her daughter's answering machine, claiming she was locked out of her house. But why would she be calling Carol, who lived some distance away, rather than resorting to her next-door neighbors—who had a key—or someone else closer by?

Gertrude Johnston

When Carol checked the caller ID, she discovered something even more perplexing: her mother had apparently made the call from *inside* the house. Did this mean Gertrude was confused, ill, delirious with fever perhaps? Or was she under some kind of external duress—maybe caused by a burglar whom she had discovered looting her home?

At the time Carol received Gertrude's message, she had a three-year-old child in her care with whom she had just spent Valentine's Day. The child's mother was due to pick her up shortly, so Carol needed to stay at home until the mother arrived. After phoning the Jaeckles, Gertrude's next-door neighbors of forty years, and asking Dr. Jaeckle to go over and check on Gertrude, Carol waited for his report. He called her back fifteen minutes later to say that he had walked around the house and seen nothing but a small light burning through a back window. So he had called out through the window, "Trudy, it's Jerry from next door." Then he received a disturbing reply: "Get away! I don't know who you are, but get away, my daughter's coming."

Next, Carol called a friend to meet her at her mother's house. Then, after the three-year-old was collected by her mother, Carol telephoned the police, who summoned an EMS vehicle and staff to Gertrude's address while Carol hurried over to join them. When she went around to the back and stood listening under the windows, all she could hear were moans. With the police already present, the friend gained entry to the house by wriggling through one of the windows. Once inside, he unlocked the doors and let Carol in. She found Gertrude lying on the floor of her bedroom in her own urine and feces with a broken leg. Gertrude was dehydrated, malnourished, and in a mild state of shock.

But she was overjoyed to see Carol and her companions.

"I'm so glad to see that the pilots have gotten the plane landed!" she exclaimed. Then she looked up at her daughter. "And I am so happy you were on this flight, Carol."

"Well, so am I, Mother," Carol replied. "Let's get our baggage and get out of here."

Her mother's words suggested the extent of her shock. But the elderly Gertrude had been slipping into occasional forgetful lapses for some time now, and her frugal and reclusive lifestyle didn't help. On her way out of the house, Carol noticed how dirty and cluttered the rooms had become. The refrigerator was full of mold, showing the extent to which Gertrude had declined. Silently Carol vowed to come back and clean once her mother was out of danger. It wouldn't do for Gertrude to return home to such an unhygienic, disheveled environment.

After the ambulance carried Gertrude to Northeast Baptist Hospital and Carol got her mother settled there with physicians in attendance, she went home in a state of exhaustion and emotional fatigue. Later that same night, she herself succumbed to a severe case of flu.

The next morning, too contagiously ill to visit the hospital and too weak and debilitated to accomplish anything else, Carol phoned her only female cousin, Joanie Cunningham Rives, daughter of J. W. Cunningham, for assistance. Joanie loved her Aunt Trudy, and the two of them had a special relationship. Gertrude often visited Joanie and her family. Joanie had many times been the means through which Gertrude and Carol communicated during the worst years of their estrangement. In Carol's words, "Joanie has a heart as big as a watermelon," and her dependable sanity and warmth would prove invaluable for this emergency. Joanie could be counted on to fly in immediately from Louisiana and nurture her aunt while Carol remained incapacitated. Gertrude, too, would be delighted to see Joanie—a bonus aspect of the arrangement. But there were other relatives who should be informed as well. So Carol called J. W.'s home in Dallas, telling her Aunt Joy what had occurred so that she could relay the news to J. W.

The first to arrive in San Antonio were J. W. Cunningham and his younger son, Jay Paul. (Joanie would arrive later.) That day, Gertrude was transferred to Park Lane, a rehabilitation center located on the Fort Sam Houston Army Base. Neither J. W. nor Jay Paul indicated a desire to visit Gertrude. That evening, Carol and the two Cunningham men had dinner together. Neither, throughout the whole conversation, inquired once about Gertrude's health—a detail that struck Carol at the time. J. W. did inform Carol that he had her mother's power of attorney. He requested that Carol get him an appointment with the bank the next day, so that he could get on Gertrude's bank account in order to pay bills and handle other matters while Gertrude was indisposed. So Carol contacted her bank officer at home and requested her to assist J. W. the following morning. J. W. also requested Gertrude's checkbook. Because Carol had always carefully dis-

Gertrude Johnston with her brother, J. W. Cunningham

tanced herself from her mother's financial and personal affairs, so as to avoid the pitfalls inherent in such knowledge, she felt too unfamiliar with whatever arrangements Gertrude might have made to challenge or doubt J. W.'s demand. It was not her place, she decided, to question him. Carol agreed to go home, where she had left her mother's handbag after the ambulance took Gertrude to the hospital, and get the checkbook and bring it to him. At this point, J. W. and his son informed Carol that they wished to spend several days and nights in Gertrude's house.

Although she felt hesitant, remembering how deeply Gertrude disliked even a housekeeper's or her own daughter's presence in her home, Carol also understood the depths of fondness Gertrude reserved for her younger brother. "Dub" was the person whom she had defended for so many years; Dub, who had been done wrong by Luby's, who had been compelled to leave his Harlingen home and go back to Dallas to start his own business when Charles and Bob had nudged him out of the company. And at this time, Carol was just as ignorant as her mother of the precise details of that fracture, since her father had never been willing to discuss it with her or disclose the truth. But there was more: Dub was also the brother who had championed and comforted Gertrude after her marriage fell apart—who had upbraided his brother-in-law's so-called callous desertion of Gertrude when Charles separated from her, at least in conversations with Gertrude. So Carol consented, giving J. W. and Jay Paul permission to stay in

Gertrude's house while they remained in San Antonio. Thinking matters were well in hand, Carol went home.

Then Joanie arrived, and both Carol and Gertrude were very happy to see her. When Carol accompanied Joanie to Gertrude's house in order to fetch her mother some extra clothing for the transfer home, she noticed again how dirty the house was and determined to clean it before Gertrude's hospital release.

Shortly afterward, Carol received a phone call from a Broadway Bank employee, who described J. W.'s and Jay Paul's bank visit to add J. W.'s name to Gertrude's checking account so he could withdraw money from it. The employee expressed astonishment and a little alarm that Jay Paul was giving his father the instructions and making the decisions, rather than J. W. simply carrying out his own mission without advice. He also kept publicly and audibly scolding his father that "he wasn't moving fast enough." The fact that J. W. was wearing a surgical back brace at the time *might* explain Jay Paul's impatient urgings, Carol thought; but the way J. W. continued to avoid her eye during his several day stay prompted her uneasiness. Just what, she wondered, was he not moving fast enough *about*?

A day or so after their bank visit, the Cunninghams went back home to Dallas. Joanie Cunningham Rives also departed for Louisiana. But ten days after Gertrude's initial hospitalization, Jay Paul Cunningham returned to San Antonio with a carpet shampoo machine "to help clean Gertrude's house." While staying in Carol's guest room over a five-day period, he fretted vocally about Gertrude's bills, remarking that he wanted some recent roofing work paid for quickly because, he said, "We don't want to end up with a lien on the house." This preoccupation flabbergasted Carol. What business of Jay Paul's could it possibly be as to when her mother's bills got paid, or whether or not the extremely unlikely event of a lien ever clouded the house's title?

Although Carol was still recuperating from the flu the day after Jay Paul's arrival, she still felt the need to fulfill her private vow. Knowing her mother's reclusive and private nature, Carol did not want to hire a cleaning crew, so she asked a friend to assist her in tackling the job of cleaning her mother's home themselves. Returning the next day to perform that chore, she discovered Jay Paul already in the house. He seemed obviously unhappy to see her and her friend. The dining table was now littered with Salomon Smith Barney financial statements, surrounded by piles and boxes of more papers—her mother's business records. Jay Paul warned Carol not to touch the papers. But when she asked him to break down and remove some old empty cardboard boxes from the garage that were harboring cockroaches and rats, he suddenly lost his temper and began to yell.

"Damn it, I have no intention of breaking down those boxes! And neither will you!" Then he began waving his arms. "You mother doesn't *want* them removed. Get your ass out of my house!"

Astounded, Carol gaped at him. So did her friend.

"What do you mean, 'your house'?" Carol asked. "This is my mother's house!"

"This is *my* house," Jay Paul replied. "They've given it to me."

"Given it to you?" Carol's emotions began to swing from bewilderment to fierce indignation. "*Who* gave it to you? What about my mother?" she cried.

"She'll be put in a nursing home in Plano," Jay Paul answered coldly.

Shaken, Carol went home, leaving her vacuum cleaner at her mother's. When she returned to pick it up, she discovered the locks had been changed. Now deeply frightened, she consulted her own bank officer. The officer reminded her that her uncle J. W. had Gertrude's power of attorney—an old one, it was true, but one that he had presented to Broadway Bank, and that the bank had been compelled to honor. If legal trouble was looming between Gertrude and her brother, it seemed advisable for Carol to hire an attorney to advise her on what steps she could take to protect herself. The bank officer then promised to make arrangements for Carol to consult with an attorney who specialized in these matters.

Carol's disquiet had initially been triggered by Jay Paul's unabashed rudeness. If Jay Paul and J. W. had behaved smoothly, matter-of-factly, with courtesy, she would have paid scant attention to their movements. And as she had always considered her mother's finances to be none of her own business, and subject entirely to her mother's discretion, she never would have bothered to look into anything that Gertrude had done or documents she might have signed. But now the bald-faced takeover of the thrifty, home-loving Gertrude's house, complete with instructions from Jay Paul to old friends and neighbors that Carol was not to return there or be given copies of the new keys, troubled and upset her even more than his abrasive retorts and dumbfounding announcement had done. She felt protective of her mother's interests. And news of Jay Paul's current denunciations of Carol to the neighbors—calling her a bad daughter whom her mother couldn't stand—put the final cap on her first intentions. She felt a deep foreboding. Clearly, if Jay Paul's blurting was any true indication, J. W. had *already* found a way to gain control over Gertrude's money and assets.

But how?

For a short time, Carol could only speculate. The evening after Carol learned the locks were changed, she called Joanie and unloaded all of her fears, concerns, and anxieties. Joanie and Carol were very close, and that night Joanie Cunningham Rives confessed to Carol that the previous January, less than two months before, her father J. W.'s attorney had sent her a set of "estate-planning" papers to sign relating to Gertrude's assets and holdings. These included a tax-free gift distribution of $10,000 to each member of the Cunningham family, as well as an unspecified cash gift to Carol's son Scott—a gift to everyone in that circle, in fact, except Carol. Joanie, at the time, had felt uncomfortable with the inexplicable "gift," and therefore had refused her consenting signature. Also in the papers was a trust document detailing a substantial trust that was to pass to Joy Cunningham, Gertrude's sister-in-law and age-old antagonist, upon Gertrude's death. Joanie had protested; to her mind this seemed both unethical and improbable, given the rancor the two women had always directed toward one another. So she told her father she wished to go talk with Gertrude and determine her wishes before signing any agreements.

Gertrude's accidental fall, however, had precluded this action.

This stunning news was the first indication that J. W. Cunningham, the beloved younger brother whom Gertrude had championed to her marriage's detriment, and who had cast such a shadow on the Luby's organization, had escalated his larcenous appetites from cafeteria blueprints to a more personal attack.

The attorney Carol now consulted warned her that until they could determine what papers her mother had signed, and whether they were signed in ignorance of content, no action could be taken. Even then, it was up to her mother. Carol had no real right to seek legal representation to probe into her mother's affairs; and the lawyer couldn't represent Gertrude either, because she had not been hired to do so. Their hands were tied.

The next day, while visiting the hospital, Carol casually asked Gertrude, "Mother, when did you give your home to Jay Paul?"

"I have *never* given him my house," her mother replied, amazed. "I don't want him in my house." Then she repeated emphatically, "I have never given him that house."

Carol patted her arm reassuringly. She recalled Jay Paul's phrasing, how he had announced that "they" were the ones who had given him the house. So, drawing a deep breath, Carol told her mother what Jay Paul had said.

Her mother reacted with incredulity. "Oh, no, I don't think Dub would do that. I don't think he would give away my house. But I have no idea what is going on."

"Well, Mother, something is," said Carol. "Jay Paul is staying at your house."

At that, Gertrude began to grow angry. "I don't want you in my house. I don't want Jay Paul in my house. I don't want anybody there. You know things have disappeared in the past, Carol. I am going to ask Jay Paul to change the locks so nobody will go in there, including him."

But Carol, unwilling to inflict any more stress upon her recovering mother, knew that such a move was already too late. For in addition, Carol learned that during a visit from J. W. and his wife while Gertrude was still undergoing therapy in the first hospital, the Cunningham couple had told Gertrude that they wished for her to sign over her half of the lake house they had all bought together in partnership, thereby divesting herself of her ownership.

After Carol left the hospital and drove home, she paced her kitchen floor for the next several hours. Her own helplessness over her mother's dilemma appalled her. Could her uncle legally move her convalescing mother to a nursing home hundreds of miles away? Did he now have guardianship authority? Might Carol's uncle and aunt exercise complete power in the future over where her mother went and what happened to her?

Was it possible that the very fate her mother had supposedly designed for Charles after his first stroke, when she had attempted to obtain a legal guardianship over him, was now being thrust upon her by the very people she had trusted for so long? Was this merely karmic justice? And just who, in fact, had been the real author of that earlier plot in the first place? Who had advised the legally unsophisticated Gertrude to take such a step against her estranged husband?

During her restless trudging, Carol began to recall moments in the past when her uncle had voiced frustration at her mother's frugality. Throughout the years, he and his wife Joy had expected Gertrude to pay half of whatever expenditures they made for various family members—such as the cost of new drapes and clothes they had bought for their ailing sibling Hubert Cunningham, for whom Gertrude had already purchased an entire new house. Their response to her refusal rang loudly resentful. Another time, they had wished to solicit Gertrude's donations to a church, and had asked Carol for suggestions about exerting persuasive pressure on her mother. When Carol replied that she took no part in Gertrude's decision-making processes, J. W. gazed out of the window, his face betraying his dissatisfaction. "I wonder what it is going to take for her to let loose of that money?" he mused aloud. Now Carol began to wonder if he had perhaps been referring to all Gertrude's money.

Joanie returned to San Antonio in early March, and accompanied Carol to Gertrude's hospital room. From there they telephoned J. W. to try to get to the bottom of the mystery. Carol asked him point-blank if the house really belonged to Jay Paul.

"Yes, it does," J. W. replied. "Carol, why can't you just be nice and go along?"

Joanie, taking the phone receiver, pleaded with her father to listen. His response was to call her a "whore who was siding with Carol." Weeping, Joanie grasped that through sheer loyalty and family feeling she had achieved a pariah's status with her own parents whom she loved. She couldn't comprehend how they could be doing this to her Aunt Gertrude. Gertrude's reaction to the scale of her brother's nefarious scheme was one of horrified distress. Begging Carol to help rescue her, she explained what had happened over the last few years. She was unaware that she had signed over her entire fortune to the control of her brother, J. W., as well as her nephew John W. III and a management company. She had thought she was merely signing estate planning papers J. W. had recommended. But then, she had also never known how he had stolen from his Luby's employers and despoiled the moral integrity of Luby's Cafeterias, Inc., back in 1959.

The legacy of Luby's first loss of innocence now came to full fruition. In this instance, it was no irony that the medieval Scottish crest of the Cunningham family bears the motto "Over, Fork Over." For J .W. Cunningham and his wife apparently believed that Gertrude's money was due to them—due because they had once been the victims of an injustice committed by Charles Johnston and Bob Luby, when these men did not grant J. W. the management position he felt he deserved. The old grudge had been nursed by J. W. for so many years that now he used it to justify anything he did. He and his wife seem to have convinced themselves— and their sons—that the money was really theirs by right.

Such is the power of the stories we tell ourselves. Such, as well, was the ultimate price of Charles Johnston's silence.

But Carol knew how to recruit important assistance for her mother that would extend even beyond the necessary legal tactics of hiring lawyers and accountants and demanding proofs and embargoes on funds from brokerage houses. She needed friends whom her mother would believe and trust. She called on the "Canasta Cavalry," made up of Luby's pioneer wives, who had been meeting monthly to play cards since the 1960s. Helen Lee, a member of the canasta group and the wife of the late Luby's pioneer John Lee, and Pat Barnett, wife of Bill Barnett, sedately marched into the hospital, spoke at length with Gertrude to determine as far as possible what had happened, and then the friends asked Gertrude what her real desires were. Only after they did this did they discuss options and finally submit a power of attorney form for her to sign in Carol's favor so she could proceed to act on Gertrude's behalf and discover what the Dallas "estate planning" papers actually contained. Additionally, Helen Lee contacted John Banks Sr., the lawyer that most of the old Luby's executives, including Charles Johnston, had always consulted, and enlisted his help. Luby's, one more time, in its usual fashion, took care of its own.

The battle was on.

The canasta players, 1982

□ □ □

Over the next few months, the tensions between the Cunninghams and the Johnstons stretched so taut as to become almost unendurable.

In mid-April Carol drove her mother from the rehabilitation hospital to her now-spotless home. But while getting her mother settled, Carol very quickly noticed that the previous clutter seemed a little too thoroughly removed. For all the business records, boxes of documents, and Salomon Smith Barney statements, among others, were missing from the premises. Even a box containing more than $3,000, which Gertrude obviously kept squirreled away in case of emergency, had vanished, never to be seen again.

No papers relating to the assets of Gertrude C. Johnston and her decisions remained in her home now. Neither she nor Carol nor their allies had any access to business records, transaction accounts, or copies of documents she might have signed in the past. The Cunninghams' raids had stripped the house as completely as army ants defoliating the crops on a

Brazilian plantation. Every day Gertrude grew increasingly more agitated to think that her brother and his family were, in essence, in the act of embezzling her fortune and her home from her ownership. Her paranoia magnified to include a fear of kidnapping. What if they abducted her from the hospital or the rehabilitation center (where she had to stay after she took an additional fall and broke her other leg) and secluded her in a nursing home, out of her own daughter's and grandson's reach?

Carol began to help her mother supervise the caregiver needed during her recovery at home. Her mother had even placed Carol as a signer on her checking account so that Carol could pay Gertrude's bills. The trust pendulum had now swung completely to Carol. Gertrude felt that her daughter had saved her life, and she rewarded that act of devotion and rescue with her trust. Fortunately, the Cunninghams had not yet given a change-of-address to the bank, or had Gertrude's mail forwarded to them. Shortly after Gertrude was back at home, Carol had asked her banker to come over and look at the mail and assist her. The amount of mail was daunting. While the two were paying bills and opening envelopes, a Salomon Smith Barney statement was discovered. Upon review of the statement, the banker was astonished. A total of $5 million had been transferred from Trudy's brokerage account to another account.

Carol tried to explain to her mother that the inconceivable was indeed happening. J. W. Cunningham was in control of Gertrude's money and was taking it away from her. For years, Carol had asked her mother, John W. III, and Joanie about the $750,000 educational trust that Gertrude and Charles had established for the benefit of their grandson. Carol's questions had been disregarded, ignored, or misdirected. This trust, which had terminated years earlier under its terms and thus should have been delivered outright to Scott, had also been sequestered from Scott by the Cunninghams. The bulk of Gertrude's money had only quite recently been shuffled into a limited partnership account in Dallas, under both Gertrude's and J. W.'s names, named the Johnston Special Investment Trust. Apparently the original plan had been to move it slowly, bit by bit, into this account, so as to promote the appearance of thoughtful, gradual investment revisions. Although there had already so far been an annual gift distribution that the Cunninghams had paid themselves from her estate, the main stake had been left alone until now. But Gertrude's fall and its aftermath had prompted the untidy haste; J. W., according to his own son's criticisms, had up until then simply not been "moving fast enough."

Carol and the banker placed a call to John Banks Sr., who telephoned the brokerage firm to freeze the funds. No further damage should have been able to occur, but this was only the beginning.

In addition to Banks, Helen Lee also advised her friend Trudy to start using Robert A. Gilliam, her CPA and formerly Charles Johnston's CPA. Gertrude had broken with these Luby's advisers shortly before Charles's death, and started using advisers in Dallas at her brother J. W. Cunningham's suggestion. Her Dallas CPA had died sometime after Charles's death, and she had turned to her brother for another recommendation. Thus had Gertrude become the client of Ken Sibley, CPA, and Ray Jordan, an attorney and longtime friend of John W. Cunningham III.

So Gertrude, during a formal meeting in late April, insisted that J. W. show her and her CPA, Bob Gilliam, copies of all documents and financial instruments that she had supposedly signed. When J. W. opposed her by retorting that he held her power of attorney, which was all he needed, she protested to him that *any* documents she had wittingly or unwittingly signed for him should be considered null and void, and should get destroyed. "I want you to return my money to my accounts and my control," she pronounced. A major skirmish was brewing, and it began with new powers of attorney drafted by John Banks and signed by Gertrude. Recognizing that she needed assistance, Carol agreed that Bob Gilliam should be the new holder of the power of attorney. He would understand better than she the documents and brokerage statements, and be able to trace where the money had gone.

But J. W. and his family were apparently reluctant even to show Gertrude Johnston whatever documents they did have in their possession. Every request she extended to J. W., asking that he meet again and materially demonstrate and justify his claim that Gertrude had willingly entered into a legitimate "estate-planning" arrangement under his control was deflected, avoided, or ignored. Bob Gilliam's power of attorney was ignored. Carol and her mother still had no idea what Gertrude might have signed; neither did Bob Gilliam, nor did John Banks Sr., the family attorney who did his best to help the situation by contacting the brokerage house and getting a freeze put on the limited partnership account before more money could be transferred from Trudy. Meanwhile, J. W.'s own daughter, Joanie, continued to ask him and her two brothers what exactly was going on, and to implore her family, in writing and during visits and telephone calls, to abandon their attempts to usurp control of Gertrude's money and return what they had already taken from her. But eventually it came to light that all conversations, telephone or face-to-face, that engaged Gertrude with any member of the J. W. Cunningham family or involved any of Gertrude's business affairs were being tape-recorded by the Cunninghams. This surveillance even extended to Joanie, who felt hurt and outrage when she learned of her family's treachery.

After weeks of efforts to legally rectify the situation, including drawing up a new will, Gertrude on June 15, 1999, grew tired of signing new papers and refused to sign another formal letter to be mailed to her brother. Instead she wrote a letter in her own handwriting to J. W., repeating her desires in simple terms. "I am upset," she wrote, "at what has happened to my money. I want my money returned. I request that all of you come to my home for a meeting to discuss this situation. I am requesting that Mr. Gilliam coordinate matters as I have requested. If this situation is not resolved to my request I will take matters to court. I hope to resolve this matter soon with your sincere cooperation." She gave this letter to Mr. Gilliam, who mailed the original to J. W. and copies to everyone else.

But the father-son Cunningham contingent of Dub and John, whom Gertrude ultimately loved, and in whom she had spent a lifetime confiding her trust, returned to San Antonio June 17. Theirs was an informal expedition that caught Gertrude while she was alone. According to J. W., they had come in order to give her their response to her requests. According to J. W., he *couldn't* return her money to her any longer because *she* had revoked his power of attorney and given that appointment instead to Bob Gilliam. This meant, he claimed, that he, J. W., no longer possessed the authority to retransfer the funds.

But, he went on to explain, it so happened that he had there in his hands at that very moment several papers that she could sign to assist him in remedying his powerless state. These would revoke Bob Gilliam's power of attorney and terminate the professional services of John Banks Sr. as her legal representative. Then everything could at last get straightened out the way she wanted it. He also reassured her that her cash, along with her jewelry, was untouched, and resting in her safety deposit box at Frost Bank.

Elderly people, while not necessarily stupid or gullible, are often easily befuddled. Their vulnerability, their longings for appreciation and tender care, can sometimes resemble that famous reversion to childhood—even when they're not off wandering amongst memories of their kindergarten days. Thus Gertrude once again placed her belief in what her brother was saying. She signed the change of power of attorney, reinstating J. W. as her representative, and thereby disassembled the structure she and her advisers had spent the last three months so carefully and painfully constructing.

But she had no clue of the magnitude and ramifications of what she had just done.

□ □ □

At last, on June 21, Carol Johnston could bear the scheming and stonewalling no longer. In a letter addressed to the Cunningham family and copied for the benefit of everyone else involved, Carol expressed her concern for her mother's "emotional and physical well-being":

> This letter is being sent with her approval and full knowledge. All parties of the Johnston and Cunningham families are now aware of the actions, documents, and legal instruments that have been created in Dallas, Texas, over the past ten years.
>
> Since her fall and subsequent hospitalization in February of this year, my mother has received an additional professional explanation of these legal instruments. She has expressed a desire to her San Antonio attorneys and CPA, her friends and neighbors, and me, to re-create the division and direction of the distribution of her assets. She wrote a letter dated June 15th, 1999, which each of us has received a copy of, in which she expressed a desire to have her funds returned to her. I hope that the confusion and efforts to please everyone that have been so stressful on all of us can now subside.
>
> Although she is appreciative of her brother J. W.'s efforts to assist her, she wishes her assets to be placed in a financial trust institution where professional, objective, accountable parties can invest, manage, and disburse

finances as deemed appropriate. She wants to be fair. She is saddened by the pain and conflict the present situation has caused and that her family has been torn apart and is in crisis.

Unfortunately, Carol Johnston's letter failed to achieve the results she and her mother desired. Even shortly thereafter, when J. W., who had recently endured spinal surgery, portrayed every semblance of surrender in a meeting with Gertrude and wearily signed the papers necessary to forfeit his "estate-planning" control of her money, their hopes got dashed. It took less than forty-eight hours—from Saturday to Monday—for him officially to renege on his agreements, rescind the freshly signed documents, and instruct Salomon Smith Barney that they were not to honor them. Gertrude was only informed of his reversal on Monday morning when she went to the brokerage house to effect the transfers, and George Mirsky, the Salomon Smith Barney official who had overseen the Cunningham-engineered transfers and transactions, told her they couldn't be done. Hearing this, she announced to Mirsky her final conclusion: "Then I guess I'll just have to sue."

So the "day in court" that the Luby's cofounders had so conscientiously forestalled for the sake of their company and Gertrude's feelings was now, at last, about to dawn. On that day, J. W. Cunningham would finally be forced to answer for his fraudulent conduct—to answer to the very person who had remained protected from its truth, who had been preserved from its devastating legal consequences, and who never would have believed it if she had merely been told. But that day, so long deferred, would cost Gertrude and her family far more than the sum of her fortune. Certainly it would exact a fee more punitive than the settlement that would be only one of its several outcomes. Before the day was over, the worm that had begun its meal four decades before would wind up feasting on Gertrude's health, her welfare, and her heart's most cherished ties. And by nightfall, a wall was erected between her and her closest loved ones that none of them would ever lawfully be allowed to scale again.

□ □ □

The lawyer Gertrude hired to pursue her case was named Frank Ikard. The location of his practice in Austin, Texas, required that Gertrude, Carol, and their companions travel the hundred miles from San Antonio to confer with him on a hot day in August. After much discussion and a thorough verbal examination of Gertrude and Carol, as well as John Banks Sr., and Bob Gilliam, Ikard agreed to take the case and said he felt confident of winning it. But he specified that he would only accept the suit if a receiver was appointed by the court. His concerns were based on the history of undue influence J. W. Cunningham had been able to exercise over Gertrude. There must be no repeats of her previous confusions and vacillations.

So Gertrude's complaint got formally presented before the probate court. The judge who reviewed the case then assigned Arthur Bayern, another attorney, to act as receiver and guardian for Gertrude. As receiver, he would withhold the monies under dispute from all the concerned parties until such time as a conclusion should be gained.

Immediately after speaking privately with Gertrude in order to ascertain that this complaint did indeed accurately represent her genuine wishes, Bayern declared himself satisfied. Then, acting on her behalf, he proceeded to file suit in the Dallas County Courthouse against J. W. Cunningham; his son John Cunningham III; Kenneth Sibley, CPA, and his firm; Raymond Jordan and his law firm; George Mirsky of Salomon Smith Barney; and the entire Salomon Smith Barney brokerage and investment house.

The die was cast.

During this period Carol, who had been granted a medical power of attorney on her mother's behalf, naturally felt a growing concern for her mother's physical needs. Gertrude had now recuperated from two broken legs in less than a year, and it was essential to obtain the right care for her. Once she got checked out of the Warm Springs Rehabilitation Center, professional nursing and care assistance was required at home.

But in addition, Gertrude needed a friendly hand to accomplish ordinary, routine tasks like bill paying and correspondence. When she expressed envy of Carol's friendship with a woman named Gloria Utay Solomon, whom Carol had known for many years and who had just, with Joanie's additional help, guided Carol through a tricky diplomatic chore, an idea was born. Gloria, a professional party planner who lived in Dallas, offered to enter Gertrude's employ. She told Carol that for $1,200 per visit, she would come to San Antonio every thirty days and do whatever needed to be done. This way, as Gloria pointed out, Carol could not be accused of "undue influence" or manipulation of her mother during the course of Carol's performance of these jobs. Then Gloria also offered to help secure adequate geriatric care for Gertrude.

The following Christmas, 1999, was expected to be a comparatively happy time. Carol, Gertrude, and Carol's son, Scott, on leave from the navy, drove to Lafayette, Louisiana, to join Joanie's family in the holiday celebrations. But on Christmas Day Joanie placed a holiday telephone call to her mother. Joy informed her that her father was critically ill with a post-surgical staph infection that had entered his bloodstream and gone to his brain. His possible death was projected. Joanie decided to leave immediately for Dallas.

Although he did not die, J. W. left the hospital only to enter a nursing home, where he resides to the present day, for some time in a *non compos mentis* state. But Gertrude, a few months afterward, was herself diagnosed with the early onset of Alzheimer's. Now the only competent antagonists left in the ring to contest the slippery trust arrangements were Carol and her son, Scott; and to defend them: Carol's two male cousins and Joy, her aunt by marriage. Gloria Solomon, who was by this time the chief conduit to Gertrude, reported only to Arthur Bayern, the court-appointed receiver and financial guardian—the sole person authorized to make all hiring and firing decisions as to Gertrude's care.

Soon after these developments—in particular after Gertrude suffered a heart attack and her caregiver Michelle Green had no one to advise her other than Carol as to whether she should take Gertrude to the hospital— Carol attempted to improve her mother's living conditions by asking the court to consider replacing Gloria with a local care administrator who could be more available. Carol had already been warned by her attorney that, due to the delicate legal status of Gertrude's estate case, any actions she personally took regarding her mother's care might leave her liable to a lawsuit. But the fact that Gloria was only on hand for a visit lasting two or three days a month presented a serious problem.

It was during the review of her mother's care in the Probate Judge's office that Carol made the full discovery of just how unprincipled and deceptive people can become when tempted by the helpless circumstances of a solitary, wealthy elderly individual. For this was when she found out that Gloria Solomon was now getting reimbursed not $1,200 but $5,000 per month to lend her mother an occasional helping hand and oversee the dubious geriatric care she was receiving. But that was not all; she also was being paid an additional $500 per month in travel expenses, plus another $250 for "daily supplementation"—a vitamin plan Gloria sold to Gertrude on the side. The total take of $60,000 per annum struck Carol as exorbitant. When she complained to Arthur Bayern, he simply remarked, "Well, it's not like your mother doesn't have the money." Bayern had only recently hired an additional lawyer to "look after Gertrude's interests," the job he was himself appointed and paid to perform. By this time, the officially incompetent Gertrude, no longer in a position to fend for herself, was feeding four separate attorneys on her payroll. Carol Johnston and her son, Charles Scott, also had their own lawyers to represent them and to recover Scott's educational trust, remunerated, of course, not by Gertrude but by the clients. The Cunninghams, however, had requested that all their legal fees be paid from Gertrude's estate. Added to which, Gloria Solomon refused to resign her administrator's position.

Thus it became time to fill the courtroom for the final battle.

□ □ □

However, in these days of ready lawsuits, when the adversarial stance has become a common posture in American life, the path to litigation runs more smoothly and predictably than it did a century ago. Settlements so often preclude the old-time joust that for many trial attorneys the art of negotiation must replace the skills of the lance, and the majority of civil cases never make it to a courtroom at all.

The same was true of *Johnston v. Cunningham et al.* The depositions given by John W. Cunningham III lacked dignity, included a shrill, mocking imitation of his aunt, and ultimately reinforced the Johnstons' contention that Gertrude had never wanted her fortune to get converted to the

Cunninghams' profit. A tentative settlement was reached in October 2000, in which Frank Ikard would receive over $4 million in contingency fees based on Gertrude's $18 million estate worth, the Cunninghams would receive Gertrude's half ownership in the jointly purchased lake house, and Scott would be granted control of his educational trust and later be appointed as his grandmother's legal guardian, within certain strict limitations and stipulations. Also, Gloria Solomon would retain her lucrative administrator's position, and Arthur Bayern his financial guardianship. At first Carol Johnston protested the court's distributions, most particularly Frank Ikard's fee, since she had understood Ikard to have promised his payment would be based on the suit against Salomon Smith Barney for acting in conspiratorial concert with the Cunninghams in the knowing misapplication of Gertrude's funds, and not against the actual recovery of her mother's money—which because it was already Gertrude's anyway, was not actually "recovered" money. But after Ikard lowered his fee by $200,000, the settlement was accepted by all parties. And so, in mid-December 2000, just as the Luby's stockholders began steaming to their peak of open rebellion against the board of directors at their annual January meeting, the bitter two-year combat that had shredded Charles Johnston's family to pieces was finally declared over.

20

LEFTOVERS

□ □ □

In late December of 2000, just days before the annual stockholders' meeting that would climax in the failed revolution, an unexpected shock wave quaked through Luby's Headquarters. Apparently unbeknownst to the executive officers and board members, someone had been quietly buying up Luby's stock. In fact, very large amounts of Luby's stock. Between the dates of October 16 and December 22, two business-minded brothers whose names few people had ever heard of had acquired a total of 1.3 million shares sold under the LUB stock symbol. This was a holding that comprised almost 6 percent of all shares owned. As a result, these two men now wielded enough proprietary clout in the company to be able to negotiate for possible board seats, further investment, and an active role in its management.

Before this acquisition, no individual or conjoint interest since the founders' generation had owned more than 5 percent of all shares. But now it seemed a corporate takeover bid had sidled in silent as a cat burglar through the back door, just at the time when Luby's stock, at $3.56 per share, was practically worthless and the company was down on its knees. In the past, such takeover offers had been politely but firmly rejected by

Bob Luby and Charles Johnston—particularly back in the late 1970s, when the company was near its zenith and in its most productive years. Nevertheless, these two brothers from Houston had invested their own money, not corporate funds, to leverage themselves into the captains' seats. In other words, they could now effectively proclaim themselves the proud new owners of two hundred cafeterias.

On December 22, 2000, brothers Christopher and Harris Pappas filed a document required by the SEC reporting their newly gained 5 percent–plus ownership. This filing was the first notice anyone had received of the slow, steady, and until that date anonymous purchase of such a large amount of shares. The moment the revelation swept through the Luby's offices and the financial community, everyone felt stunned. News of this kind always generates a sense of drama and excitement—and more often than not, dismay, especially if the tactic denotes hostile intentions—but this ambush was especially piquant, given the troubles besetting the company and the anger presently roiling and seething among the minority stockholders. It wasn't as if these strangers had entered the fray to seize a fat plum off the money tree. Instead, they were shouldering a heavy wad of debt, buying into a losing streak, enthroning themselves in a kingdom that was unraveling at the seams. And although the Pappases also told the SEC that they harbored no current plans to seek voting control of the company or force any other change in the board or corporate structure, this was hard to believe if reformatted in the future tense. For although the Pappases had never owned any cafeterias before, they were most emphatically "food people." Unlike anyone serving on the board just then, they had very strong ideas not only of what might have gone wrong at Luby's but also of what they could do to make it right again, and what the heck they were investing in. This was because they already happened to privately own more than fifty different restaurants, specialty places that sell a variety of dishes from Creole cuisine to Mexican plates to seafood to barbecue to steak. The Creole restaurants are called Pappadeux's, in a clever marriage of Cajun patois and the brothers' Greek surname. The Mexican units sport the name Pappasito's Cantina. The barbecue and steak houses were left with a simple Pappas. Each of these eateries has plenty of theme atmosphere and can seat large numbers of customers—and each of them, scattered as they are across Texas and several northern states, wound up packed to capacity every single day and night, with waiting lists sometimes one or even two hours long for tables. So although the operational requirements of such types of establishments lay a wide field away from those of a cafeteria, the Pappas brothers indeed knew how to run a successful dining chain. Even more to the point: they knew how to cook truly delicious food—a knack for which the management at Luby's seemed to have developed amnesia.

What's more, the Pappases enjoyed a very similar heritage to that of Bob Luby and Charles Johnston. Their grandfather, H. D. Pappas, had come to America from Greece in 1897 to follow his aspirations and take *his* part in the American Dream. He realized his dream by opening cafes and restaurants—in Tennessee, Arkansas, and finally Texas. His passion for quality and service had borne a strong resemblance to Harry Luby's, who had, after all, achieved his own version of that same American Dream. So H. D. Pappas's grandsons Chris and Harris approached their legacy with a similar devotion and sense of integrity—revering it as a family heirloom, and conserving it with sharp business savvy.

But the crowning factor in this business-driven conquest was simply one of loyalty and respect. Those bedrock virtues sustained for so long within the Luby's organization now lay seemingly abandoned like empty husks. It might be safe to surmise from its members' behavior that the present board nurtured no real respect for the already-indignant stockholders who threatened mutiny, and regarded them as pesky gadflies without much actual sting. But it's possible the two canny brothers from the tightly knit, closely guarded Houston Greek community felt that the only way to resurrect these old virtues was to take their deserters by surprise. The Pappases had ties to Luby's that stretched back to their youth, and their own respect for the company's traditions and product remained untarnished by the current post-Parker fiasco. Luby's was part of their history; what was more, Luby's had already contributed to their industry expertise. For Harris Pappas had actually attended the Luby's Management Training School, graduated, and then spent nearly a year working in the Buffalo Speedway Luby's in Houston right after he finished earning his accounting degree from Texas A&M University. He knew far better and more intimately than any of the board members except George Wenglein just what it takes to run a cafeteria—and to run it the old Luby's way. And he had always found the loyalty that Luby's inspired in its employees to be a valuable commodity, one that should not be treated lightly. Even if he and his sibling needed to modify and readjust some of those old ways to fit the demands of the new marketplace, they understood what had gone into Luby's culture and they wanted to make sure it wasn't lost forever. As for Chris, who holds an engineering degree from the University of Texas: "He knows everything there is to know about equipment," no small compliment coming as it does from one of Luby's chief operations veterans. Far from eliminating Luby's as competition for their own businesses, they determined to retrieve it, set it back on its feet, and keep it alive and thriving.

The one item they didn't have on their experience list—the sole facet of leadership they weren't accustomed to—was that of running a publicly owned company.

So the conversation bubbling through stockholders' groups at the January meeting was peppered with speculation. What did the new buyers intend? What were their plans? How would the board react? Most of all: would the brothers instigate changes that might turn things around?

"I know for a fact that the Pappas restaurant chain is a well-managed restaurant chain," said Tom Palmer, the Tyler investment manager who was seeking a board seat at the meeting. "I'm a customer myself. We would think that they'd have a lot to offer Luby's, but the question is, will [Luby's] listen?"

Stock analysts were more optimistic. "This is exactly what the doctor ordered for Luby's," Bill Baldwin of Dallas-based Baldwin, Anthony & McIntyre told the *San Antonio Express-News*. He suggested that the insurgents should step aside and let the Pappases go to work on the company. The revolting committee members, he added, "don't bring any more to the part than what the current board does, but the Pappases do. They bring a wealth of experience and success and credibility to the party."

But the Pappases were famed for their privacy, for playing their cards close to the chest; they never shared their thoughts or advertised their plans before they were ready. Their refusals to speak with the press remained consistent. Both had reputations as stern visionaries. Both were shrewd entrepreneurs accustomed to turning their self-generated ventures into gold. As one Houston lawyer has put it, the Greek community in that city keeps itself to itself. Fraternizing outside its boundaries is cordial but limited. And apparently these brothers approached business the same way.

Nonetheless, they were already receiving encouragement only a few days after the initial revelation. In a public statement to the *San Antonio Express-News*, David Daviss, the board chairman and acting chief executive officer until a replacement could be found for Barry Parker, indicated how the board felt toward the authors of the recent surprise upheaval. "Although discussions are at a very early stage and no understandings have been reached, we welcome the interest of the Pappas brothers, who have an excellent track record in the restaurant business." Whether this statement was merely politic or betrayed the fatigue of a struggle-worn and starving people gratefully laying down their plowshares and embracing the conquering invader—either way, it didn't matter. A fait accompli had taken place, and the Pappases were there to stay.

By the end of the first week of March 2001, the shareholders' questions got answered. During a meeting with the board, the Pappases proved their absolute commitment to the company in the best way possible: they announced that they would accept stock options as compensation for their new positions as president and CEO (Chris Pappas) and COO (Harris Pappas). In addition, their pledges to infuse the ailing enterprise with "a significant level of their own capital"—i.e., $10 million in exchange for notes that would be convertible to common stock—put them squarely in the time-honored bootstrap camp of the old pioneers who had nourished the company with their hard work, sweat, personal funds, and dedication. As well as assuming the chief officers' roles, the Pappases took seats on the board of directors. Then, slowly, they began reversing the direction of the juggernaut that the board had launched in the 1990s. Inch by inch, they tugged it backward, erasing its former progress and restoring as best they could the previously existing conditions that would nurse the company back to health.

But every juggernaut leaves behind a trail of churned earth, debris, and destruction. Before too much longer, the course grew clear: in order to get out from under the prodigious debt while resuscitating what was left of Luby's, a large number of stores were going to have to close. And their personnel were going to have to lose their jobs. In this way the full penalty of Luby's wild nineties expansionism was finally levied.

□ □ □

The last of the Luby's pioneers, George Wenglein, retired from the board of directors in 2000. It was only fitting that he do so at the historic stockholders' meeting that introduced so much fermentation and change into the corporate structure. John Lahourcade, a director since 1970, also took his final bow into retirement at that meeting. The final chapter of the old Cafeterias, Inc. closed with the century in which its concept and philosophy had first seen the light, and the new millennium's hope of a return to those former values at Luby's, Inc. opened.

Since their 2001 takeover, the Pappases have made huge changes to the Luby's chain. More than fifty stores have been closed since the spring of 2003, completely eliminating the Luby's presence in all but five of its previous eleven states. The Luby's in Mississippi, Tennessee, New Mexico, Florida, Missouri, and Kansas are gone, the circle of cafeteria operations drastically contracted to 136 stores. Chris Pappas, in one of his rare statements, explained it to the Associated Press: "We are confident," he said, "that with this new business plan, Luby's will be in a stronger position to focus on our core Texas markets and continue to provide our customers with delicious, home-style food, value pricing, and outstanding customer service. Luby's has a great deal of capital in its real estate; and by closing and selling unprofitable stores, we can realize some of that capital."

One store was not on the new closure list. The Killeen Luby's, site of George Hennard's murderous rampage in 1991, had already fallen victim in 2000 to the earlier unit closures recommended by the consultant firm the board hired for advice. The promises of the departed Pete Erben—that the store would re-open after the massacre and *stay* open as an employment haven for its personnel and a renewed and safe gathering place—only survived for nine years. Now the twenty-four deaths are commemorated only by a memorial that was erected at the same time the store was rebuilt—both constructed as sources of great community pride, and regarded by Killeen citizens as a joint demonstration of their town's ability to respond effectively and with a positive attitude to tragedy. But the memorial won't be found at the old cafeteria's location. It is instead situated on the grounds of the local community center a couple of miles from the cafeteria site.

In a number of the remaining stores, a new style of restaurant service has succeeded the old cafeteria format, with serve-yourself all-you-can-eat buffets (a few of which Barry Parker instituted), an eat-here-or-take-home entity called Luby's Buffet Xpress (designed to compete with modern high-end supermarket delicatessen fare and other quickie family restaurants that have sprung up all over the country), and menus meant to sate the consumers' appetite for more contemporary and exotic food, such as Asian and Greek salads. Determined to revive the sagging corporation, the Pappases have implemented their own operational systems, which, in the assessment of one old Luby's hand, may not always work very effectively in a cafeteria line. These specifically involve more paperwork (causing further loss of tenured employees). They also include the practices of cooking small amounts, à la carte kitchen style, in rapid increments that result in emptying the serving pans too quickly; serving fish that looks good when first offered but suffers visually under 30 minutes' exposure to the line's heat and light; hiking prices and increasing portion sizes—thereby discouraging longtime elderly customers, who feel they cannot consume everything they're paying for. Also because the brothers are more accustomed to the à la carte system, the old Luby's veteran feels that they lack the ability to utilize and re-serve run-offs, or ROs, otherwise known as leftovers. So too much waste takes place in an environment that used to be justly famed for its efficient thrift with resources. The Pappases' exertions, though, are apparently unflagging, their determination strong.

However, the losses from declining sales that began badly dogging the company by 2000 had continued their downward spiral throughout fiscal 2003. And starting in November 2002 and continuing through January, April, and May 2003, Luby's repeatedly defaulted on an outstanding $80 million loan, driving the amount up to $108 million, then $115 million. Because of the structuring and purposes of the debt, in May 2003 the Pappas brothers were forced to call in their $10 million loan to Luby's, which the company also defaulted on. The struggle for survival was, as of that moment, touch and go.

Some turnarounds take longer than others. And some organisms require a near-death experience before they will evolve into a newer, fitter incarnation. The Pappases had announced to the shareholders in 2001 that there would be no quick fixes to their situation, and had committed themselves to an emphasis on fundamentals. This commitment is now redeeming itself. At the end of its third fiscal quarter in 2004, the Pappases were able to announce an earning increase of 4.8 percent from the same quarter

Gertrude Johnston, Carol's son Scott, and Carol Johnston

of the previous year, with a net income that was in the black for the first time since 2000. In June 2004 they also refinanced their outstanding bank debt and cured the defaults by continuing to pay down the debts owed through the sale of closed-store real estate.

"I'd say that aircraft carrier has turned," Jeff Dabbs, an analyst with San Antonio's Kercheville and Co. who has tracked the ups and downs of Luby's closely for many years, said at that time. "They're getting pretty close to break-even. . . . If they continue to keep comps going in the right direction, they may have turned a corner."

And he was right. As of August 1, 2005, with one year left in the Pappases' current contract to administrate the course of Luby's, the stock had climbed to $14.60. The stock was by then already considered by brokers and stock pickers as a highly recommended turnaround stock. And according to a feature article published on July 10, 2005, in the business section of the *Fort Worth Star-Telegram*, Luby's was making money again—three quarters in a row.

□ □ □

For ninety-five years, the name Luby has been synonymous with public dining with the true public in mind—the great congregation of Americans who have found in the Luby's establishments a democratic distribution of good food at cheap prices. For fifty-eight years, the creation of Bob Luby and Charles Johnston has fed the citizens of this country. During that time it has flourished, gasped, and climbed slowly back up for air. But it still serves people today with the same attention to the quality of food it offers as when the founders first set up shop in a San Antonio basement back in 1947.

Few things are more American than a cafeteria, and no cafeteria is more representative of that concept than Harry Luby's brainchild. A century's worth of middle-American life can be viewed in microcosm through the telescope of its serving lines. People have come in as newborns and toddlers, grown up, loved, married, grown old, and died there. Some have grown rich under the company's wing; some have lost everything by trusting in the permanence of that wing's integrity.

Some, like Gertrude Johnston (who died in April of 2005, seventeen days after her sister-in-law, Joy Cunningham), perished under the wing, reaping the tragic harvest of its first moral downfall. Some have left the past sadly behind and moved on to a separate destiny.

But the last word in this hymn to a classic embodiment of the American Dream must belong to Herbert Knight, the sixteen-year-old farm boy without a college education who started his vocational life as a busboy in the Main Street, Dallas, Luby's in 1943 and wound up, a hardworking hero, as the retired vice president of the largest cafeteria chain in the nation.

Ina Faye and Herbert Knight

The Luby family, 1940s

In 2000 Ina Faye Knight, the fellow busgirl with whom the sixteen-year-old had fallen in love and whom he eventually married, was diagnosed with terminal cancer. At the same time, Luby's stock, upon which the majority of the Knight assets were based, was dropping so quickly that everyone connected to the corporation could only stand helplessly by and watch their hard-won retirement savings disappear. Ina Faye, hearing the news of the plunge from some of the other worried Luby's women, turned to Herbert.

"Should we sell our stock?" she asked.

In a fashion typical of the Luby's that Harry Luby, Bob Luby, and Charles Johnston had first forged, Herbert replied. "We've got more important things to think about. Besides, I believe in Luby's itself. Look back at all we've done. Look at the people we've worked with. Even if the stock price drops to zero," he said, "it doesn't matter. We've had the life."

EPILOGUE

□ □ □

In the years since the Pappas brothers shouldered their chief administrative positions, they have continued to carry out the traditions of good citizenship initially established by Harry Luby, Bob Luby, Charles Johnston, and the Luby families. Their commitment to these traditions can be observed in their recent conduct while meeting the 2005 Hurricane Katrina and Hurricane Rita crises.

Following the Katrina disaster, Luby's offered a 10 percent discount statewide for one month, and collected donations in all their stores for the Bush-Clinton Relief Fund. Luby's employees also donated to the Red Cross, with the company matching each donation to double the final total. In addition, the company sent several hundred cases of water to the Astrodome shelter, and catered food for the Kelly Air Force Base shelter.

During the days preceding and following Hurricane Rita's landfall along the coasts of Texas and Louisiana, Luby's reopened a closed store in order to assist officials coping with the massive evacuation effort. They made the store's facilities available for the use of officials and emergency personnel, as well as provided an air-conditioned oasis for the general public traveling on those hot, steamy highways. A local grocer and a nearby Wal-Mart donated fruit, drinks, candy, water, and other provisions to hand out to travelers. One local official estimated that over five thousand people stopped at the site and availed themselves of Luby's generosity. The City of Burleson recognized Luby's contribution with a special commendation. In Orange, Texas, Luby's allowed FEMA and the Red Cross to set up camp at another closed cafeteria. These aid workers used the Luby's parking lot as a headquarters for six weeks, passing out relief checks there and bringing mobile homes and restrooms for evacuees' use.

Although one Luby's store in Port Arthur, Texas, was completely destroyed by the storms and a second was severely damaged, the organization still managed to mirror the behavior of civic-minded personnel during Hurricane Carla, in 1961, when Luby's became the very first public food provider to reopen premises in the Houston and Beaumont, Texas, areas and to feed the cities' hungry populations.

As far as growth in the business is concerned, the Pappas brothers are determined to bring the turnaround in Luby's fortunes to fine, full fruition. The stability that has already come back to the business "through tremendous execution by our employees" has led to the announcement to investors that the Pappases plan to open two new stores in 2007, as well as to implement upgrades and innovations in facilities and services in already-existing stores. They have also instituted programs to "develop talent," offering improved recruiting and "a better quality of restaurant life" to their personnel.

In early March of 2006, Luby's stock price at last broke the $15 per share mark. So now it can truly be said that Luby's has turned out to be a prime example of that rarest of occurrences in the business world: a genuine revival.

Harry would be pleased.

Carol Johnston

□ □ □

Standing still, looking over my shoulder at my history, my life is a marvel even to me. While most folks would be comfortable reflecting on their life singularly, for me to do that would do an injustice to the truth. My life has been integrally woven with so many other people's lives, and is a small part of an incredible social history and family story. To speak of my life experience without sharing the gamut of family members and others who preceded me—their work and their interactions both personally and professionally—would be leaving out the very influences on the person I have become.

Over the course of my lifetime my association with the Luby family and the members of its business organization has been a wellspring of joy, pride, and satisfaction to me. Prior to 1998, the virtue and integrity of the organization that I was born into were sources of both amazement and respect to those standing in line to enjoy a delicious meal, to those operating the cafeterias that catered those delicious meals, and to the business community at large.

My childhood was one enviable by even the most pampered of babes. I was surrounded by chicken-fried steak or a small portion of fried fish, the creamiest mashed potatoes with an occasional lump that made your taste buds smile, cream gravy made with real cream, macaroni and cheese with lumps of warm cheese as an occasional delight for chewing thoroughly. The crisp fried okra, perfectly seasoned collard greens with a bit of bacon or ham, cornbread so fresh and moist that it seldom needed more butter, and a glass of "sweet milk" were some of my favorites. For dessert, let's see—yum, we could have sweet rolls with big pieces of pecans, raisins, and filled with cinnamon and a caramel topping or a small slice of cherry, peach, Dutch apple, or chilled cream pie—chocolate, coconut cream, banana cream, or the vanilla custard pie known as the "Luby's Special."

My parents worked together first in the Dallas stores and then later moved to San Antonio, Texas. There they teamed up with those who saw the opportunities that the split from Dallas could bring.

Today's human resource expert was yesterday's "people person." I believe it would be fair to say that of all the degrees from all the colleges and universities, the only parchment that cannot be earned or granted is the one for educating, training, or recognizing a person on the basis of his or her ability to care about another human being. My father was such a man, as were most of the initial business partners who gathered to develop and enlarge on the concept that Harry and Julia brought to the table. They were people who cared about people in both a business and personal sense. The restaurant business takes a lot of people to turn out a good product, and the idea was to have everyone want to pull equally, according to their abilities or interests, so that the managers and employees who would later follow this business strategy would do so knowing that they would be able to reap the rewards of a solid business philosophy and work foundation.

Few people have had the opportunity to see and experience the closeness, the collaboration to succeed and to profit together, that was a win/win proposition for executives, management, and employees and finally to build a business that was founded on a rock of reward for those assuming responsibility whether as a partner or as an employer. Those willing to train, transfer, and work hard were compensated generously. Business was not "as usual"—not at Luby's.

The life was good; the uniqueness of its business philosophy and practices had put Luby's Cafeterias at the top of its industry. The Luby's marquee was a beacon to customers wanting to savor a fresh, nutritious meal at affordable prices. The story of the business that Harry Luby built—this "Merchant Boy" along with his family members, pioneers, and partners—is worth sharing. When the direction of the company that I believed was founded and built as solidly as the steel beams that held those marquees began to shift, crack, and falter, I knew it was a story that had to be told.

My journey to find the right partner to assist me in this massive project was a long and bumpy one with frustrating breakdowns, dead-end streets, and detours that have taken well over four years to bring to completion. Writer Carol Dawson was the person who agreed to partner with me to tell the history of my family, the Luby's organization at large, and my life's personal experience as part of that history.

Carol has done a colossal job of sifting through a vast amount of information and has in the pages of this book briefly given an overview of a business with ninety-plus years of providing "Good Food from Good People."

The Luby's of yesterday is no longer. The cafeteria line that once was filled with the patient, hungry family members and loyal patrons that returned generation after generation to meet and eat at Luby's has shortened. The business has adapted to a more common philosophy of business or business as usual.

This story of a dynamic family is dedicated to those individuals that I remember from my childhood, the men and women and their descendants who dared to try to build the invincible. A business that partnered with all who came to Luby's—whether as a person who dreamed of the responsibility and rewards of a manager's position, as a long-term food-service employee who was rewarded with tenure and benefits, or as a customer who is just looking for a friendly face and a hearty, luscious meal.

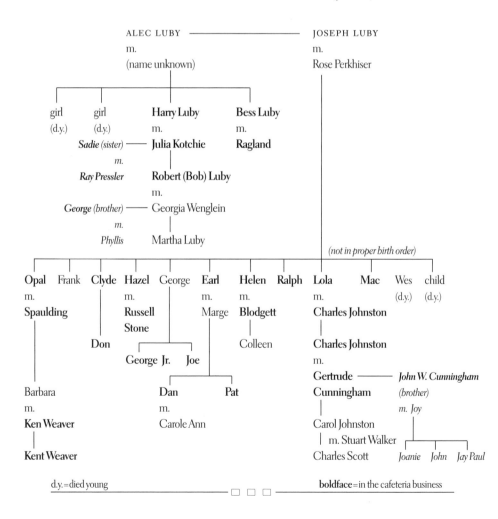

LUBY FAMILY TREE *(partial)*

ALEC LUBY —————————————— JOSEPH LUBY
m.   m.
(name unknown)   Rose Perkhiser

girl   girl   **Harry Luby**   **Bess Luby**
(d.y.)   (d.y.)   m.   m.
              Sadie (sister) ——— **Julia Kotchie**   **Ragland**
              m.
              Ray Pressler   **Robert (Bob) Luby**
              George (brother) ——— **Georgia Wenglein**
              m.
              Phyllis   Martha Luby

(not in proper birth order)

Opal   Frank   **Clyde** **Hazel** George   **Earl**   **Helen** Ralph   **Lola**   **Mac**   Wes   child
m.   m.   m.   m.   m.   (d.y.)   (d.y.)
Spaulding   **Russell**   Marge   **Blodgett**   **Charles Johnston**
                          Stone
                          Don   George Jr.   Joe   Colleen   **Charles Johnston**
                                                                                                      m.
Barbara   **Dan**   **Pat**   **Gertrude** ——— *John W. Cunningham*
m.   m.   **Cunningham**   *(brother)*
Ken Weaver   Carole Ann   *m. Joy*
                                                                                    Carol Johnston
Kent Weaver   │ m. Stuart Walker
                                                                                    Charles Scott   Joanie   John   Jay Paul

d.y. = died young   ☐ ☐ ☐   **boldface** = in the cafeteria business

ACKNOWLEDGMENTS

□ □ □

I would like to express my deepest gratitude to all the people who so kindly cooperated by sharing their memories, experiences, and knowledge in
order to contribute to this book: Herbert Knight, George Wenglein, Phyllis
Wenglein, George Luby, Barbara Luby, Dan Luby, Carol Ann Luby, Har-
old Day, Mike Day, Kent Farmer, Robert Gilliam, Wendelyn Wilkes, John
Lahourcade, Becky Geiger, Kenneth Weaver, Kent Weaver, Genevieve
Hayes, Tommy Griggs, Barbara Griggs, Elizabeth Allen, Elisse Jones Freeman, Rick Gozaydin, Craig Gannaway, Juanita Gonzales, Ralph "Pete"
Erben, Ruth Pennebaker, Tracy Gieselman-Holthaus and the Springfield
(Missouri) History Museum, and countless others. Staff members at the
University of Texas Press have been peerless in their support and profes-
sionalism; in particular, I wish to thank Bill Bishel, Lynne Chapman, and
Dave Hamrick. My agent Nick Ellison did a splendid job of facilitating
the book's existence; David Marion Wilkinson supplied the masterstroke
of liaison for the authors; and my father, aged ninety, provided true inspiration with his memories of dining at Luby's from his childhood to the

present day. He especially praised the chocolate Swiss roll, so delicious to an eight-year-old in 1924.

Finally, I will never cease to thank the people who have supported me throughout this process with their patience, belief, and love, and without whom the book could not have been written: Jeffery Poehlmann, Rebecca Brumley, Sarah Bird, my children, and all my friends.

CAROL DAWSON

□ □ □

Without the patience, encouragement, personal time, tears, and laughter of Wendelyn Wilkes, there would have been no effort on my part to create this work. Thank you, Wende.

My appreciation, love, and prayers will always be there for Joanie—my cousin who did the "right thing" at a time that was filled with betrayal and tragedy. May God grant you peace in knowing the truth.

My thanks to writer Paulette Jiles, without whose hours of listening and looking for just the right person with whom to collaborate, the co-author would not have been found.

Thanks to my son Scott, a young man who refused to quit trying to make the quality of life better for his grandmother, without reward or reservation and regardless of the mandated circumstances.

My gratefulness to Patricia Villasenor for the assistance and order that she has provided for these past few years.

Enormous kudos to the family and friends who have been supportive to us.

CAROL JOHNSTON

SELECTED SOURCES

□ □ □

INTERVIEWS

George Wenglein
Phyllis Wenglein
George Luby
Dan Luby
Carol Ann Luby
Harold Day
Kent Farmer, Austin Luby's Manager
Carol Johnston Walker
Robert Gilliam
Wendelyn Wilkes
Kenneth Weaver
Kent Weaver
Tommy Griggs
Barbara Griggs

Herbert Knight
Elizabeth Allen, *San Antonio Express-News*
Elisse Jones Freeman
Rick Gozaydin, former Luby's manager and private nurse to Charles
  Johnston
Cathy Howell, RN, and Judy Cohn, nurses for Gertrude
Dr. Craig Gannaway, forensic psychologist and expert on mass murder
  and terrorism
R. Matt Dawson, Luby's customer since 1924
Juanita Gonzales
Genevieve Hayes
Ralph "Pete" Erben
Wallace O. Chariton
John Lahourcade

□ □ □

PUBLISHED SOURCES

Newspapers and Magazines

Fort Worth Star-Telegram
Houston Chronicle
Nation's Restaurant News
The New York Times
San Antonio Express-News
Scene in *SA Magazine*
Texas Monthly
Waco Tribune-Herald

Books

Barnhill, Steve. *The Luby's Story: Good Food from Good People*. Edited by Ivan Fitzwater and Alice Evett. San Antonio, Texas: The Watercress Press, 1988.

Batterberry, Michael and Ariane. *On The Town In New York: The Landmark History of Eating, Drinking, and Entertainments from the American Revolution to the Food Revolution*. New York and London: Routledge, 1999.

Diehl, Lorraine B., and Marianne Hardart. *The Automat: The History, Recipes, and Allure of Horn & Hardart's Masterpiece*. New York: Clarkson Potter/Publishers, 2002.

Foote, Kenneth E. *Shadowed Ground: America's Landscapes of Violence and Tragedy*. Austin: University of Texas Press, 1997.

Gladwell, Malcolm. *The Tipping Point: How Little Things Can Make a Big Difference*. Boston, New York, London: Little, Brown and Company, 2000.

Langdon, Philip. *Orange Roofs, Golden Arches: The Architecture of American Chain Restaurants*. New York: Alfred A. Knopf, 1986.

Mariani, John F. *America Eats Out: An Illustrated History of Restaurants, Taverns, Coffee Shops, Speakeasies, and Other Establishments That Have Fed Us for 350 Years*. New York: William Morrow and Company, Inc., 1991.

McElvaine, Robert S. *The Depression Years, 1929\-1941*. New York: New York Times Press, 1989.

Spang, Rebecca L. *The Invention of the Restaurant: Paris and Modern Gastronomic Culture*. Cambridge, Massachusetts, and London, England: Harvard University Press, 2000.

Internet Sites

www.cliftonscafeteria.com/home.html
www.furrs.net
www.lubys.com
www.piccadilly.com

Annual Reports

Luby's Cafeterias, 1975–2002

INDEX

□ □ □

Page numbers in *italics* indicate illustrations.